BY ANY MEANS
NECESSARY

BY ANY MEANS NECESSARY
THE TRIALS AND TRIBULATIONS OF THE MAKING OF MALCOLM X . . .

SPIKE LEE

with

RALPH WILEY

New York

Library of Congress Cataloging-in-Publication Data

Lee, Spike.
    By any means necessary : the trials and tribulations of the making of Malcolm X / by Spike Lee with Ralph Wiley.
        p. cm.
    Includes screenplay.
    Includes bibliographical references.
    ISBN 1-56282-913-0
    1. Malcolm X (Motion picture : 1992) 2. X, Malcolm, 1925–1965. Autobiography of Malcolm X.   3. X, Malcolm, 1925–1965—Film and video adaptations.   4. X, Malcolm, 1925–1965—Drama.   I. Wiley, Ralph.   II. Title.
PN1997.M256633L4   1992
791.43'72—dc20   92-34037
                                                            CIP

First Edition
10 9 8 7 6 5 4 3 2 1

. . . (while ten million motherfuckers are fucking with you!)

ACKNOWLEDGMENTS

All praises due to the following for the support of this book and film: Monty Ross, Ernest Dickerson, Jon Kilik, Wynn Thomas, Preston Holmes, Ruth Carter, Barry Brown, Denzel Washington, Terence Blanchard, Ntshavheni Wa Luruli, Robi Reed, David Lee, Bob Little, Wilfred Little, Omar Azizz, Yvonne Little Woodard, Minister Louis Farrakhan, Bob Haggans, Dr. Henrik Clarke, Marvin Worth, Captain Yusuf Shah, Benjamin Kareem, Dr. Betty Shabazz, Leslie Wells and the staff at Hyperion Press. And a special shoot out to Ralph Wiley for hooking me up.

The white man wants you to remain a boy, he wants you to remain a lackey, he wants you to remain dependent on him, wants you to come looking to him for some kind of advice, some kind of teaching. No. You teach yourself, and stand up for yourself, and respect yourself, and know yourself, and defend yourself, and be yourself, and you will be recognized as an intelligent person.

. . . Our people are waking up!

Malcolm X, 1963

And if, to protect my relations with the many good white folks who make it possible for me to earn a fairly good living in the entertainment industry, I was too chicken, too cautious, to admit that fact when Malcolm X was alive, I thought at least now, when all the white folks are safe from him at last, I could be honest with myself enough to lift my hat for one final salute to that brave, Black ironic gallantry, which was his style and hallmark, that shocking zing of fire and be damned to you, so absolutely absent in every other Negro man I know, which brought him, too soon, to his death.

Ossie Davis, 1965

Wake up!

Spike Lee, 1986-88-89-90-91-92

CONTENTS

P R E F A C E

For me the title says it all. That's exactly what's it been like trying to make this film. The static, the resistance came from everywhere. From Warner Brothers, the Completion Bond Co., the Teamsters, High Minister of Black Culture and Ethics Amiri Baraka and his gang, the media. Everyone got in some swings. But you know what? This is the only way the film could have been made. We had to fight tooth and nail, fight like hell to get what we wanted on the screen.

All human beings are periodically tested by the power of the universe. Whether you're an athlete, entertainer, businessperson, etc., how one performs under extreme duress, how one performs under pressure is the true measure of one's spirit, heart, and desire. And most importantly, the WILL TO WIN. Sometimes, I think that may be more important than talent.

I hate and refuse to lose. I had been given the opportunity of a lifetime to attempt the life story of Malcolm X, one of the most important people of the twentieth century.

We had to win on this one. No ifs, ands, or buts. We needed a W, no tie and definitely not an L. We went through the fire on this one, we got singed here and there but we were stronger for it. I find myself constantly alluding to sports when talking about cinema, but for me it's the same thing.

Presently in America a war is being fought. Forget about guns, planes and bombs, the weapons from now on will be the newspapers, magazines, TV shows, radio, and FILM. The right has gotten BOLD, bolstered by their squashing of Ice T's *COP KILLER,* any piece of art that doesn't hold the party line is subject to attack. It's war in the battleground of culture (i.e., Quayle–Murphy Brown–Bush, Simpsons vs. the Waltons). At stake is the way to control the way people think or not think, act or be passive. Which brings us back full circle to Malcolm X. In this war, it's gonna come down to the artist. What is she/he trying to teach us? Entertain us. If their art moves us it's because it's about the HUMAN SPIRIT.

Artists have been blessed with God-given talents that must be allowed to flourish. It's their life, that's why they were put

here on the planet, they have no other choice. Wynton and Branford Marsalis have to blow their horns. I feel it's as simple as
that. I'm an artist. I live, breathe, and will die for my art, for
CINEMA. *Malcolm X* is my artistic vision. The film is my interpre-
tation of the man. It's nobody else's. I do not want to sound
egotistical either. I stand behind it all the way and everyone
involved has contributed to a great piece of cinema. As Malcolm
often said, "All credit is due to Allah, the lord of all the worlds
and only the mistakes have been mine."

Spike Lee
Brooklyn, N.Y.
September 5 in the year of our Lord 1992

INTRODUCTION

I've been watching Black men for a long time. Particularly the young ones who don't seem to have a clue as to what being a real man means. I am the mother of an eight-year-old son. When he's asleep at night I look at him long and hard. At how innocent he is. How smart. How beautiful. How vital. But sometimes I look at him so long that it makes me cry. I squeeze my eyes and behind them I see this kaleidoscope of hundreds of young brothers I've seen hanging out on street corners in L.A., Oakland, Detroit,

Manhattan, and Brooklyn, to name a few. I look at these young men very hard, too. I watch them make deals. I watch them drink from swollen paperbags. I've watched them packing their shit. I've watched them rap to young girls and disappear inside pissy project doors because their rhetoric worked. I watch them bop, boast about how much pussy they're getting and still "she can't claim me as her man." I watch the teenage mothers of their children watch the fathers of their children from the windows of small hot cramped apartments. They chain-smoke, feed the baby while the young fathers do everything and anything they so desire except be fathers. Because they don't know how. Don't want to. And I watch young brothers wear red or blue and give themselves a name and terrorize the very neighborhoods we used to feel so safe in. I watch how they rob, kill, hurt people whose skin is the very same color as their own, and I watch how there is no remorse, there is no guilt. I watch these young boys pretend that they are men. They are so proud of their big dicks that they boast about its power. The boys who wear colors and brag about how many casualties fill their lists.

I sit on the edge of my son's bed and look at how much he's grown already and realize one day I'll blink and he'll be twenty years old. When I pull the covers up and kiss his small forehead, I know that no matter how much I love him, no matter how much I try to teach him self-respect and respect for others, that when he goes out into the world, he's going to be the kind of man he wants to be. I just pray that he won't be one of those young men in red or on the corner or hitting the pipe or making babies without bearing the responsibility. And I think of Malcolm. I pray that when he grows up that he has one-tenth of Malcolm's courage, insight, wisdom. That what I am able to teach him and expose him to will deter him from the bullshit in the streets because he'll be more interested in being a real man by making something out of himself and adding something to our community instead of being a burglar of Black life in all its shape and forms. I hope that he will make me proud. I hope he'll grow up to be a role model for somebody. I hope he never grows up wanting to kill or hurt anybody. I hope he grows up knowing that being a Black man in America is going to be hard, but he will know from history that men are made, not born. I hope he will be strong enough to say no to anything that will strip him of his power. I hope he will worry about the moral fiber of our community. I hope that he will grow up knowing that if he is not an asset to anyone other than himself, then he will be a liability. I hope he knows how hard moral debts are to pay back. I hope that in the morning when he wakes up that he has dreamed once again about solving the world's problems. I want to continue to hug him for being brave even in his dreams. So that one day when he walks out my front door and waves and gets in his car, I hope that all the young men whose mothers are worrying about them right now, who cannot sleep, who ache inside because they are afraid, I hope that one day when I walk down the street I will see these young Black princes helping old ladies across the street, protecting our neighborhoods, reading a book, doing their home-work, writing letters home from college, and realizing that man-hood is not measured by anything that's visible with the naked eye. It's the work you do inside yourself that makes you on the outside a man.

—Terry McMillan

PART ONE

THE WELLSPRING

September 1990

It's big. I mean *Big*. You understand big. Well that's what I see. You gotta have the vision first. You gotta have it, you gotta go through school daze, you gotta do the right thing, and maybe, if you're lucky, you'll get mo' better. But you have to have that vision first. I started seeing it before I was attached to the project, before we made *Mo' Better Blues* and *Jungle Fever*, before *Do The Right Thing*. If I'm diming on myself, giving up the tapes of my own mind, too bad. I've been seeing this film all along in

my head. I'd be lying if I said it hasn't been there a long time:
Malcolm X.

Back then I knew the time wasn't right. I wasn't ready and
neither was anybody else, probably. But this was the picture I
was born to make—this was the reason I had become a filmmaker. I learned a lot making those earlier films, my NYU student film, *Joe's Bed-Stuy Barbershop: We Cut Heads* and *She's
Gotta Have It* and *School Daze*. There was always a connected-
ness to this movie that was vague, somewhere off in the future.
But one day . . .

Everything I've learned up until now made me feel able,
ready to do what needed to be done. *Malcolm X.* Big in scope. Big
in scale. Blow it up to 70 millimeters, put it on a thousand plus
screens. And no doubt about it, big problems, big headaches to
go along with it, but in the end, still a Spike Lee Joint, ya-dig
sho-nuff, a film that's gonna be right on top of you, right in your
face every minute, frame by frame. I'd always done small stories, but this story had to be more. Much more. I knew it had to
be done by an African-American director, and not just any African-American director, either, but one to whom the life of Malcolm spoke very directly. And Malcolm has always been my man.
I felt everything I'd done in life up to now had prepared me for
this moment. I was down for it, all the way.

I grew up in Brooklyn, in various neighborhoods—Crown
Heights, Cobble Hill, and Fort Greene. Saturday afternoons in
Cobble Hill was when all the kids, big and little—everybody in
the neighborhood who wanted to—would go to the Lido Theater
on Court Street for the matinees, the double features, and of
course for candy, popcorn, and soda. I can remember my
mother, Jacquelyn, taking me to see James Bond movies. She
liked them. I used to like old 007 myself. I remember seeing *Help!*
with the Beatles and *A Hard Day's Night.*

My mother was always taking me places to see performing
arts. I was grounded in the arts. I can remember so clearly how
she took me to the Radio City Music Hall one Easter Sunday to
see *Bye Bye Birdie.* I also remember her taking me to Broadway
to see *The King and I* with Yul Brynner when I was four or five
years old, and how I cried until she took me home because I was
too scared. Either the music was too loud or I didn't like our
seats—last row in the balcony. I'm still afraid of heights. The
point of it was this: All this exposure started my interest in visual
arts. My siblings and I were exposed to the arts, all of 'em. This
happened about as soon as we could walk. I believe exposure
makes all the difference in the long run.

Soon I was going on my own to the Lido Theater. One Saturday when we were there checking out the matinee, some construction was going on right next door, and somebody drove a bulldozer through the wall during the movie! I don't remember the movie, but I remember that bulldozer coming. I guess in a way it was prophetic because the Lido is no longer there. And maybe that's one reason I ended up being the kind of filmmaker I became. I figure the competition might be a bulldozer coming through the wall, and I've got to keep my audience involved, or one day I won't be around, either.

Becoming aware of any love of cinema came very late to me. I was not one weaned on Oscar Micheaux or David Lean or anybody else, Black or white, not in any sense that I was conscious of at the time. In fact, way back then, before I read *The Autobiography of Malcolm X,* back in '69–'70, when I was at P.S. 294, Rothschild Junior High in Fort Greene, I had been daydreaming of playing second base for the Mets, of being like my man Joe Morgan (that guy should be a manager in the major leagues!) of the Cincinnati Reds, or maybe like my Brooklyn homeboy, Willie Randolph, who was on his way to eventually becoming the every day second baseman for the Yankees. That was Willie Randolph's daydream I was having.

But then I read the autobiography and—well, just put it this way. I read it and thought, "This is a great Black man, a strong Black man, a courageous Black man who did not back down from anybody, even toward his death. The Man. Malcolm." And then I woke up to other things that were going on around me that had nothing to do with the arts. People had pushed Dr. Martin Luther King's philosophy and his legacy to the forefront—they were both dead by this time, around 1970. Dr. King had gone to Morehouse College in Atlanta. My father Bill Lee was King's classmate there. I would go on to Morehouse myself, in 1975. And Dr. King was chosen for a national holiday. And there are times when Dr. King is a vehicle for my true feelings about the racial situation. But from what I read of Malcolm X, I immediately knew that what he said was much more in line with the way I felt. So it wasn't a question of school loyalty or fellow alumni or knowing I would do a movie about Malcolm X one day. At the time, it was a question of being drawn to his intelligence. So I put King's and Malcolm's respective quotes at the end of *Do The Right Thing.* Many people (white people, that is—it's interesting the things white people question you about that Black people don't) were asking me at that time why I put those particular quotes there,

at the end of a film, and which one did I favor more, King's quote
or Malcolm's? Here are the quotes:

**Violence as a way of achieving racial justice is both
impractical and immoral. It is impractical because it is a
descending spiral ending in destruction for all. The old law
of an eye for an eye leaves everybody blind. It is immoral
because it seeks to humiliate the opponent rather than win
his understanding: it seeks to annihilate rather than convert.
Violence is immoral because it thrives on hatred rather than
love. It destroys community and makes brotherhood
impossible. It leaves society in monologue rather than
dialogue. Violence ends by defeating itself. It creates
bitterness in the survivors and brutality in the destroyers.**

—Dr. Martin Luther King, Jr.

**I think there are plenty of good people in America, but
there are also plenty of bad people in America and the bad
ones are the ones who seem to have all the power and be in
these positions to block things that you and I need. Because
this is the situation, you and I have to preserve the right to
do what is necessary to bring an end to that situation, and it
doesn't mean that I advocate violence, but at the same time
I am not against using violence in self-defense. I don't even
call it violence when it's self-defense, I call it intelligence.**

—Malcolm X

What do *you* think?

People asked me if I was advocating violence like Malcolm X
did. I laugh at that. What do *you* think?

Is that all Malcolm X was advocating? Or was he advocating
a total Black self-respect, a mind to do whatever was necessary
to better yourself or uplift the race! Remember that when he
came along, Black people were being beaten and lynched and
strung from trees by the double digits, brutalized all over the
map, treated like the bald-headed stepchildren of America. And
Malcolm X was having none of that. He didn't want to hear that.
So he said, okay, first things first. By any means necessary. You
gotta be alive in order to get ahead, in order to get your rights,
don't you? So many times white people have said to me:

"Oh Spike, why did Mookie throw the garbage can through
the window of Sal's?"

But I've never, ever had a Black person, an African-American, ask me that question. Not ever, it's understood.

About the quotes at the end, I told people who asked me (by telling me) that they were not really reading that Malcolm quote, which probably meant they had never read or known the man and never wanted to. They said the name, they thought "Malcolm X, oh shit," and they thought violence or nigger or radical or whatever they thought. It doesn't matter. That quote, if you read it thoroughly, it was all about self-defense and that's a lot different from random violence. And it's also important to look at that still picture I used. Malcolm X and Dr. King are shaking hands and smiling. So when I put those two quotes there, it was not a question of either/or, not for me, anyway, just a choice of tactics. I think they were men who chose different paths trying to reach the same destination against a common opponent.

There are a lot of books and tapes and articles out now about Malcolm X. Some of them are revisionist histories, but there was one book I wrote a preface for, called *Malcolm X: The FBI Files,* that I felt important for the public to see. It really showed just how much the government, and especially J. Edgar Hoover, head of the FBI, *hated* Black folks. *Hated* us. With a passion. What he did to King was pitiful. Just pitiful. He would audiotape King, his sexual escapades, and then he let King know he had him on tape. Hoover went in for that sort of thing. Hoover told Dr. King that if he didn't attempt suicide, he was going to send the tapes to his wife Coretta. Dr. King said, "Go ahead." And Hoover sent the tapes to Coretta.

It would be hard to trap Malcolm X like that. He was not like that from what I've been able to learn about him. Once he turned his life around, he was on the straight and narrow. He had been to the bottom, the dregs, and when he rose up, he rose up righteous. Strong. Could not be had just for the asking. Could not be bought by anything or anybody. And Black people, they *sense* that kind of sincerity. He *speaks* to them. It was that evolution that fascinated me about Malcolm X.

They both, Malcolm and King, had eerie premonitions of their deaths. King said, "I've been to the mountaintop, I might not get there with you but we as a people will get to the Promised Land." Malcolm said, "Now is the time for martyrs." So they both knew what they had gotten into for the dignity of their people. That they had to die for what should be a natural human right is the terrible thing. And Malcolm knew he was going to die. He knew. I also think Malcolm was just beaten down. He was tired. He was tired of running, tired of looking over his shoulder, tired of being chased, tired of endangering his family. I've heard there were a couple of times when brothers from the Nation, the Nation of Islam, were waiting for him in front of his house with knives, and he had to jump over bushes to get into that house. His own house, in Queens. There's a tape from after his house got bombed on the Sunday in February of 1965, the week before he was assassinated. The next night, Monday, he had to speak in Detroit. I've heard this tape. Malcolm is practically incoherent, and he was never that. The clothes he wore still had that burnt smell and were full of holes, I've been told. People who had been his fellow ministers were now ordering him dead. If Hoover didn't care for Martin Luther King, Jr., you know how he would have felt about Malcolm X. So, you know, my man was almost friendless, and completely worn out. They had won. For a minute.

People should try to learn from both men. They were different, they might have had different means, but they were after the same end. Simple dignity and rights for Black people, and all oppressed people. It's something we could apply to ourselves today, to make it work for today, for the world we live in now. King had his detractors, but Malcolm had many more. I think it was important they came along at roughly the same time, because if King had been the only one out there, there would have been a lot more resistance to him. But it was really white people who had the choice. Malcolm talked about this choice all the time. He would say, "You know, I think I'm helping brother King a lot because it's either me or him. I don't think they want to deal with me right now, so they're more willing to deal with King." They were both after results.

I was definitely not inspired by the blaxploitation film era of the late sixties and early seventies. Except for Melvin Van Peebles's *Sweet Sweetback's Baadasssss Song,* I didn't even watch those films back then, although I've seen almost all of them since. But not back then. I can't explain it; I'm not saying I was a fully developed film connoisseur back then. I suppose it was because I had been weaned on not just art, but the purer forms of art. My father, Bill Lee, is a jazz musician, and he has never played electronically amplified music in his entire life. In some ways I'm like him, in terms of the integrity of my art. In other ways, I'm not like him. My father was never really a businessman. And I'd have to say he really helped me by not being one.

What I mean by that is I understood from being my father's son that talent alone is not nearly enough. My father has always been a greatly talented musician, but it takes more than that. You've got to have business sense, too.

I learned that from just seeing how it was with my father. You can't function well as a starving artist—at least, I knew I never wanted to try and do that, and this was long before I became a successful filmmaker. My father would come home with a suit, let's say. He'd say, "Look here, I got this suit for four hundred dollars," swearing he got a bargain. My brothers and I would look at each other and say, "Man, that suit cost fifty dollars. You got robbed! Aw man, Daddy. Not again . . ."

That's my father's story. He was always getting beat. Always. One reason for this is that money never really had any meaning to him. Didn't mean anything to him unless some creditor was asking for it from him. If he had it, fine. If he didn't have it, it was like, well, we'll get some money tomorrow. It doesn't matter. We'll get it. Uh-huh. That's what something in me would say. Uh-huh. And I never wanted to put myself in that position. So I think I take after my grandmother, Zimmie Shelton, in that I look for value, I'm looking to save, I'm looking to run a tight ship. And since my art turned out to be film, it was also important I wasn't a selfish artist, the kind who is just doing my art for myself, and it doesn't matter if anybody sees it or understands it or not. Film is not really that kind of medium, I don't think. That shit costs too much money for you to just be making films for yourself, unless you're financing it yourself and are a fool who doesn't care about throwing away his or her money. Now if you're a painter or something, that's fine. Cut off your ear, paint for yourself only, suffer in silence.

But film is a different sort of medium. You share in film. So eventually I knew who Oscar Micheaux was, and Gordon Parks, and Melvin Van Peebles, but I didn't become a filmmaker because of them, not at all. I became one because of me. Nothing else was the inspiration for me, and I don't say that with any lack of humility as much as I say it as a statement of fact. My life itself was my artistic inspiration, and my life came from my parents and grandparents. It was what I was s'pose to do. For me, it grew from something I happened to do one summer while I was at Morehouse College, in Atlanta. The summer between my sophomore and junior years there was when I began to love film.

My mother had died the year before of cancer of the liver. I was an undergrad student at Morehouse, and I had chosen mass communications as my major. Mass communications encompassed print journalism, television, radio, and film. I bought my first camera, a Super 8. I didn't have a job, so I began shooting a lot of stuff in New York City so I'd have some stuff to play with when I got back to campus and began to concentrate on the major area of study. Shooting a lot of stuff became shooting all summer, and that's where my love began, I think. Now, that summer just happened to be the summer of the blackout. So I shot that, or people's reactions to it, and felt I was on to something. That was also the first summer of disco and everybody was doing the Hustle, a new dance craze. You could look anywhere in New York City and there was a block party—all these DJ's had their turntables out, right in the street, plugged into the street lamps at night, playing disco music. Folks were doing some serious Hustling! I filmed a lot of those block parties, and then I sort of put those elements together and came up with something I called *Last Hustle in Brooklyn.* I still have it on quarter-inch tape. My co-producer Monty Ross has seen it. It was Monty and myself who sat on my grandmother's porch back when we were in college, eating her fried chicken and drinking her iced tea, visualizing everything we're doing now. So we inspired ourselves. I have to put it that way. And my love of the cinema grew from there, from those spots. When I graduated from Morehouse I realized I still needed more skills to become a filmmaker, so I set out to further my education.

I still live not far from where I grew up. I went to NYU film school (it's a three-year program) after graduating from Morehouse. I won the Student Academy Award for my senior thesis film, *Joe's.*

My first feature film was to be called *The Messenger.* It never got made in spite of intense preparations and borrowing. That almost broke me. But I stayed on the case, and *She's Gotta Have It* was made on a shoestring, $175,000. It came out in August of '86, after being entered in the Cannes Film Festival that May. Then *School Daze* in '88, *Do The Right Thing* in '89, *Mo' Better Blues* in '90, and *Jungle Fever* in '91. But it is *Do The Right Thing* that people seem to remember, or so I've noticed. When I walk the streets in Brooklyn or Manhattan, or go to the Garden for a Knicks game, the people yell to me and say, "Yo, Spike! Do da Right Thing!" That title is going to haunt me to my grave.

I did not put those quotes from King and then Malcolm at the end of *Do The Right Thing* to promote myself as director of

Malcolm X, necessarily, but it was because of *Do The Right Thing* that a man named Marvin Worth—who had the rights to the material on Malcolm's life—sent me a letter saying that he wanted me to direct the film, or would at least like to discuss with me the possibility of doing it. I never did receive the letter, but he later showed me a copy of it. He had bought the rights to the story from Betty Shabazz, Malcolm's widow, and from Alex Haley, who co-wrote *The Autobiography of Malcolm X* more than twenty years ago. But for one reason or another, they had gone through four or five scripts and the film never got made. I believe there were more than a few reasons for that, and not the smallest is that I believe it wasn't *s'pose* to be made until now. That doesn't make me arrogant. It makes me fortunate.

Later, people at Warner Brothers suspected me of being behind a letter-writing campaign protesting Norman Jewison directing the film. At that time, right after *Do The Right Thing,* during the shooting of *Mo' Better Blues,* I had made pointed statements in the press about Jewison, the director, who had signed on to the project for Warner Brothers and who'd optioned the rights from Worth. The star of the title role was Denzel Washington, who was brought in before Jewison on the project. Norman and Denzel took a walk on the beach and negotiated a deal. But I never was behind any letter-writing campaign.

I did have serious reservations about a Caucasian directing a film this important to our existence in this country. Playwright August Wilson had the same problem with it. He wrote an article in an issue of *Spin* magazine that I had edited about the same thing, how he wanted a Black director for the movie version of his play *Fences.* Marvin Worth had taken the property from Columbia to Warner Brothers some time ago, and Norman Jewison had signed a deal with Warner Brothers. Norman had asked them at the time what kind of properties they owned. I'd heard he turned down *Bonfire of the Vanities,* but he saw *Malcolm X* and thought it would be a great movie, became very interested in it, and hired Charles Fuller to write a new script. Norman and Charlie are tight because they worked together on *A Soldier's Story.*

Marvin said Norman felt he needed the Black credibility of Charlie to get Betty Shabazz on his side. Norman wanted to feel wanted by the Black community. When it got out that Norman was going to direct this film, that's when I started to speak out about it. So Marvin had gone after me before Norman even came on the scene. Marvin wanted me, Warner Brothers would take me, so it was a matter of how we could make the deal, and let it be Norman's decision to leave, to save face.

I never received the letter from Marvin Worth, and, since he didn't hear from me, there was a long time span when he felt I wasn't interested and didn't know how much I wanted to do the film. Until he started to read statements by me in the paper. And I did go off when I heard the project was up and Norman Jewison was directing it. No way I was going to let it go without saying something about it in public. Let the people know. So eventually Marvin called me and said I really had to stop saying things in the press about Jewison directing. He asked me about the negative mail. Jewison and Warner Brothers thought I was behind it. Like I said, my name is Bennett and I wasn't in it. Marvin and I sat down and talked about me doing the film, and if I was to do it, how to gracefully replace Norman Jewison. Warner Brothers talked to him and, finally, there was a meeting between me, Norman, and Marvin. While all this was happening, Norman was waiting on another draft of a script by Charles Fuller. Norman said he didn't particularly like the second draft of the script, so he just outed with, "I don't know how to do this film, I can't lick it," and then he just wished me luck with it. Just like that.

We didn't want it to seem as if we just Bogarted him or bum-rushed or steamrolled over Jewison, who is a fine director who has done good work. But at that point there was nothing for him to feel attached to with Malcolm X. For me it then became only a matter of choosing which script I wanted to do, whether I wanted to rewrite Marvin Worth's existing script by James Baldwin and a collaborator named Arnold Perl, or one of the others, or whether I wanted to start from scratch, or what. I knew about Malcolm X, but I would have to really get to know him, and those people who knew him intimately, much better before I could feel comfortable shooting the film. I felt that was the only way to do the matter justice.

Why was Warner Brothers willing to make the film? Well, for one thing, Malcolm has been dead for so long, a lot of white folks are less threatened by him—those who are old enough to remember him when he was alive. So I think it had become time for the film to happen, and I give credit to rappers like Chuck D. of Public Enemy, who had given Malcolm X visibility in his music (that was Malcolm saying "No sell out!" at the beginning of *Bring the Noise* back in '87). And, more than twenty-five years after he was murdered, people, especially Black people, still responded to what he was saying, and young people went completely wild over him. I know the challenge in front of me. Malcolm X was so many things to so many people, and then there are the people who think they know all about him, but they don't know anything that's true. And I also know for a fact that around ten million motherfuckers are going to come out of the walls saying that they were down with Malcolm, and that's bullshit. Malcolm X causes a reaction, so there is no way the film won't do the same thing.

The story of Malcolm X belonged to Black film, and there was no other way to look at it. Too many times have the lives of the Martin Luther Kings and Nelson Mandelas ended up as made-for-TV movies. Too many times have the Steven Bikos ended up minor characters in feature films that were supposed to be about them. Too many times have white people controlled what should have been Black films. And there is a reason for this. They still feel—I'm talking about the major Hollywood studios—that white moviegoers here in America are not interested in films with Black subject matter. But, if the major studios are going to finance Black films, for the most part it's two genres: You have the homeboy shoot-'em-up drug movie or you have a hip-hop musical comedy. I think Black film should be broader than that. Don't you?

But the studios have no respect for the buying power of the Black market, no belief that other people are interested in the films we make. They would like for us to believe that the people who are interested in, say, a Spike Lee film, have no idea that they together form a market. We have to prove the same thing over and over to the studios, again and again and again and again.

So as filmmakers we face the same glass ceiling that our brothers and sisters in white corporate America face every day. You've got to be into how much money a studio is going to spend to make your film—unless you're Eddie Murphy—and then how much money they're going to spend to market it effectively. This is not to say Hollywood doesn't want to make Black films at all. If they can keep making *Boyz in the Hood* for six million and take in $57 million, they'll make those forever. But what happens if you want to make films that are beyond those allowable genres? What happens when we want the same amount of money on the production budget, on advertising and marketing our films as for films done by the white boys? That's when we have problems. To this day, I've never had a film that's been in as many as one thousand theaters. The most we had previously was seven hundred, for *Jungle Fever.*

Racism permeates the whole fabric and structure of America, so why should the entertainment industry be unscarred by that? We could go to the Hollywood studios and go right down the line and see how many Black executives there are, number one. Number two, we could see how many Black executives there are *who can green light a picture.* Fox, Universal, Warner Brothers, MGM, Touchstone, Tri-Star, Columbia, Paramount—how many Black executives do they have, and how many can green light a picture? Well, if you did that, and then asked them point-blank, is it racism, they will say no, it's not because of racism, it's really because Hollywood is built on a network, an old boy's system, blah-blah-blah. But you know what the deal is—not to say it's 100 percent racist top to bottom, but that has to account for something there. At least a major percentage of it. So what we have to do is—we as a people have to stop bullshitting and start coming up with financing. I mean, I would love it if some Black investors or foreign investors would totally finance this film. It's a drag, you know, begging.

I don't mean just begging for a reasonable budget for what you want to do. I mean getting to do what you want to do in the first place. Creative control. Black cinema is written, produced, and directed by Black folks, and usually all three of them have to be Black for the film to stay Black. For instance, the motherfuckers behind *Soul Man* think they were giving us a social statement. C. Thomas Howell with blackface. To me that film was an insult to Black people because there is no way any real Black person in that film would not have known this was some idiotic white boy with shoe polish on his face and an Afro rug on his head. It was the same thing with *True Identity,* almost, only reversed. That's Van Peebles's old film *Watermelon Man* being done again and again. That shit is old and tired. *True Identity* was directed by Charles Lane, a brother. I liked his film before that, *Sidewalk Stories,* a lot. But why he wanted to do a film at Touchstone in the first place—now that's a real plantation over there. I would think that with Charles being an independent filmmaker, he'd get room. But they have motherfuckers on their sets every day, checking in. When you finish a shot, they're calling the studio. "All right, they're done with that shot, all right Charles, let's go." That's the way I've heard they make their movies over there. Fuck that.

So Black film is still in a kind of embryonic stage, I believe, partly because of the lack of work opportunity. I mean, it doesn't cost a million dollars to record a song if you're a singer, but the financial needs of a movie have tended to cut us out of the picture in the past. Right now we're just really at the beginning, where we're starting to make our entrée—not to say there weren't Black filmmakers before, but now there seems to be a more concentrated effort by African-Americans to enter this last frontier called movies, cinema, film. The further we move forward, hopefully the better the products will become and we'll have better and better filmmakers eventually. If we could make filmmaking as enticing as some of the other arts, or as popular as sports, we'd get there quicker. In film we haven't produced any Duke Ellingtons or John Coltranes or Michael Jordans or James Baldwins or Zora Neale Hurstons or Ella Fitzgeralds yet. We'll get there, but it's going to be a while coming. And it's only going to happen and happen steady and stay that way when you start to have more and more filmmakers who love cinema, who've seen movies, who know cinema history. If you don't love it, maybe you'll get lucky and make some money, meet some people, bone a leading lady, whatever. But I feel those are not really the right reasons to be in cinema, and it will become obvious in your work. Sooner or later your shit will be exposed as WEAK.

If *She's Gotta Have It* wasn't a hit, there would have been no way I could have made *School Daze.* Not with studio financing anyway. There would not have been this succession of films I've made. Five films in six years would not have happened, and I would not now be doing *Malcolm X* as number six. Or, if I had been doing it, I wouldn't have been doing it as well because my experience and budget would have been more limited. So it was luck, timing, and talent, a combination of those for me. I'm just one writer-producer-director. We've got to have more. We *do* have more.

Daughters of the Dust by Julie Dash is a fine film. And so is *To Sleep with Anger* by Charles Burnett, with Danny Glover. I think Charles makes a kind of art-house movie, which is fine. We need that. But it's like this—Jackie Robinson was not the most talented ballplayer when Branch Rickey picked him to integrate the major leagues. He saw that Jackie had been in the Army, had gone to college, was very disciplined, and he was *fast,* and so they chose him. History chose him. My problem is that a whole lot of those guys who were maybe more talented than Jackie Robinson in the Negro Leagues, instead of supporting Jackie, they were like, "Well, *I'm* better than Jackie." But you can't worry about it. I'm happy for John Singleton and *Boyz in the Hood,* and I hope he gets nominated for Academy Awards for director and screenplay. He should. He's like me in that he came along at the right time.

It's great that we got together, John and I, and found that we saw eye-to-eye on many levels. The reason John and I get along so well is that we recognize good cinema when we see it—we both love cinema, bottom line. And we're too smart to let people try to set us up against each other in any way. I wish I could say the same thing for Matty Rich, who directed *Straight Out of Brooklyn.*

Matty, I think, got some bad advice from some people. I mean, I had just met the brother, and he was telling me how the system was opening up. Opening up? So I was trying to help him. He didn't even know what distributors he could go to. The people he wanted to use, or had been told to use, Samuel Goldwyn, had distributed Charles Burnett's film and I felt they had bungled the release. So I said, "Look Matty, you should call Charles first." This was when he called me before his film was going to come out. I was glad, and glad to talk to him about it. Then Matty told me they were opening his film on the same day as *Jungle Fever.* I told him that was a little crazy and he ought to try and have the date of his opening moved. We'd be splitting the market, and it would hurt his film more than it would hurt mine. The next thing I know, I'm in the *New York Post:* MATTY RICH STEALS SPIKE LEE'S THUNDER. I couldn't believe it. He bought into that shit and came out swinging, attacking me. Was quoted saying I had a big fight with him and was yelling at him and was trying to find out when his film was going to open because I was worried he was going to steal my thunder, and that I had a lot of influence with the selection committee at the Cannes Film Festival and that somehow I had kept him out of the festival. It would take more than Matty's word to get me that kind of power. Matty was tripping.

It doesn't matter, because in my opinion, Matty's not going to be around long as a filmmaker unless he goes into the wood-shed and learns his craft. Matty don't love no fucking movies. He don't love cinema. I mean, he brags that he's never taken a class, that he's never been to film school, I ain't got no education in film, I ain't got this, I ain't got that. His movie reflected that shit, too. Not to knock him totally, because anybody that gets a film made should be commended for that, especially at his age. At the same time, I would advise my brother: You'd better go back in the woodshed and learn how to make a movie. Learn the craft of filmmaking.

It's like some of these young Black people run around talking about how doing well in school, or even *going* to school is "acting white." I think it's gotten critical now where you have—I want to say millions, but I'll say a lot of young African-Americans across the country, especially boys, who fail classes on purpose because of peer pressure. Speak "dems, dese, and dose," only because of peer pressure. Seems the fashion is that if you're intelligent, if you do well in school, then you are "acting white." But if you fail classes, if you hang out, if you get high—then you're Black and you're down. That's where ignorance is championed over intelligence, and that's not where we want to be. That's definitely not what Malcolm X was talking about.

It goes back to a value system, and I don't mean a white man's lip service value system either. I mean our own value system, our inherent value system, which doesn't include a lot of meat-eating, incest and disease, and lack of respect for women. Our inherent system of values, down from earliest civilizations in Africa, is not like that at all. So when I say value system, I don't mean Father Knows Best, because father is an alcoholic and is feeling up little Peggy. I mean our own value system. But our whole value system is, how else do I say this, fucked up. It's just completely fucked. When young people will fail classes or belittle their own intelligence to fit in with the rest—what can you say? It's gonna take some strong motherfuckers to say, "You might think I'm trying to be a white boy, but I'm going to get these A's if I can get 'em, and you can kiss my Black ass two times two, which is four, you ignorant-ass motherfuckers!"

They're just going to have to stay strong and not bend to peer pressure. Whether it's staying off unsafe sex, or drugs, or going hard after education, whatever. You just can't be doing shit because everybody else is doing it. And it's bullshit to put it on anybody but ourselves. Malcolm said we're the only ones who are gonna do something positive about our lives, so we have to take responsibility for them. You can't blame it all on the white man—that's part of our problem too. In fact, I think education of our younger brothers and sisters is totally on us and up to us now. You've got to own up to some of this shit we're doing. Sometimes, more often than not in some of these places in the United States, we're the ones killing ourselves. I guess whatever I'm thinking always ends back up with Malcolm X for the time being. By any means necessary. If a book or a film is the means, use it.

My means is filmmaking, and I don't think Warner Brothers knows what they have with this film. The anticipation of it is so high. Somehow they don't know that, or will act like they don't.

Everybody was asking me, even before we started shooting,

"When's the film coming out? Spike? When? When? When? I'm going to be there!" White and Black. Cabdriver to mogul. Recently, this one brother on the street asked me when the film was coming out. I told him at that time I thought it would be coming out next Christmas. He told me, "Then I'll be there Christmas Eve!"

And it's not just Black people who want to see this film. It's not just Black people who should see this film. I believe this is going to be a huge, huge film. Big. People have told me some people at Warner Brothers believe this will be their Academy Award film. And they'll probably tell me the same thing. Now let's see if Warner Brothers will back that shit up with money to shoot, promote, and market *Malcolm X,* and I'm talking about the same kind of money they spend on a film like *JFK.*

MONTY W. ROSS
Co-Producer

I think what Spike and I envisioned a long time ago, back in college in Atlanta, majoring in mass communications, sitting on his/our grandmother's front porch during summers, was knowing between ourselves that the day would come when Black culture could be represented in its truest forms in cinema, and that we could be the ones to represent that culture. All media, including film, as popular as it is, has been one of the slowest outlets in allowing Blacks to control the reflected image of their culture, to control the expressions of themselves. They always want to censor it to their liking, or to water it down. And what we envisioned was to be able to say, look, if we contribute 250 billion dollars or what-have-you to the United States every year, some of that money should be directed to us as investors in controlling our own destiny as it relates to the media.

We were taught in our college media classes that we were embarking on something that was very, very important. Therefore, strive to be the very best, get a job that is important, try to make some changes, and if you do become an entrepreneur in media, remember to look back at your own culture.

Hollywood was no different from any form of media. But we felt that the day would come. We had some examples.

Ossie Davis and Ruby Dee did it. Ossie said he thought his phone was going to ring off the hook when he was a younger man and they had gotten married and done a successful Broadway play. They thought certain other things would happen for them. When it didn't happen like that, they created their own avenues with Black people. They had to stay with Black people.

Consequently, as they grew, Black people around them grew, and that's what has to happen. That's what happened in Black entertainment back in those days. The Peacock in Atlanta and the Apollo in Harlem always had their place. You had Black spots all over the country, even the boondocks. Black musicians didn't really have to depend on the record companies because the record companies were ripping them off. So there was a circuit for that, just like there is a circuit for everything in our culture.

Now that has been wiped away and everything has been watered down and pushed to the side, yet we still have to survive within that mainstream which is now the only stream. Berry Gordy of Motown was another example. They were heroes to me because they were Black. I was trained on Malcolm X, I believe "by any means necessary," and I think I understand what it means. It's not that hard. Like all of Malcolm's statements, it's pretty clear. At Motown, the cats were calling their shots. What went on behind closed doors there I don't know, but I assume there was a lot. However, if you look at that roster of talent for that segment of music, that roster has never been duplicated since. So that's what we envisioned, to be able to put together a project that will represent our culture in the best sense of those words, that would be full of spirit, that would motivate people, that would be educational, yet at the same time be entertaining, so we could stay in business, so we could employ people at the same time, and take advantage of all our opportunities. And that's a big job. Last year, 1991, there were nineteen Black films, and people made a big fuss about that. This year, 1992, so far, how many . . . five? Six?

So, otherwise, unless we've got our own base to build from and do deals from, we're at the mercy of the system of Hollywood, not individuals. The individuals are fine. But what the system says comes out of individual mouths. And the system might say, "I've been looking at these statistics and I'm looking at your cost reports, and I don't know; it just seems like the Black films you people do, people aren't looking at them anymore, you know, guy?" And you have to be able to rise above that kind of thinking. Only the cream can rise to the top.

And all of those young people who are aspiring filmmakers, who are out there hustling because they've been inspired by what we might have been able to do so far, where do they go without a base? If we haven't created some kind of system of our own, where are they going? They go back out on the streets, throw their hands up in the air and then they say, "Let me go be a salesman at Macy's, I got a family to feed." I know. I've been there.

I have to listen to a Malcolm X tape every once in a while, and I'm talking about long before we started doing this film. I've always had to do this, just to remind me. It's like a father figure saying, "Okay y'all, it's gonna be hard, but this is what we're gonna have to do." You put that tape on and it's like, no matter how bad things are, it's like your father saying, "Hey man, you can get it done." And you calm right back down. He's the man, you've got to give it up to him. My problems now are not what Malcolm's problems were then, or what any father's were in a previous generation. But he laid it out for me, the path. He laid it down and he made it. He lived it, under much harsher circum-stances than what I've had to deal with. We are going to put down a representation of it, but he lived it, and at a time that in any moment he could have been killed, but he stood up strong and tall and didn't back down.

So, I'm just a child. A child who has been given a gift. Now I'm either gonna play with it, or do the right thing with it.

To me, you can't take this man's life (anybody's life, really, but most especially his) and mistreat it. Even though you are selling tickets to an entertainment event, it's still a man's life. There were many, many people who are now fifty, sixty, and seventy years old who actually lived through this too, and put their lives on the line. You don't want to be cavalier about that. They didn't know anything about a civil rights bill changing their lives, they didn't get a chance to grow up with Lyndon Johnson's War on Poverty in effect, they didn't know anything about that when they were out there getting their heads whipped. So you can't re-create that any way you choose, write them out of the equation. Nobody knew what was going to happen then. All these people just said, "Well, *something* has to happen." So you can't sell tickets on that. You can't think, "This is really going to advance my career, to work on this film, *Malcolm X.*" It will work against us if we think that, because you are taking the blood, sweat, and tears of people who didn't know what was going to happen. How could you take that and commercialize it only, and then sit back and say, "Well, I'm going to be a great so-and-so behind this." Can't do it.

You've got to let the spirit come through you instead. You're just a vehicle. You've got to get out of the way of it. If you're in there selfishly, it's going to work against you. I hope everybody who works on the film understands that. Selfishness is not what these people lived for, man! And some of them lived to see us as younger people tell a story, to use the camera, to go to school, and they are proud we have acquired this knowledge and expertise so that we can sit down with a $30 million budget, or whatever, and say who's gonna get this nickel and who's gonna get that dime and have all that paperwork together. They are proud that we can write the script. They are proud that we can run the production. Some of them still alive are proud that we can read and write, man! So we have to make them proud. If we make them proud, then I'm all right. Then I can go and celebrate because my job will have been well done. Then I can say I'm outta here. And going into this thing is something that Hollywood and everybody else really better take into consideration because they are losing sight of the spirit that could make this a great film if they keep talking about money. It's not always about money. We know how to make a profitable production. That's what we do. I just hope they recognize that. I feel people want to come out to see this film because they want to hold onto the art. In this case it would be something unfiltered, something uncensored, and when people have this, we want them to be able to say, "I've got my copy of the masterpiece, got my book, got my videotape, I've got my ticket stub to the first ever showing at so-and-so! I saw it happen, for once in my lifetime, and I want to hold onto it."

And as far as where I'm coming from personally, well, every now and then, to remind myself about where I've come from, I have to put on one of those Malcolm tapes. Have to put it on.

People will need to see this. The Rev. Martin Luther King was a middle-class Black minister who was dissatisfied with the social conditions around him. But Malcolm was from the streets, from the bottom of society, and he belonged to the have-nots, the miseducated, the uneducated. And he made his points just as clearly, his points were just as undeniable. So if we don't make this picture-perfect, it might do more harm than good.

Spike is ready for this. He's ready in every sense. You watch. Spike is going to get out of the way, he's going to check his ego at the door, he's going to let the spirit come through him because he knows Malcolm belonged to the people, and he knows how great the story is. Spike's thing right now is in taking his vitamins, riding his bike, getting into physical shape, because the way he makes films is physical, it takes a toll. I don't know how many people really realize that about him. He gives it all he has. Right now, I can see him getting into his thing, beginning to concentrate. Concentrate. Spike's on a mission. We all are.

PART TWO

THE PROJECT

January 1991

While we were shooting *Jungle Fever* in late 1990, I made up an initial design for the ''X'' cap. I'd already decided I had to do *Malcolm X,* and marketing is an integral part of my filmmaking. So the X was planned all the way out. I came up with a simple design—silver X on black baseball cap. The colors could be changed later on as the campaign advanced. It looked good. I started wearing it, and we began selling it in our store, Spike's Joint, and in other places. I gave them away strategically. I asked Michael Jordan to wear it, and he has. Then I asked some other stars to wear it and, what can I say, it just caught on. Then the knock-offs started appearing. These X caps are coming from everywhere now. It's raining X caps, X this, X that, sometimes without the wearers knowing the story behind the X. The word of mouth is beginning to pick up on this already.

See, I realized that being a Black filmmaker, I'm never going to have the same amount of money spent to market my films as I would if I was a white filmmaker with the same number of notches on his gun, the same amount of success. And I don't want to duplicate what happened to a lot of the Black filmmakers of previous generations in front of me—and some from today as well. They were artists and not businessmen, or at least more artist than businessman. I'd already been warned about that, not by a lecture but by life experience. When I was in film school, I would see these guys who had spent four or five years, and sometimes even longer, trying to raise money for their films. And these were often good films. But they were seen, if they were seen at all, as nothing but a blip on the screen before the public. If anything, we'd end up seeing them at a screening at a museum, or at a university, or during Black History Month, and that's all. But I knew I didn't want hundreds of people to see my films. I want millions of people to see my films.

I have to film and market and act accordingly. I want my films to be seen by as many people as possible, and I know a lot of that comes down to not only the quality of the product—which of course has to be good—but marketing. There are many good films that haven't been seen, or have been seen by fewer people than should have seen them. It comes down to marketing in the end, and my activity comes from knowing that nobody is going to spend $20 million advertising and promoting my films, at least not to date.

So I knew I had to get the necessary image out there, do the interviews, make the people know about this film. Then they would want to come see it, once I had. And marketing is something I'm very proud of—the only person who does marketing better than me, as far as artists go, is Madonna. She's the Champ.

I had hard experience from when *Do The Right Thing* came out in 1989, the same summer that *Batman* came out from Warner Brothers. We spent a lot of time figuring how we were going to combat that, to get our little share of the audience. *Do The Right Thing* did $28 million—pretty good for a film that cost

$6.5 million. It didn't just happen like that. Today, Horatio Alger would have to book promotional dates and understand multilevel marketing. We had to plan how to get ink in the face of *Batman* and all that paid-for hype on television and radio and with toy companies and other promotions with retailers. One thing we figured we could get for free—editorial space in the newspapers. That's why controversial or political subject matter can work well at the box office. I'm used to getting out there and pushing my films in any way I can. Film content is always in my plan. I try to show excellent taste in what I do, but I also do try to make thought-provoking films that are entertaining. It's a hard juggling act, balancing what is good business and good art, but it can be done.

It's time to round up my crew—the usual suspects. Monty, co-producer; Ernest Dickerson, cinematographer; Jon Kilik, line producer; Wynn Thomas, production designer; Preston Holmes, co-producer; Ruthie Carter, costume designer; Barry Brown, editor; Robi Reed, casting director. We'd been together a long time on projects now, some off and on, and I'm happy to see everybody getting other work because of solid successes we had as a group. Plus, we knew each other's moves, and I wanted that complete familiarity on *Malcolm X.* There was so much to do, we didn't need that little extra added attraction of having to break in anybody new on the fly. And luckily, everybody was down for it, everybody was available to work, although Ernest, photographer extraordinaire was getting ready to direct *Juice,* his first feature.

The largest budget I'd had up until that time was $14 million for *Jungle Fever.* Jon, Monty, and I originally submitted a budget for *Malcolm X* at $38 million. The people at Warner Brothers, Terry Semel, the president and CEO, and Bob Daly, the chairman and CEO (two CEOs, don't ask me), immediately said, "You're crazy." They told us to come back again with another budget, and they also told us they weren't going to spend a red cent over $18 million themselves. They wanted the total cost of the film to be $20 million at first, and I just remember thinking, "This film is going to cost way more than any $20 million to do it right. And I ain't doing it wrong." I was ready to get up then. I would get back to them on budget later. I had to decide on the script.

From talking to Marvin Worth, I knew the story of how there came to be so many scripts in the first place. Marvin Worth had known Malcolm back in the days when Marvin was a musician in New York—Marvin still wears snazzy threads and dark glasses, I asked Marvin if Malcolm was dealing when he knew him—this was long before Malcolm went to prison. ''Yeah, grass,'' Marvin said. ''That's all I knew about.''

''You know, Spike, I didn't even know there was a book called *The Autobiography of Malcolm X* when I got the rights. The idea just came into my head.'' Malcolm wasn't still living when I had this idea? ''No, no, no, no. He was dead. I got the rights in sixty-nine.''

Marvin said he had made calls to Alex Haley and Betty Shabazz, and that Alex was cool, although Marvin said he had to convince Betty. But what helped Marvin with Betty was that he was friends with James Baldwin, and he went after Jimmy to write the first script, using the autobiography as sort of a guide. Marvin said he also had made a deal with Alex to option *Roots*, which wasn't a completed book back then. But Columbia passed on that deal (!) and David Wolper got the rights to *Roots*. Somebody at Columbia caught hell behind that one, I bet.

Baldwin wrote the first script. At the time he was really drinking heavily, and eventually another writer named Arnold Perl helped him finish it. Perl was a writer who was blacklisted in the McCarthy era. Of all the scripts I read—a Baldwin-Perl script, a Calder Willingham script, a David Mamet script, a David Bradley script, and then the Charles Fuller script—no question, Baldwin's was by far the best. But it fell down in the third act, and I think I know why.

At the time James wrote that script, the Honorable Elijah Muhammad, the head of the Nation of Islam, was still alive; there was still a lot of bad blood between what was left of Malcolm's camp and the Nation. There was a split in the Nation itself. One of Elijah's sons, Wallace, formed a splinter group called the American Muslim Mission. Minister Louis Farrakhan had become head of the core Nation of Islam, still following the precepts of the Honorable Elijah Muhammad. And there were other more localized and independent splinter groups, different factions. There still are today. But at that time, James didn't feel he could really get into it too deeply. Some things weren't as clear then. The passing of time only helped me out a lot, because more and more people had come out and talked about Malcolm's split with Elijah and the assassination and that whole period of time more freely.

Marvin said there really had been no director under the Baldwin-Perl script. They brought in Michael Schultz for a minute, but they couldn't do a deal. Also—this is fifteen or so years ago, remember—Denzel wasn't around then, but Marvin said he had been thinking about Dick Anthony Williams in the role of Malcolm. Marvin had seen Dick in a stage play back then called *Big-Time Buck White.* Just a couple of years ago, Dick played the role of Big Stop, Bleek's (Denzel's) father, in *Mo' Better Blues.*

"It was just taking James a long, long long time to finish the script," Marvin said to me. "I don't know if you noticed in the script, but Jimmy had big problems with what happened behind closed doors with Malcolm and Elijah after Malcolm accused him of, you know, the thing about the babies. And Jimmy got scared, you know, he said how can we prove any of this? Jimmy called Arnold for help at the time to try to get the screenplay in order. But Jimmy worked a long time alone. He worked at Columbia, before we moved it to Warner's. Jimmy never worked at Warner's."

No shit Jimmy was scared. Fornication and adultery were two of the biggest offenses in the Nation, and Malcolm found out about all these young, beautiful intelligent sisters who had Elijah's babies. Elijah's weakness was young women. It came out later. Now, it's not like I would be making up this part of the story. I figured I could straighten out that third act.

Marvin said nothing was wrong with the original script but the third act, but that Columbia wasn't moving because the screenplay was too long. That's when the project was moved to Warner Brothers, and all these other scripts slowly came about. Calder Willingham, who co-wrote *The Graduate* with Buck Henry, wrote another Malcolm X script. I saw it; it wasn't the one, either. I'd heard that when Betty Shabazz read it, she looked up from her dinner and threw food at Willingham. Not that this means anything. She may want to do that to me. Then there was a script only Marvin had, by Joseph Walker, but Marvin said he couldn't find the only copy he had of that one. A few years later, Sidney Lumet got interested in the project, and he wanted to do a script written by David Mamet. This must have been around '78 or '79, because Sidney had just finished doing *The Verdict* from a Mamet script.

"Mamet wrote it pretty fast," Marvin told me. "We got the screenplay and disagreed with a lot of it—so did Warner's. My feeling was, the power of the speeches wasn't there. It would've been like doing the life of a singer without him singing a song. Malcolm was a guy who talked, who spoke, aside from all these other things. Without him speaking, it would be like doing the life of Elvis without what he sang. It would make no sense. And his character didn't jump off the page. Why, you can't name movie stars today with more charisma than Malcolm X had.''

Sidney Lumet didn't say no to any of this back then. He and Mamet went away for a while and came back with something else. But Sidney Lumet wanted Richard Pryor to play Malcolm. Richard Pryor? Marvin said Mamet's last script was, ''like, the great American liberal's civil rights dissertation, so I said, 'Let's go get a Black writer who's been there somehow.' I didn't want somebody who was just in awe. I wanted someone who had been there, if only a little. Someone who could feel it.''

Marvin had read a book called *The Chaneysville Incident* by a Black writer named David Bradley, around the same time he saw *Ma Rainey's Black Bottom,* August Wilson's play, at Yale. We must have been in the middle '80s by now. Marvin met August in New York, then at the Warner Brothers studios in L.A. August wanted to do it, but Marvin said he found out it takes August a long time to do his plays, he never had any experience with the screenplay form, his latest play, *Fences,* was coming to Broadway, and he had another one called *The Piano Lesson* in the typewriter. But Bradley had a script for the life of Otis Redding that Marvin liked, even though he said it wasn't shootable. So Marvin made some kind of deal with Bradley, who also took a long time to write a script because he was teaching. Marvin said he felt Bradley's script had authenticity in the Harlem and Boston street stuff, and his ear was pretty good for the dialogue, but that he didn't like the Alex Haley character.

''The Haley character took over the thing,'' Marvin said. ''It became more about this reporter, it was more about his life. He became the star.''

Yeah, that was sure right from what I saw. That's something I definitely did not want. What I definitely didn't like about the Bradley script was that he had the Alex Haley character in it. I felt it wasn't needed. No offense to Alex Haley, but I didn't feel he should be in this film. It's not a story of the book being made; it's a story about Malcolm X's entire life. I mean, I love Alex Haley and he did a great job, but I didn't feel his presence was needed in the film. I'd also heard that Eddie Murphy had read that particular script and he really wanted to play the Alex Haley character. If Eddie Murphy wanted to do it, it's a wonder that shit wasn't made right on the spot! But Marvin said that even though Paramount probably would have let Eddie do it, Jewison didn't want Eddie. Marvin said Norman told Eddie he was a movie star and Denzel was an actor. Marvin said Eddie wasn't real pleased with Norman saying that.

After I was brought on, David Bradley came out in an interview saying, "There's no way they'll let Spike have the final cut on *Malcolm X*." Why? Because I didn't want to do your script? Just because they didn't want to make *your* movie?

Finally, Denzel had been brought on by Warner Brothers. You probably know that Denzel had portrayed Malcolm in a stage play, *When Chickens Come Home to Roost,* around ten years ago. I heard Denzel wasn't particularly happy with the Charles Fuller scripts either, but I knew they had all worked together on *A Soldier's Story.*

James Baldwin knew Malcolm X; they were acquaintances—even good friends, I've come to believe. Also, I don't think there has ever been a writer to better capture Harlem and its people better than Jimmy Baldwin. Baldwin was brought up in Harlem, he was an African-American, a human rights advocate, and a great writer. So he had all the ingredients. The only place the script was lacking was in the last act, where we should clearly see defined the split between Malcolm and Elijah. So I had read five scripts: James Baldwin–Arnold Perl. David Mamet. Calder Willingham. David Bradley. Charles Fuller. There were good parts in all of them. I just felt that the last four didn't hold up. I also thought that those scripts were too short.

So, I went through the Baldwin-Perl script. I got it retyped and threw out everything I didn't need. Then I had a better sense of the length. I again went through the script, filling in holes. And in the end, I knew we had something that was worth shooting.

All I had to do was decide which script I wanted to do: rewrite or start from scratch. But I felt, "Why should I start from scratch when the best script, the Baldwin script, is right there for me?" As I've said, the last act was weak because of the uncertainty of how to portray Elijah Muhammad in the context of the film, but I knew I could work that out now, at least creatively. How Minister Louis Farrakhan would react, I didn't know. I just needed a little more feel for that whole situation, which would come from interviews.

Then came more negotiations between us and Warner Brothers. I flew out there in December of 1990, me and Monty and Jon Kilik. We sat with Lucy Fisher and Terry Semel and Bob Daly and Mark Canton, who had sent us a letter. I could see right there that they really didn't know what they had in *Malcolm X,* even though Daly said he wanted it to be their Academy Award film for

'92 and all this blah-blah-blah. And also they definitely did not want to spend the amount of money I needed to shoot the film. Yet I knew it needed to be made, and would be a success. I told them. I told them right at the meeting. I said, "This is a movie of three hours, for around $33 or $34 million, minimum." I don't know who shit first in that room. Well, you know how it is. This was the first official meeting and they didn't want to start anything; they still wanted to keep relationships good, so they all started smiling and saying, "Well, Spike, let's not talk about that right now. Let's not talk budget. Why don't you finish with the script and let's let the lawyers talk about all that other stuff. Let's not let that complicate our friendship."

They were like, we'll come to that bridge when we cross it. Right from the beginning, they kept putting the budget off.

During my very first meeting with Warner Brothers, I had tried to explain to them that this was a big, big film, that this was an epic film. Epic in period. Epic in length. And epic films cost money. To make a film look good, you need time. To make a film look great, you need lots of time. Ernest Dickerson is a great cinematographer who needs time to work properly, and time means a longer schedule. Plus, by working with the Baldwin-Perl script, the film had stretched into three hours plus. And in that script the whole trip to Mecca is only three pages, and that's three out of a 184-page script. But I'm seeing the trip to Africa as around fifteen minutes now. A 190-page script. All this means more money to do the film—which will pay off in the long run.

But no studio likes long films. The theater owners want to get as many showings as they can into each day. If you have a three-hour film, that's one less showing per day. And that's lost revenue, as they see it. But there had been cases over the last couple of years that showed length didn't mean much if it was a good film, an exceptional film. *Dances with Wolves* was a three-hour-plus film. There is no way a two-hour *Dances with Wolves,* or a two-hour *JFK,* which Oliver Stone was shooting, would be as good. And it would be the same thing with *Malcolm X.* We didn't want to shoot it in a cut-down, cut-back, second-class version.

The brass at Warner Brothers and I never saw eye to eye on the magnitude of the film. They still don't know who Malcolm X is. What scares me is that these are the people that are going to have to market the film, too. And that's why we had Paul Lee, a scholar on Malcolm X—been studying him since he was fifteen—come out to Los Angeles and give a seminar to Warner

Brothers, to their marketing staff, about Malcolm X. Because for the most part, let's be honest, Hollywood is predominantly male and Jewish, and all they think is that Malcolm X was anti-Semitic and hated white people and advocated violence. Now, if our own marketing people believe that, how are we going to effectively sell the movie? That's why we want to do what we did at Universal, which is bring in skilled Afro-Americans to help sell and promote the film, because we're going into uncharted waters with people we're not familiar with.

Warner Brothers is not endearing itself to me through this entire process so far—not that they care a gnat's ass about that. I think it's important to consider the relationship I had with Universal Pictures and the progression of the three films I did there. It was a learning experience for all of us, but we got along with Universal. We had our disagreements and our fights, but there was a mutual respect and I don't know if we ever got that respect from Warner Brothers. I'm sure we didn't. It was adversarial from the beginning, and I don't know if I will ever go back to Warner Brothers to do another film. It's funny, though. John Singleton wanted to get together with me over a Black Panther property that Warner Brothers owns, and they had to meet over there at the Warner Brothers building, which definitely looks like an old-time plantation with those white columns out front. They were telling John, "Johneeeey, don't believe anything Spike says, ha, ha, ha, ha." Right. John's sharper than that.

Corporations do business. I'm usually able to get along with the people I do business with. I have a relationship with them, like at Universal, but that was not the case at Warner Brothers. Their offices are run very differently. Universal is really a good situation for me because it's a hands-off situation. They let me alone. They let me make my films. And they never failed to turn their profit. I've never had somebody meddle as much as Warner Brothers has with me so far, and we haven't even started shooting yet. Of course, I realize I never made a $33 million film at Universal, either. So the higher the stakes, the more the studio wants to have a hand in the creative filmmaking process. I'm quite aware of that, but I can't afford to let them prove a point with *Malcolm X*. That's where you can blow it, especially on a film like *X*. This is important because I think that I would have a lot fewer headaches all along if Warner Brothers and I had gotten along better from the jump. But it's just the way they do things, or, you might say, the way I do things. It doesn't seem to mesh.

In fact, we wanted Warner Brothers to sell the project to Universal, but they weren't gonna do that. No . . . way. And Universal would have taken it off their hands, too, for the right price, I'm sure of it. I always knew, in spite of all the problems, we'd get the film made somewhere. It was going to be a profitable venture.

But we have to lead Warner Brothers by the hand and say to them, "This is what you have to do." They really don't know how to market to Black people. Not to say *Malcolm X* will appeal only to Black people, we hope everybody will go see it; well, not everybody, but all people who want to be enlightened about their history in this country. But Warner Brothers didn't seem to have a clue. We had to tell them, and we had to tell them again.

It always came back around to money, because there are two standards, the old double standard—there is the amount spent for a Black film and a different, much higher, amount spent on a white film. Same with marketing the two films. Unless you're Eddie Murphy, if you're Black, forget about it. That's why we're really gonna be in Warner Brothers's ass knee-deep all the way through the project, and I'm sure they'll be on ours as well. But when it's finally all over, I know we'll be vindicated. I know that. And when it's over, I'm *definitely* not going back to that plantation again! I'm hooking up with Harriet Tubman and taking that Underground Railroad to the Promised Land.

I'm so grateful to Oliver Stone, because he really is setting a precedent for us by doing *JFK*. Because the big battle down the line, outside of money, is going to be over the length of this film. Oliver was about to finish his film, and I was on the phone calling Warner Brothers asking, "How long is it? How long is it?" They didn't want to tell me. It wasn't until later that I found out the length of the film, from Oliver himself. He also told me how much they spent, how many prints they had, all this stuff. We admire each other's work, and he doesn't want to see me get the shaft, but he still has his own picture to finish and he does have to deal with Warner Brothers too, so he can't be diming on them too heavy. But he kept giving me enough to get by on.

And we're going to kick and scream if we don't get the same motherfucking shit they give Oliver Stone and *JFK*. This movie is just as important, or even more important, from our perspective.

We have a story to be told here, and we're tired of being slighted, where we have to take the short end of the stick again and again. How can they keep doing that? They always try and say, "Well, Spike, Oliver Stone has made more than $100 million with *Platoon,* and *JFK* might make that, and Denzel Washington's not the truly great movie star that has the box office appeal of Kevin Costner." I've heard this from them, that's their feeling, and it's bullshit, and the reason I know why is because they will spend $45 million on a film directed by Dan Aykroyd, *Nothing But Trouble.* Dan is a funny comedian, good actor, nice guy, and all that, but how is a first-time director going to get $45 million to direct a movie like *that?* How much money is that movie going to make either in primary or secondary markets? Look at *Bonfire of the Vanities.* How much money did they spend on that screen gem? Over $50 mil? What did it do? Bomb! And what about *Havana.* A $60 million bomb! Tickticktickticktick————BOOM! *Radio Flyer.* And we can go on and on and on.

When Jon Kilik had to slash the budget, he was really just marking stuff down. The budget was not realistic. It was always a $33–34 million film. Jon had cut the budget, we came in low, around $31 million, and we knew all along that Warner Brothers was not going to budge from $18 million, $20 mil tops, and that would include all contingency monies. By this time we were getting ready to go to Cannes with *Jungle Fever.* We wanted to see what they'd get for the foreign rights. We didn't know what Jim Miller, the guy who was supposed to sell them for Warner, would go for. Claude Berri, the famous French director, called me up at my hotel in Cannes and said he had just seen *Jungle Fever* and right away he asked how much it would take to buy the foreign rights to *Malcolm X.* So at that point, he was going to come in at around $7 mil, but then Largo, which is owned by Larry Gordon, came in with a larger offer—$8.5 million. Claude was only going for 7. He wasn't budging. I think Warner Brothers could have sold the foreign rights for much more. The foreign buyers see an $18 million budget, they think around $7–8 million for foreign rights. So the comparatively low budget hurt us again.

Now, there's also a clause in all my contracts which states that my films cannot be distributed in South Africa. When Largo bought the rights, they didn't know this fact. Warner Brothers didn't tell Larry Gordon he wasn't getting the South African rights, and I think when it finally was pointed out to him, he wanted to get some of his money back. Then there was this big fight, and it was decided those South African rights were worth a half-million, so we were back down to $8 million for foreign rights, a $26 million budget, total, to do a $33 million film. That plantation mentality. I'm starting to look for Harriet Tubman to come and rescue me. Harriet, where are you?!

In the end, Warner Brothers never budged from this: "Spike, we're giving you eighteen, and we'll sell the foreign rights, try to get as much as you want for them, but that's it." I said from the beginning the film would cost around $33 million. So going in we had a choice. We could try to get all the way down for whatever we could piece together, or wait another twenty years for this movie to be made, or go forward knowing that we are going to come up a little short in the end. But we will have the film in the can. Maybe we can try and get some outside investors to come in later.

You would think that would be the case, that Black investors would step up, but then again, there was nothing really there to offer them because Warner Brothers had the rights and the profit lines were drawn. They weren't going to cut their share. It comes down to this: We never had the money to shoot the film we wanted to do from the beginning. And that is what made it tense. But this was *always* a $33 million film, and when I make a $33 million film it's actually a $50 million film, because you *know* we have to know how to cut corners and do all kinds of stuff on the cheap or the quick without compromising the work. Black people have to do this all the time, making do with what you have.

You always have to stretch everything double. Everything!

What kills me is, all it's going to do is make money for Warner Brothers in the end. You got to spend money to make money. We don't want to be nickel and dimed to death on an important project like this. This film is too important. We had momentum. It would be a crushing blow to everybody in-volved—especially me—if this film were not to happen. As long as we're saying we're going to do it, and the momentum is behind us, let's go, we have to stop waiting for that pie in the sky when we die. So I said to myself, "Hell no! No delays over money-haggling. We're going to shoot this film by hook or crook. By any means necessary."

So all during these negotiations, from January of '91 right up until the time we started shooting in September, I was sitting down with different people who had been in Malcolm X's life. This was one reason I felt it was imperative that an African-American director do this film, because it required a lot of re-search, and I'm not just talking about academic research.

The research I'm talking about is talking to the people who

knew Malcolm intimately, who knew his life. Talk to his brother Wilfred; his brother Philbert; his sister Yvonne; Captain Yusuf Shah, who had been his first lieutenant and the security chief at Temple No. 7; Benjamin 2X, whom Malcolm converted; Charles Kenyatta; Minister Louis Farrakhan; many others who had been in the Nation or who had known Malcolm X.

No way would most of these people open up to someone who was not Black. There was no way you were going to get any sort of cooperation from current and former members of the Nation of Islam with a white director. No way possible. These Black folks just don't trust white folks. There is just no way. There's no way Farrakhan is going to let just anybody come to his house in Chicago. There's no way the Saudi government is going to approve a Hollywood film crew to go into Mecca for the hajj, the holy pilgrimage. It was not going to happen. So there were these certain things we had to utilize for our production. Clout!

These interviews would help me find out the essence of the man, and I had to talk to a lot of people to do that. With all these people still out there who knew Malcolm, this research would be invaluable. This process will take six to nine months. I'm sure—I hope—that I can get several revealing anecdotes out of this that will work their way into the final script.

Betty Shabazz has stayed far in the background on this so far. On numerous occasions she's been asked for documents, for clothes, for pictures, for access to Malcolm's home movies. She really hasn't come up with anything. Frankly, at this point she's been very sometimey. One day she would be all lovey-dovey—"Oh, I love you, Spike"—and the next day I'd be nothing but a cursed-out bum. Lately she's been asking to see the script. I'm hesitant, because there's an art to writing and reading a movie script. A layperson might have a hard time knowing the difference between what's on the page and what a shot looks like, or what makes up simple, effective narrative drive. I didn't want to give her a script until we actually started shooting the film in the fall.

So I started interviewing. Kicked it off with Benjamin 2X, Benjamin Karim, who is a character in the script. I sat down with him at the Parker-Meridien Hotel in Manhattan just as New Year's 1991 came in. He is called Benjamin Karim now. He had converted to the Nation of Islam right after a showdown in the streets of Harlem when Malcolm got a Nation of Islam brother who had been brutally beaten by the police out of jail and to a hospital with a show of force. Benjamin Karim had just been a kid growing up in Harlem then, but after he'd heard about it, he was so impressed with what Malcolm had done that he'd idolized him and joined the Nation after that. He became a brother based at Temple No. 7 in Harlem, Malcolm's temple, until Malcolm's split with the Nation. He'd stayed with Malcolm through his split with Elijah, then his assassination. Benjamin had been like Malcolm's son, and he had his own son with him when we met.

"I learned a lot from Brother Minister, I really did," Benjamin said. "He was an exceptional person. But he could be difficult. His eyes were warm when he was being humorous and felt amiable, but when he fixed his eyes on you, it was piercing and they were like ice. He had those grayish eyes, the man had eyes of ice. When he was teaching his eyes just . . . I don't know. I've never seen anyone else with such a penetrating gaze. He was private. I mean very private. I mean that to know him publicly is to see the outer person, but the inner person was really only expressed when he was with Muslims, when he relaxed and unfolded and opened up and joked. I was surprised when Fuller told me that there were brothers who said Malcolm never smiled. Man, that man used to have you rolling on the floor! And he could admit if he made a mistake or a wrong judgment. And he would do it with a teaching.

"There was this one sister who worked in one of our restaurants. She never smiled. He told us one day that most of a waitress's salary was tips, and she would get better tips if she smiled. So I told her this, and she told me the reason she didn't smile was because her teeth were bad. We went back and told him. And then later, he told this story, a lesson, a parable, about a man who was looking through the window of a building and saw a man lying prone on a table and another man sticking a knife in him, drawing blood from his stomach. The man outside ran and called the police and told them he had witnessed a murder. The police told him, the building you're looking into is a hospital. The man lying prone is a patient. The man with the knife is a surgeon. He's not killing the man, he's saving his life. And then, Brother Minister took up a collection for the sister, so she could go to the dentist and have her teeth fixed."

Benjamin had been there, all right. I asked him if he'd traveled abroad with Malcolm and he said no, he hadn't. Abroad, Malcolm usually traveled alone. Benjamin also said he believed Malcolm's famous "chickens come home to roost" quote about the Kennedy assassination was just a means of gaining some separation from Elijah Muhammad, that he never thought it would escalate any further. I didn't know about that. It was difficult, even after all these years, talking to Benjamin about the assassination. He was a little evasive at first, but he had good information. Later on, so would people like Charles Kenyatta, Earl Grant, and A. Peter Bailey. They'd been there. Benjamin told me Captain Yusuf Shah, one of Malcolm's No. 1 men, the head of the FOI (Fruit of Islam) had not left the Nation of Islam when Malcolm did, as Karim had, and that this was key to Malcolm's demise.

We went over the floor diagram of the Audubon Ballroom that fateful day. Benjamin had introduced Malcolm to the crowd. He told me two women were there, women who were pivotal in Malcolm's intricate understanding of the U.S. government and geopolitics. He said one of those women works for "major television" now and would probably not admit she was loyal to Malcolm, even though she was there the day he was assassinated.

The week before, Benjamin said he had convinced Malcolm to take his rifle, an M-1, to use to defend his house in Queens— this was before it was bombed. Benjamin said Malcolm only had a 7.62 bolt-action rifle—ironically the same kind of rifle that supposedly killed Kennedy. Benjamin told Malcolm that bolt-action was no good, too slow, that he couldn't get off but a round at a time.

To ease things up, we went back to happier times.

"Malcolm drank milk with his dinners," Benjamin said. "He drank a quart of milk when he ate. And he could eat too, he could eat five banana splits, one behind the other . . ." That made me think about the autobiography. Malcolm made those banana splits for his first girlfriend, Laura. She had loved them. Malcolm was guilty all his life about Laura, saying he had "wrecked that girl" by exposing her to nightlife in Boston.

I eased Benjamin back to the assassination. I could see that to talk about it still affected him. But I needed to know how it actually was, as close as possible. The assassination would be one of the pivotal sequences in the film. It had to be done right.

"Malcolm could walk across the floor and you couldn't hear him if you weren't looking, all right?" Benjamin said. "So he had walked out of the dressing room and I didn't know it. I walked out to look around the crowd. And I felt this thing, man, I really did. I kept noticing there were two brothers—Malcolm always said that whenever Muslims came in, let them stay regardless of where they came from. But there were these two brothers sitting down front . . . I would give it twenty seconds between the time

I left that stage and the time that Malcolm was lying on that stage dying . . . all of a sudden I hear these firecrackers, pow-pow-pow-pow, and heavy explosions, voom-voom. When you're hit with a sawed-off shotgun, man, you're knocked off your feet . . . The doctors later said he was medically dead before he hit the floor . . . brother Reuben shot one of the guys trying to escape . . . I was just looking at Brother Minister. And the way he was staring, you know, he was just—I knew he was dead."

Ease up for a minute. I asked Benjamin if they were allowed to watch movies, and he could only come up with one. *Lawrence of Arabia.* So I asked him, "Would he critique it, or was it just for enjoyment? Would he show it as an example of a white man's version of history, or was it just supposed to be enjoyed?"

"Oh," Benjamin said, "there was never anything presented for enjoyment in his teachings without a lesson."

Back to the job. I told Benjamin I had spoken to the lawyer William Kunstler, and to Thomas Hayer, also known as Talmadge Hayer, one of the assassins, who has been out of prison for two years now. Through research we feel that there were five assassins. Hayer had a .45, one guy had a sawed-off shotgun, another one had a Luger, and they were all from Mosque No. 25, a New Jersey Mosque of the Nation of Islam. Hayer made me think of those other four guys. One is dead, the other three are still around, and not one of those guys ever spent a day in jail. "If it did come down that way," Benjamin finally said, "it would have had to come as an order from the officials in Chicago. They could have never done that without their sanction. They would've never done that."

I asked him if he thought this was a case where the Nation and the U.S. government had colluded. Benjamin said if that was the case, it would have had to be filtered through John Ali, a member of Temple No. 7, who always talked about the FBI.

"What would Malcolm think of the state Black people are in now?" I asked. "Would he be sad?"

"Yes."

"What would be his biggest disappointment?"

"He was a fanatic for education. He once said that the Black college student would be very instrumental in the liberation of Black people. He would always try and surround himself with people who had academic knowledge. He had great respect for it. That's why he sorta liked James Baldwin. Malcolm knew Baldwin was an intellectual, but he also knew Baldwin wasn't brainwashed."

"Did he know Baldwin was a homosexual?"

"Yes. He knew Baldwin. He might make an allusion to it, but he respected Baldwin. I once asked Brother Minister what was the strongest urge in a human being. You know what he said? He said the urge to eat. He said, 'If you go without eating for a week, and then bring in your wife naked and a plate of lamb chops . . .' "

I laughed and wished I could find a way to use that.

"The brothers close around Malcolm weren't afraid of anything," Benjamin said. "Brother John. Brother Ivory, a few others . . . they all had been trained. I mean trained in deadly hand-to-hand combat. One night, Sensei took us out for training and told a brother named Cyril to get in his car and drive toward him at precisely 60 mph. He would just stand there. Cyril balked, said, 'Naw, Sensei.' So Sensei ordered him. His job was to train the FOI, the Fruit of Islam, so Cyril being a young brother, he had to do what Sensei said. Cyril got in the car and gunned it toward him. Sensei just stood there. He just stood there. Then he jumped, folded, barely touched the roof of that car with his feet. When he came down he was squatting with a pistol, and the sight was on that car. This was Sensei."

Me, I was kind of skeptical, so I said, "He was like James Bond, eh? Or more Like Action Jackson."

"Like? No, Mr. Lee. Brother Minister used to say one never needs to read fiction because the truth is stranger. Sensei was a real person, an exceptional person. I asked him one night at the restaurant if he was going to teach the other brothers the martial arts. He said, 'No. I'm going to teach them death.' "

Benjamin Karim said this Sensei character, even though he had trained many Muslim bodyguards, almost met death himself after Malcolm's assassination. Some of Malcolm's group plotted to kill him because they suspected he had something to do with it because much of his training stemmed from the Oriental martial arts methodology. And one of those arts was something Benjamin called Chung Fa, I think it was, and one of the legends of that discipline is the legend of the five archers sent to assassinate a statesman. There were five people involved in Malcolm X's assassination, and the people involved in it were very well trained. So I asked Benjamin if this Sensei was a Muslim himself, and he said yes. "He knew the Koran almost by heart," Benjamin said. "I believe his mother was Oriental and his father was Black. But he was a brother, believe me. And the way he appeared to have no use for whites was hardened in him. As a matter of fact, even when we met him years before this, we were the ones in the Nation, and he was the one calling them devils.

"But Malcolm, Spike, was not just a revolutionary, man. He was a philosopher. This man absolutely studied deeply. And toward the end just before the 'chickens come home to roost' thing, I began to sense something in him that changed. That's why I wasn't surprised when he left. Naturally he was suspended by Elijah Muhammad, but he may have maneuvered this himself.

"He was an expert in etymology. Once we went to the Barry Farber Show. There was man working there and Malcolm asked him if he was Greek, and the man said yes, and Malcolm started speaking to him in Greek. Gave him a saying. Malcolm would take the word and take you so far back with it, take you to the history of that word. It was astounding, man. His knowledge of root words was really astounding. And he had a very, very deep understanding of natural law, the behavior of creatures as it applies to man. Because he understood, he used to go into that in order to give us a yardstick of how to measure things that change against things that don't. Like the leaves, the trees, they appear dead in winter, but they come back to life. The living from the dead and the dead from the living. Change and the unchangeable. These things were constant in what he taught about. This is how he taught us to measure human behavior."

Malcolm's mother, Louise, had died only the year before, 1991, at the age of ninety-five, up in Michigan, where she had been living with one of Malcolm's sisters, Yvonne. I asked Benjamin if Malcolm had ever talked about her and he said no, he hadn't.

"You know," said Karim, "he was hit sixteen times."

"Did you go to the funeral?"

"Yeah I was there. Sensci was there too, sitting right there at the end."

"He was there?"

"Yeah."

"To make sure he was really dead, huh?"

"I always thought he had something to do with it."

I asked him if he felt I should talk to Minister Louis Farrakhan. Karim told me to turn off the tape, then he said, "Yeah, you talk to him. You do that. Get his view. But listen, Spike, don't have Malcolm shown doing drugs or running around with white women. For your sake, whatever you do, don't do that."

I didn't say anything. I knew all that was in our script. And I knew some people would have problems with it. Benjamin Karim would not be the last person to talk to me about my own security in relation to doing this project.

When I talked to David DuBois, the son of the late, great writer and Black intellectual, W. E. B. DuBois, David said the same thing, but he was more blunt and meant it in a much different way than Benjamin 2X had. He was coming from a different place.

DuBois had lived in Ghana for some time, and then in Cairo. He had been there when Malcolm came through, and he'd met him. He said Malcolm looked very calm and thoughtful when he met him, not haggard at all, not like he was hunted, although by that time he *was* hunted. David was working as a journalist at that time.

"Cairo and Accra were two independent African capitals in sixty-three and sixty-four, near the high point of African liberation," David told me. "Both cities hosted and welcomed and supported the liberation organization representatives from all over the continent. Maya Angelou and I sort of worked as the liaisons between the African-American members of this mission, the U.S. mission in Cairo, and the liberation organizations. Maya was a great hostess. She would give these fabulous functions to welcome the visiting African-Americans.

"It was this mood of liberation that Malcolm attached himself to when he came to Africa, this euphoria of African liberation. I'm sure it impacted him tremendously."

DuBois said Malcolm was under U.S. government surveillance by this time, but he had protection from the Egyptian government—two Egyptian security men outside his door twenty-four hours a day.

"Malcolm brought this consciousness back to America, and in one important way he still survives," said DuBois. "African-American studies is now aimed at correcting that weakness, that failure in the educational system. I'm not talking about Black being superior, the beginning and end of all existence, where Black people are somehow the new pharaohs. It has to do with a recognition, number one, that European education has deliberately ignored and aborted Black history, African-American history, and African history long before that, to face reality. There is a knowledge now, a consciousness, an awareness of Africa as part of world society, as contributor to world culture, as valid and older than European contribution, as old and valuable as

Asian culture. To suggest that all culture, all society, all intellect had its origins in Europe and is superior is ridiculous. Untrue. And in that context, what happened to Malcolm X prepared him to launch these kinds of questions and ideas on African-Americans.''

David looked at me.

''But efforts have been made to destroy any possibility of Africans and African-Americans coming together in any kind of way. They don't want this. Any leader who starts to talk about Africa and African-Americans, watch out. And that's one thing I want to raise with you right here and now. Be careful about your own security, Spike. You've got to be careful about security.''

Me?

''Yes, you.''

Because of the movie?

''Because of this movie in particular.''

Anybody who knows me knows I travel around by myself a lot. I don't have bodyguards and all that. For what? I haven't had a need for it. But I did hear what David DuBois had said.

I went up to see Bob Haggans, who took many photographs of Malcolm and was seen by many as his unofficial photographer. Bob lives up in the Bronx. The only time I go up there, usually, is to turn out for a game at Yankee Stadium. It had been a while.

''Earl Grant and I worked together, mostly,'' said Haggans. ''It was Earl Grant who shot the picture of Malcolm lying on the floor, not me. But everybody thinks I shot those pictures because I sold them to *Life* magazine. I was the one who made the deal.

''I was the one who tripped Thomas Hayer. It was chaos. But then Malcolm came down the stairs on a stretcher, and I looked at him as he went past. His mouth was open, eyes rolled back in his head. And as he went by, I thought, 'He's not gonna make it.' ''

Bob showed me a lot of old photos that he had—some of it was very fascinating stuff. ''This picture with Farrakhan and Malcolm together has caused a lot of problems for me,'' he said as he spread the photos out in front of us and picked one up. ''The clients who buy my pictures, mostly white people now, like from, say, *Cosmopolitan* magazine or from European magazines or whoever, they always ask if I can cut Farrakhan off the picture.

''Malcolm didn't have a dime for himself that I knew of. He

wasn't that kind of leader. Half the pictures I'm showing you I paid for out of my own pocket. Paid for 'em myself. Boy didn't have no money. Didn't have a dime. He had given over every dime he ever collected to Elijah.

"Malcolm called me from Miami right after the Cassius Clay–Sonny Liston fight in Miami in 1964. I'm the first person that Muhammad Ali spoke to on the phone after he won the world's heavyweight title. Malcolm called and said, 'I want you to speak to the Heavyweight Champion of the World.' I said, 'Who is it? Who's there?' Then I heard Muhammad Ali say, 'Assalaam-alaikum, brother.' The next day, I met them both at the Hotel Theresa. When I walked into the room, Malcolm was sitting on the bed. Ali was hiding behind the door. I didn't see him. When I walked in, I heard this voice say, 'Put your hands up. Stand over there. I heard what you said about me behind my back.' It was Ali. He says, 'Put your hands up. You're gonna do five minutes with me!' So—man, this cat was throwing punches! Playing of course, but I had to stand stock still because I knew he wasn't trying to hit me, but if I ducked, I might duck right into one of those punches and be knocked out. All I could do was stand there, smile, and hope that his aim was good. I could feel the wind as they went past my head. And Malcolm was sitting there, laughing. He said, 'You can take him, Haggans, go on. Do four rounds with him.' Finally I said to myself, 'I'm gettin' outta here.' We all went downstairs and then we took a walk through Harlem together."

Mob scene, I bet. He showed me pictures. Yeah!

"Oh yeah," he said.

"What's this guy's name, Haggans?"

"Oh, that's a brother from New Jersey. They cut his head off. They found it in a garbage can."

"Yeah?"

"Yeah. I can get his name for you from Earl."

"What did he do?"

"He said something."

I laughed then, but Haggans didn't. "Man, say the wrong thing and you were in trouble. I'm telling you. He said something out of line and the next thing you know . . . this is Dick Gregory right here . . . the fat Dick Gregory."

Pre-Bahamian diet.

"This is Malcolm telling Muhammad Ali what to say and what not to say. I gotta be careful what I'm saying to you, today. This is Captain Yusuf Shah."

"He was Malcolm's bodyguard, wasn't he?"

"No, he was captain of the FOI—the Fruit of Islam. He was much higher than a bodyguard. He was close to Malcolm."

"Didn't he go with Elijah when Malcolm split? I'm asking."

"Yeah, you are asking, and now you got that on tape, too. Leave that one alone. You can put two and two together. Somebody on the inside had to set him up. I'm not naming nobody. That's not my job. I'm a photographer. I take pictures.

"But I'm gonna tell you something. I learned an awful lot from this man. He changed my whole life. He changed my attitude about myself. He changed my attitude in relation to other Black people. He said the average Black man don't know what time it is, that's why he can't keep time, he don't know what time it is. He said the first thing you gotta do in the morning is find out what time it is. Then find out how the world is and your relationship to that world. What role do you play. Then you can understand how and who you are. If you don't know who you are, you can't do much.

"People come to me sometimes and want that picture of Malcolm with his fist balled up. I got rid of that a long time ago. Malcolm told me, 'Brother Haggans, I can get anybody to do that. Why should I pay somebody when I need a picture, if all you are gonna do is project the image that all the rest of them are projecting, do what the rest are doing to me? I don't need that.' Man, I felt like two cents when he told me that."

I laughed.

"He told me show him as a human being, and from that day on, that's exactly what I did."

Haggans gave me one more thing I could use. He was at the Audubon Ballroom when Malcolm was shot. He told me he had seen that the anteroom was filled with cops.

"Hell yes," he said, "it was filled with cops. If I took a guess, I'd say twenty-five. It was filled with cops. Cops who must've waited until after he was shot to file into the ballroom."

I felt I had enough background now to speak with the surviving members of Malcolm's family, outside of Betty Shabazz and his daughters. I'd already spoken to Attalah, but she and her sisters were too young to have many detailed memories of their father.

Now I wanted to hear from his much younger brother, Bob, and his older brothers and sisters. But first I wanted to speak to a historian, and who better than Dr. John Henrik Clarke. Dr. Clarke has to be well into his eighties, and he's a foremost scholar not only on the history of Africa but of African-Americans. Yet by virtue of his long life, he also had personal experiences that went beyond history books. I met with Dr. Clarke the day before I was to meet Bob Little. Dr. Clarke was a great help. First he gave me a criticism of the television production of *Roots*. He didn't think television had done such a great job with it. He also gave me some insights into Betty Shabazz, gave me some things to think about, and talked about how Malcolm had changed—and how he hadn't—at the time of his death. We also talked about Snow Hill, Alabama, because Dr. Clarke is from Alabama. My great-great-grandfather, William James Edwards, had founded Snow Hill Institute there. Dr. Clarke knew of it.

I asked Dr. Clarke which assassination, King's or Malcolm's, had been more detrimental. He said, "Both were, but perhaps Malcolm's more so. All the working-class people could feel a Malcolm X. They could hear Malcolm X, and two weeks later they could whisper back what he said. Verbatim. They could remember the way he put it, and he put it so well. The day after King spoke, they knew he had spoken well, but they couldn't exactly say what he said. Malcolm X found the language that communicated across the board, from college professor to floor sweeper, all at the same time, without demeaning the intellect of either."

Dr. Clarke told me Malcolm had turned down a million-dollar offer from the Arab world to break from Elijah and start his own mosque, which would have given the Arab world a voice in the West. "He wouldn't have broken from Elijah," said Dr. Clarke. "I think he loved that old man like a father. He had a beautiful devotion to him . . . there were a lot of people in the Nation stealing and thieving—and they knew if Malcolm took charge as successor, they could never get away from that.

"I met him in the early fifties. In 1958 I was broke, scholars are notorious for it. I was the head of an African and American exhibition, cultural director. There was a girl who was, I think, Hungarian, who was assisting me. Malcolm X and others came in to see the exhibit. Later he asked me, "Is that your woman?" I told him no. He said, "Good."

"He said that?" I asked.

"He said, 'Good,'" repeated Dr. Clarke. "He said, 'I've been down that road, brother, and it's a dead-end street.'

"A pattern of friendship developed between us until he died.

A standard joke between us was that I was a swine-eater. He said he'd give me credit for being ninety-nine percent human, and that he'd give me one hundred percent if I'd stop eating swine. He'd be proud now because for health reasons I had to get off pork. I think the real awakening of the man had occurred in prison. But that's going to be tough for you, dealing with the inner man and his moods. It's something the Japanese do very well. There are some long silences in Scandinavian and some Japanese films, when the audience knows action is taking place, but the audience hears no action . . ."

"Which doesn't go over well in American films," I finished.

"No, you're right. They want bang, bang, bang. So how can you reflect a man being reborn, transformed, and then again?"

I paused. "I told Warner Brothers that this film has to be at least three hours long, Dr. Clarke. That's how. So what are Black people to do, Dr. Clarke? With all your experience, what would you say? I know people are going to say to me, 'Well, what about *solutions*, Spike?' What do you suggest I say to them? We're waiting for another Malcolm X to come along?"

"No, Spike."

"We can't put that much on any one person."

"Right. No, you cannot. In order to have a charismatic leader you have to have a charismatic program. Because if you have a charismatic program, then where if you can *read* you can *lead*. When the leader gets killed while you're reading from page thirteen of your charismatic program, you can bury the man with honors, then continue the plan by reading from page fourteen. Let's keep on."

Umph!

I met Bob Little, Malcolm's younger brother, the next day, at Junior's, a restaurant in Brooklyn.

"There were eight children in all," Bob told me. He is a commissioner with New York's Department of Human Services. "The eldest was Wilfred. He was in the Nation. Hilda is a little more reclusive. She lives in Boston now. Then Philbert. His name is Omar Abdul Azziz now. Reginald, Wesley, Yvonne . . ." He ran it down, then confirmed that his mother, Louise, had died just a year before this, at the age of ninety-five. He said she had gotten out of a mental institution a year or two before Malcolm was assassinated, and had lived a long time with Philbert in Lansing before finally moving and living out her years with her daughter Yvonne in Woodland Park, Michigan. I would have loved to have gotten a chance to speak to her myself! Bob also confirmed that Earl Little had one eye. Earl Little was not Bob's father, though. Earl Little had a family with three children before he got divorced and remarried to Louise, Malcolm's mother.

Philbert had said some things about Malcolm to the media that I would have categorized as traitorous. "But Philbert says he was tricked into that, Spike," Bob said. "But then again, you know, Philbert has always been tricked into things, to let him say it. I think the family was very pissed off. We were hurt by it, definitely. But, and this was especially true in Malcolm's case, you don't really change a whole lot from a child to when you get to be older, an adult. I would imagine your family would say the same things about you, you know?"

"Character is character."

"Yes. And my observation from the records I've seen and in talking to people is that Malcolm was not the big-time hustler he was made out to be by Alex Haley's book. He hustled, but everybody hustled one way or another because it was about trying to survive. I think the book was heavily dramatized.

"Malcolm had—I never met anyone who knew him personally that didn't feel warmed by his presence. He was a good dude, a person you would want to hang with. He was comfortable. He enjoyed good conversation. He laughed, and liked to laugh. You know, you had to laugh to keep from crying sometimes.

"He recognized the status of the Black man, and if you understand the forties, fifties, and sixties status of the Black man, we didn't have a whole lot to be proud of, right? In fact, we didn't even like to be called Black until Malcolm came, right? So the essential part of what Malcolm did was present a strong Black male father figure who was about things, who was an organizer, who was about social justice for his people, who was about building a Nation. And he was relentless in what he was doing.

"He talked about Black people psychologically becoming reconnected to their own cultures, specifically African-based cultures, for purposes of self-respect and self-worth."

"That's happening," I said.

"Is it? Is wearing kente cloth a psychological connection or a commercial opportunity?"

"It can be both."

"I'm just a poor social worker, Mr. Lee."

"But I understand what you're saying."

So on February 2 of last year, I went to Detroit to sit down with Malcolm's surviving brothers and sisters in a group. We met at John Salley's house in Detroit. John, who played for the Detroit Pistons, had bought a huge property that used to belong to the Catholic church, or something. It's a huge house, and John was gracious enough to lend me several rooms where we could conduct the interviews. John cooked a meal; it was all very nice. Malcolm's brothers Wilfred and Philbert came, and his sister Yvonne, who started things out by saying, "My mother never cursed. She didn't use profanity. Remember that."

I asked Wilfred and Philbert if their father Earl had a glass eye. "Oh, yes," Philbert said. I asked if he could take it out. Wilfred said, "Oh sure, he could take it out and clean it."

I told them a funny story about a glass eye to break the ice: When I was at Morehouse, there was a very mean instructor in the drama department—Joan Lewis. She would just ride you, ride you, ride you. She had a glass eye. They were doing a play, and she was riding a student named Rusty Hamilton really hard. She was unmercifully hard on him. He was on a stepladder hanging a light and she was saying, "You stupid so-and-so," and kept it up until Rusty jumped down and choked her. Her eye popped out and was rolling around on the stage, looking at everybody.

They laughed.

Then Philbert said, "Malcolm liked to laugh, too. He wasn't an intensely criminal person at any point, I don't think. Every time he did something, he got caught, arrested. There's more made of that in the book than what actually was there."

I figured that. But Malcolm knew what he was doing in the book, too. He wanted to show a bigger change.

"Well, I know he was no criminal," said Philbert. "Not even in his own mind."

Wilfred said, "He was just trying to find a place."

They told me about their mother, who was from Grenada, and their father, who was from Reynolds, Georgia, originally. They'd met in Canada. They told me how, years after their father was killed and left on trolley tracks in Lansing, the state took them and committed their mother for all those years, giving her drugs and shock treatments. "My father was a carpenter," Philbert said. "He was in the building trades. He knew brick masonry, cement work. And most any house we'd live in, he'd built it. The last house we lived at in Omaha, he'd built that with his bare hands. And he'd built the one in Lansing, as well. He was used to being independent. We lived in East Lansing, then eventually he bought acreage south of the city and built 'cause he wanted to get where he could have enough land to raise his own food, have everything and be independent. He was used to being independent. 'Cause in those days if you spoke out and didn't kowtow and you were a Black boy, well, you couldn't keep a job. And wherever you worked, a committee of white people would go there and talk to your bosses and they would have to let you go. That's what happened to my father. And when he built houses for himself and his family, we were burned out. But before that we raised all our own food and my mother would can enough to last us through the winter. We had our own chickens, our own eggs, everything . . .''

''And a goat,'' said Yvonne.

''Yeah, a milk goat. And all that made us independent, and we didn't have to go along with the program that they had intended for us. The ones in town, if they wanted to keep their jobs, they'd go along with it. But us—we were called those old 'uppity' niggers that lived out south of town.''

''Called this by Black and white, right?'' I asked.

''Sure, Black people and white people referred to us like that,'' said Wilfred. ''Them Littles. Some Blacks didn't want to be known as acquaintances of my father's, as his friends, because he might put a mark on them. Because he was very active trying to get something going as far as Marcus Garvey was concerned. He would take people from Lansing into Detroit where they could meet people involved with United Negro Improvement Association, UNIA.''

''Did you ever meet Garvey?''

''Garvey came to our house in Milwaukee,'' said Philbert. ''At the time, my mother and father warned us, don't tell anybody he's been here. At the time he was moving about in such a way as to be discreet because the government was trying to deport him.''

Wilfred said, ''My mother was a secretary at the newspaper at the time, called *The Negro World.* I can remember Marcus Garvey dictating to her some letters he wanted her to write. And my mother used to write articles for *The Negro World.''*

So the need to fight for freedom, that unconquerable dissent, was in Malcolm's blood, even before he was born.

''My mother in her younger days would've looked something like Lena Horne,'' said Philbert.

''Dorothy Dandridge?'' I asked.

"You know Dorothy Dandridge?" Philbert said.

"She was nice, wasn't she?" added Wilfred.

"She was tough," said Yvonne, flatly.

Then I asked them, "When the state broke up the family after your father's death, how were you parceled out?"

This seemed to cause a little confusion among them briefly. Wilfred said all were parceled out but the two eldest, himself and Hilda. They were allowed to stay at the house. Yet Philbert said he also wasn't parceled out, but went to work for a family called the Hacketts, who paid him and boarded him for work.

Yvonne said, "It was the youngest five of us who were warded out, Malcolm, Reginald, myself and Bob, Wesley, five of us."

"Who committed your mother?"

"The state," said Wilfred.

"But someone has to sign the paper," said Yvonne, anxious to discuss this. "And this Dr. Hoffman, apparently, is the one who did. It was Dr. Hoffman and Judge McCollough . . . but there was something shaky going on there, all right . . . it was seven years after my father was killed. I was two when he was killed, and I was nine when my mother was committed . . . although they had started messing with her right away."

I asked Yvonne, "Did you sell the land you had, or did the state take it?"

"The state took it," she said, "and we need to fight that."

I asked them why their mother had been committed for so long. It was Yvonne who had eventually gotten her out, after over twenty years. I asked her if the institution had kept her drugged.

"Yes."

"Oh yes," Philbert added.

"Experimenting, that kind of shit?" I asked. I will lapse from time to time when it comes to what's called profanity.

"The Upjohn plant was not far from there," said Yvonne.

"They also gave her electric treatments," said Philbert.

"Shock treatments?"

"Yes."

"But she was strong. She only died last year, and all that seems like so long ago to me. If you spent time with her, as I did, she'd have some good conversations. I run a little store at home, so I didn't always have time during the day. But at night, we'd talk. She had a pacemaker. That helped."

"Made her a new person," said Wilfred.

"Yvonne had taken her to the doctor," Philbert said. "He'd

checked her out and found out what she needed. A pacemaker. That might have been part of her problem for a long time."

"For years," said Yvonne. "You know, as we're telling this, we want things to be done right, but I guess I have some concerns about where Betty, Malcolm's wife, fits into this also."

Wilfred agreed. "This should be said plain," he said. "How can Betty know anything about my mother? She has six children. Yet those children have never spent any time at all with us, and it isn't because we don't want to see them."

"We've tried to see them," said Yvonne.

"But she doesn't allow them to come," said Wilfred. "Except when Attalah dragged her out for our mother's funeral."

I didn't want to get in the middle of this.

We talked some more, then finally, after noticing this, I said, "Wilfred, you look like Alex Haley to me."

"Doesn't he though," Yvonne said. "They sound alike too."

Wilfred said, "I've been in airports where white people have walked up to me and said, Can I just shake your hand? I'm looking at them, and they're thinking I'm Alex Haley! I saw a picture one time where I thought it was Alex Haley. Turned out it was me!"

Wilfred was the first brother in the family to join the Nation of Islam back in the day, then the younger brother Reginald, who used to hang out with Malcolm on the East Coast, joined. It was Reginald who converted Malcolm while Malcolm was in prison.

Toward the end of my meeting with this fascinating family of people, Wilfred said, "Spike, like you said, just do the right thing. And watch the language."

"I have to admit that I'm guilty of using profanity. I mean we try to put some meaning behind the MFers in our films."

Yvonne said, "Child, ask your grandmother if that word was around then, back in Malcolm's and our day. I don't think so."

I asked Wilfred when was the last time he'd seen Malcolm.

"It was close to his death," he said. "I was talking to him on the phone and I said, 'Malcolm, why don't you take a picture of yourself and compare it to a picture taken a year ago?' I was trying to tell him he was a nervous wreck. I never accepted that, the fact that he had to die. I never accepted it because I thought he could beat it. Just get out of the way of it.

"He was my little brother."

It was July 25 when I finally got an audience with Minister Louis Farrakhan, at his palace on Woodlawn in Chicago. Also present was one of Malcolm's daughters, Gamilah. I guess from the Nation's perspective, it made things appear better. Looking back at it, it wasn't really nerve-racking at all. It was very cordial on both parts. What was surprising to me was he really didn't seem to care about how Malcolm would be portrayed in the film. He was much more concerned about how the Honorable Elijah Muhammad is portrayed. Specifically with the secretaries, and specifically in light of his role, if any, in Malcolm's death.

Farrakhan began with a statement to me: "Before I say anything I'd like to put on the record that this movie on the life of Malcolm X has the potential of becoming one of the most powerful movies ever done by a Black person, or a white person for that matter, for it is, possibly, the most consequential movie, in that the life of Malcolm is one of the most exemplary lives that shows the ability of our people to make the transition from ignorance to knowledge, aimlessness to purpose, in the span of one lifetime. However, as important as the movie could be, the consequences of the mishandling of this film could be very, very grave for all concerned. My deep concern is that while there are many who love him and desire to see his life portrayed before the world in a way that inspires young Black people in particular to take the proper course and direction in their lives, there also exists the possibility of this film being used in a very ugly and sinister way. This looms very big in my mind. The enemy of all of us in this room, all our people, in my humble judgment, would like to see this film used to make deep schisms, deeper schisms in our community. The film has the great possibility of healing wounds that prior schisms have made. With that in mind I would like to answer all of your questions. I want to also state that I asked Brother Spike not to put on any kid gloves but ask any question he so desires."

So we started with stuff I basically knew from other sources. Mr. Farrakhan had met Malcolm back in 1953, when Mr. Farrakhan was a nightclub singer in Boston at a place called Eddie Levine's. He had heard of Malcolm before then. They were introduced. Two years later, in Chicago, he became Louis X. I asked Mr. Farrakhan what he remembered most about Malcolm.

"Well, as a teacher, I never heard any Black man speak in the manner that I heard him speak. With the boldness . . ."

"Even the Honorable Elijah Muhammad?" I asked.

"Well, I was not directly under the Honorable Elijah Muhammad. I'd only heard him speak once. But Malcolm was, of course, more articulate than the Honorable Elijah Muhammad

. . . No, I had never heard anybody speak like Malcolm. And when I first heard him the thought came to my mind that if this man was not God, he was very close to it. So when I joined the Mosque, Mosque No. 7 in New York, I came directly under the influence of Brother Malcolm . . . he literally became my mentor . . . I listened to him in private, in conversations in the restaurant, or when he spoke to reporters, or when he spoke on college campuses. I adopted his style. I styled my delivery and whatnot after Malcolm. I remember him as being one of the most disciplined men that I have ever met. Exceedingly punctual . . .''

Brass tacks. I asked, in a roundabout way, what caused the split between Malcolm and Elijah Muhammad.

''In all organizations, in all of us, in all our professions, the jealousy and envy of our own brothers and sisters often does us harm,'' said Minister Farrakhan. ''I've walked in Malcolm's shoes now. I became what he was, national representative of the Nation of Islam, representative of the Honorable Elijah Muhammad. So I have walked a long way in his shoes now. Jealousy and envy . . .

''Malcolm was very stern, he was a disciplinarian, and we became the strongest Mosque in the Nation under his leadership. And people feared the FOI. They feared the members of the Nation because they knew we didn't take any foolishness and that we had come up out of the world, so we did everything people in the world might do, and more. So when you're trying to get Black people to love each other and to respect each other and not destroy each other, it is difficult. The road to get us to destroy each other is much easier than the road to get us to respect each other and follow divine law.''

But was Minister Farrakhan once jealous of Malcolm?

''No. I was not. I loved Malcolm much more than words are able to describe. You go back and look at all of the films of Brother Louis X standing behind Malcolm. When Malcolm would be preaching, I would be scanning the rooftops . . .''

Before he left the Nation?

''Yes of course.''

But I don't think you felt that way after . . .

''No I did not.''

How many wives did the Honorable Elijah Muhammad have?

''I couldn't say with truth.''

Now the two women that pressed paternity charges against him, were they his wives too?

"Yes . . . I say this to you now Spike, because I see that you have a tendency in your language and in the subtleties of your speech to view Elijah Muhammad and his wives, quote unquote, from the mind of a Christian who is not familiar with Islam nor familiar with the lives of many religious prophets. If you believe God sent Moses . . . and sent Noah and Lot and David and Joshua and all those people . . . many biblical prophets had a number of wives . . . if Malcolm was so hurt over the fact that Elijah Muhammad, now I'm going to use his language, had sex with teenaged secretaries, and left him and went to follow the prophet Muhammad, who had nine wives and a concubine who was eleven years old, how can you say you deny one man and accept another man who lived fourteen hundred years ago? So to me that is incongruent."

Why did he defect then?

"In my judgment, that's one of the reasons, but I think the thing that affected him most was thinking that Elijah Muhammad was jealous of him, was the architect of his pain and reason for his fall, when the Messenger sat him down and silenced him over the 'chickens come home to roost' remark . . . Now the responsibility is on your shoulders, Spike, but before you make this movie, you need to study the lives of the prophets."

We went over some more things, but I wondered what Sister Clara Muhammad, Elijah Muhammad's wife, would have thought of all these other "quote unquote" wives. That's what I thought.

Minister Farrakhan and I talked about a secretary named Evelyn Williams whom he believed Malcolm was in love with, and she turned out to be one of Elijah's "quote unquotes," who became pregnant, along with another one named Lucille Rosary, so that was another reason Malcolm was angry with Elijah Muhammad. Minister Farrakhan made no attempts to hide anything from me. I had the information that Evelyn was pregnant with Elijah's child, and the Minister looked at me levelly and said, "That's right. Correct."

"All this hurt him, hurt Malcolm, I'm sure," said Minister Farrakhan. "It affected him in a negative way after he'd heard it from Wallace D. Muhammad, because Malcolm had the Honorable Elijah Muhammad on a pedestal, and he felt his personal life that could have been with sister Evelyn was destroyed. Added to that were the other things that were happening to Malcolm and surrounding Malcolm, the envy and enmity of the other ministers and what-not. Malcolm had the kind of courage where he would eventually confront Elijah Muhammad, which he did.''

''Was that when Elijah quoted the Scripture to Malcolm?''

''Yes. Later, Malcolm made the statement about the chickens coming home to roost after the Kennedy assassination. I was the person selected to speak in Malcolm's place. I was brought down from Boston, where I was heading up a new mosque . . . I told Malcolm I did not wish to get in between a controversy—I did not want to call it a power struggle—between two powerful men. And when I told him that, he told me, 'Brother, there's only one powerful man,' and he was speaking of the Messenger, not of himself. I told him, 'Yes, I'm aware of that.'

''Let's face facts. We live in America. You're not—you, me, anybody—going to do big business in America if you don't have a force to go along with your business. That's why white folk will let you get so big and then they eat you up because you're so busy doing business, you don't set up that which will protect your business. Maybe you think that white folk and police will protect your business. But big business has armies. Big business *buys* armies. We don't, and we didn't have to buy one, we made one, and we don't and didn't make any bones about it. We know we'll never be successful inside America and do anything of value for our people unless you have a force that not only will protect the leader, but will defend the right of the leader to preach the truth and be willing to die in defense of that truth.''

I had to be blunt now. ''So who killed Malcolm?''

''You're asking the wrong man,'' said Farrakhan.

''Have you ever heard of Thomas Hayer, Ben Thomas, Leon Davis, William X, aka William Bradley, or Wilbert McKinney?''

''I know of Thomas Hayer,'' said Farrakhan.

''Or were they all out of Temple No. 25 in Newark, and didn't they have the reputation of doing—you know of this?''

''What was this reputation?''

''If a job needed to be done,'' I said, ''25 would do it.''

''Do you know why Talmadge Hayer stood up in the courtroom? I noticed you didn't mention him. I'm talking now about the two brothers you haven't mentioned.''

''Those are the ones that are in prison.''

''Are they those who did time for a crime they didn't commit?''

''That's why I didn't mention them . . . I want to refer to a comment you made where you said because of Malcolm's actions at the time, every member of the Nation was a potential murderer.''

Farrakhan smiled, looked at me, and said, ''Well, brother, any one of us is capable of committing murder if the right button is pushed. As peaceful as you look, you'd commit murder.

''The button for the Nation was how do you handle that man, Elijah Muhammad, that's the way it was, and I'm telling you now, brother, that's the way it *is*. I mean, that man has meant everything to us. I don't know what he means to you, but I know what he means to me, and I'm not going to stand by in 1991 or 1992 and have anybody just do to Elijah Muhammad what you want to do, because you are not interested in digging deeply enough to give this thing the balance that it should be given.''

''That's why I'm here,'' I said.

''Maybe, maybe, Spike. You spend two hours with a man, three hours with a man, maybe that's all you can spend . . .''

''I told you I'll come back.''

''This is critical. How this is handled is absolutely critical, and to be very honest with you, Spike, and I like to be quite frank, you have already demonstrated in your language the biased view when you mentioned Elijah Muhammad's extracurricular activities . . . your view is that he was kind of a low down man.''

''That's not true.''

''That's why I'm telling you, that's why I'm saying this to you, brother . . . it's been twenty years trying to put this movie out and it hasn't happened yet. It's going to happen today because they want it to happen today.''

''Who's 'they'?''

''I'm saying that because white folk have studied you, they know you got courage. They know you love truth and want to make a movie of truth, and I admire that in you too. Now, what is truth, good man? I don't know how much truth you can tell in three hours, or whatever your plan is. But I'm telling you I believe Malcolm X's life is the most exemplary life of the century. For all kinds of reasons . . . If it were not for Malcolm, Jesse Jackson and I would have gotten into it when Jesse repudiated me.''

I knew this was the infamous episode where Jesse was pressured to repudiate Farrakhan, while Jesse was running for president and had Secret Service protection. This was not long after his ''Hymietown'' gaffe. I knew before this he'd been protected, as some of our movie sets were, by the Fruit of Islam. Farrakhan kept talking, never missing a beat.

''But thanks to that lesson that I learned from that mistake that I once made, I would not fall into that trap. So when I went on a television show, with forty members of the press in another room waiting for me to lash out at Jesse, I wouldn't do it, and it just blew everything to pieces for them. I said, 'Whatever Jesse said, I'm sure he has a good reason for saying it. But we all want to see our people unite behind Jesse to send him to his Democratic convention with the strength of his people apparent.' I would never have said that if I hadn't had the past experience with Malcolm. And, beyond that I'm telling you, I'm alive now because of what I learned from that experience. So I wisely never attacked Wallace D. Muhammad. I didn't agree with him, I didn't like what he was doing, I went to him and told him straight to his face what I felt, but I knew if I had stood up to attack him, there were those in his camp poised to kill me. I'm lucky to be alive. But I'm strong now. I have soldiers now, everywhere.

''When Malcolm left Elijah Muhammad, he didn't have the soldiers. So Malcolm was more vulnerable in some ways. We all are in some ways. We all have vulnerabilities.

''When they brought Martin Luther King into FBI headquarters to talk to Hoover, and Hoover showed him what he had, King could have folded, but he was a man of great strength and courage. So he said to J. Edgar Hoover, do what you feel you have to do. And they sent those sordid tapes to Coretta King. It devastated the family. Martin was in great pain in the last days of his life, as was Malcolm. Great, great pain . . . now here we are, this is Malcolm's daughter, and I would hope and pray that somehow the wounds of our people could be healed. I would hope and pray that somehow the children of Martin, Malcolm, Elijah, Farrakhan, Tutu, and Jesse can see the mistakes of their fathers and mothers. Not to condemn, but to learn from, that these can write a new chapter in the future of our people. Today you can't say anything about me that would upset me to the point where I would do you harm. I know now why that was done to Malcolm and why that was done to me, the testing, the envy, the jealousy. You think I've not been touched by that from others? Elijah Muhammad is not here anymore. I can't call him on the telephone. I'm the most evil-spoken-of Black man in the last ten or fifteen years. I don't know of any Black man who has been eaten up by the press the way Farrakhan has.''

''The *New York Post* loves you,'' I said.

''Yeah, I'm sure. I'm sure.''

''And Nat Hentoff.''

''I've got my own brothers, Muslims, who hate me, speak

evil against me. My son is a witness. I've never allowed any believer to speak evil of former ministers of Elijah Muhammad, because one day I believe I'll win every one of them back. But today they're on my case. But you can't find any word that I've spoke against Wallace D. Muhammad publicly. I don't attack him publicly. I don't attack former ministers of the Messenger publicly. And today you will hear me say publicly that I helped contribute to the atmosphere that led to the assassination of Malcolm X.''

"So, Minister Farrakhan, you acknowledge the assassins were Muslims of the Nation of Islam, as well?''

"I will not acknowledge that.''

"You just said you contributed to the atmosphere.''

"Of course.''

"I need to know, what atmosphere?''

"Let me be very candid. Because we're going to contribute to this atmosphere too, you and I, before this thing is over. I want to be very clear I'm not talking about just the atmosphere in the Nation. Because as Malcolm and Elijah were going back and forth, there were other forces watching this. And as Malcolm attacked Elijah Muhammad and we attacked Malcolm, we were creating an atmosphere of murder not just within the Nation. The time was right for any outside force that wanted Malcolm out of the way. Which of the two would they hit first? Who was most vulnerable? It wasn't Elijah Muhammad. It was Malcolm X. If you kill Malcolm X, blame it on Elijah Muhammad, you've killed two birds with one stone. We, in our ignorance and zeal, created this atmosphere.

"In my judgment, Spike, this movie can have a healing or a terribly divisive effect. I will wait and see what is done, how it's done. Because I firmly believe, my brother, Mecca is very upset because Farrakhan has brought back the teachings of Elijah Muhammad, and now tens of thousands of our people are gravitating toward his message, which they don't believe has everything to do with true Islam. The Malcolm I know was not impressed with rituals. You couldn't take Malcolm to Mecca and show him some blond-haired, blue-eyed white man walking around a black stone and knock Malcolm out. Not the Malcolm I knew. Because that's not reality, that's a ritual. In Islam, Blacks don't have the respect and honor of whites in the religion. Racism pervades Islam as well as Christianity. I've been there and I've seen it.''

I protested this. "But his famous letter, something must

have happened. I mean those letters weren't fabricated when he said he felt that true Islam would remove racism from . . .''

Farrakhan wasn't having any. ''When the Nation sent Malcolm to Mecca in 1959, he saw that. That last time wasn't the first time he ever went. He didn't experience hajj that time, but he knew there were white Muslims and he knew Islam, and any true religion is supposed to be able to remove racism. But the question is, has it? If racism is still in existence in the Islamic world, then how has Islam removed racism? It has not.

''No, brother, Malcolm was moved by the power of Islam to bring human beings together in that ritual, but Malcolm would have loved to have seen the reality, not the ritual, because that lasts for ten to fourteen days and then that's over, it's back to business as usual, brother. So I wouldn't be moved by no ritual and Malcolm was much more politically astute than I was. And I don't think that religious ritual would move him when the political and practical reality of Black people in America is what it is. You go there now, see who their servants are. See who the people are who bring the tea and scrub the floor and wash the car. It ain't the soft-handed, light-skinned Arab, it's the Black African, or the Indian, or the Pakistani that does all the hard work in Kuwait and Saudi Arabia. And Malcolm would not have been blind to that. I first went there in 1977. There was a ghetto there in Mecca and Blacks were in that ghetto in Mecca, the Holy City. And I saw little Arab boys right around the Ka'Ba, white Arabs, throwing bread to Nubian women like they were feeding pigeons, throwing the bread in the air, and these Black women had to run and scrape for that bread. I know what I saw and I talk about it to them—I don't wait to get behind their backs, I talk straight to them, so you can't tell me nothing about Islam removing racism, not *that* Islam. It ain't happening, brother. It *can* happen, but it hasn't happened. Malcolm was a much smarter man than that. But where was he going to go? He was going to be a Black Nationalist, right? But he had to make peace with Martin and the civil rights movement. How are you gonna do that? Islam and the broad universal concept of Islam, as in Christianity, provide for all the races of man, all the colors of man, to get together in brotherhood. But what is the reality? It ain't happening. It sure ain't happening in Christianity, and it's not happening, really, in Islam. They have a better show in Islam when in reality they don't look too well at Black people. I haven't found any place, any ism, ideology, or religion where Black people are respected along the top. Islam does better, but they're a long, long way from it. So, my brother, I'll conclude this by saying, I have walked in my brother's shoes.''

By the time I got to the interview of Captain Joseph, also known as Yusuf Shah, the former head of the Fruit of Islam, the Nation's security force based at Temple No. 7 in New York, it was nearly at the end of August and shooting was imminent.

He had been once known as Captain Joseph, the head of the Fruit of Islam, and was now known as Yusuf Shah. He was a man whose affiliation with the NOI came much before Malcolm's. He had joined in 1951. He was from Detroit. He was with the Nation when it was small, when it was one, and great, and now he was still of the Nation, even though it was split into more than just two camps, as he would let me know. I'd heard he was not a man to be played with, not then, not now. I met him in Brooklyn, up in my own offices at 40 Acres and a Mule Filmworks. He was pleasant, a cordial brother. He traveled with a stone-faced man. Yusuf Shah was the one who surprised me a lot. Yusuf had a different kind of perspective. I'll never forget—instead of calling the American flag the Stars and Stripes, he called it ''the Scars and Strikes.''

''My name is Yusuf Shah. Y-U-S-U-F S-H-A-H . . .

''Fear? There was no fear. We dealt with them all. We kept the Ku Klux Klan in line. We dealt with them. J. B. Stoner, we dealt with him. It is serious business, Mr. Lee. You don't mess around, Mr. Lee. The reason that I say this to you is that you will come to realize, maybe not now—but you have a job to do. You're interested, you're filming, you have all these things you want to do and I respect that. And I honor you for that because I think that you got a forward look. But one thing you're going to see and that you must understand is that we are wrestling for the minds of our people, you see. It's a psychological war that's going on. And this is why we have to tell the truth because hundreds of millions of minds are involved in this thing. And it is necessary to tell the truth. Because why put something out for popularity, when a man's life is at stake, you see. When people's lives are at stake. Eighty-five percent of the people don't know what's happening. Ten percent of the people are those who run the government and finance. And, as the man who started the Five Percenters says—you've heard of them? We put him out of the Nation of Islam too, you know—he says that the Five Percent— that's a lesson we used to have—are the most righteous Muslims who don't go along with that mystery God, you know. They believe in the true and living God. So it's eighty-five percent, ten percent, and five percent. Now I'm with the eighty-five percent. I'm not with the ten percent, because they are the rich, the aristocrats, the Black bourgeoisie, they are all linked together. I'm not with the five percent counted as Muslims either, because they've become bourgeois themselves, they've forgotten what their aim in life is supposed to be, what they're supposed to do. They condemn their own people more than when they were lost themselves. But the eighty-five percent, they don't know, so these people have to be awakened and taught and then you'll have power. I'm among those eighty-five percent.

"You see, Mr. Lee, power is not in the gun, power is not in the pen, although they say the pen is mightier than the sword. Power is in the people, and that's what Mr. Muhammad realized. And the reason he treated Malcolm as he did was that he realized the ability of Malcolm . . ."

I interrupted: "To get more people in the Nation."

"That's right. He realized that ability."

"To build a Nation."

"And he helped, he helped, Mr. Lee."

"I hear you were a drill sergeant."

"Ha, ha, ha, don't be like that. Yes, I was the Captain, brother. In other words, Mr. Muhammad might say, tell the brothers to sell what papers as they can, but you inspire them to do better. And I'm an inspirer, brother."

We both laughed. I laughed with him, I'd say.

"How would you inspire them?"

"Conversation. I didn't have to beat them. Talk."

"They were scared of you?"

"I don't know if they were afraid or not, but I could talk, though, that's one of my virtues."

"So you were Malcolm's lieutenant?"

"I was Captain. I was the enforcer. The structure went, Minister, Captain, Secretary. The Minister is in charge of the temple; the Captain is in charge of operations and security; the Secretary is keeper of records, recorder of deeds and facts."

"Was there a power struggle in New York between Malcolm as Minister and John Ali as Secretary at No. 7?"

"After John Ali was brought to No. 7 as Secretary—he was an intelligent, college-educated man, you know. And Malcolm, he could be very devious."

"Malcolm? How?"

"He viewed everything from the point of the street, how

he'd come up in the street. That's how he saw it. Then after he viewed it that way he would come back to the righteous way, but his first view was from the street. He'd tell me, yeah, what we need to do is take a hammer and knock the teeth out of a transgressor.''

"Those orders were carried out?''

"These things did happen . . . Once some $1,700 came up missing. He ordered us to find out, take the person responsible to the river to discipline them. The only reason this person was brought back up was because they started to say, ''God is great!'' in Arabic. *Allahu Ahkbar.* And the person was brought back up.''

"They were thrown in the river? Could they swim?''

"How could they swim tied up?''

"Tied up!''

"You can't believe that, can you, Mr. Lee?''

"I believe it. So the Fruit could get physical.''

"Very much so. We had judo classes. Aikido. Everything. We had two hundred men that were killers.''

"Why?''

"Well, you see, if a man is saying what we were saying, then you're going to get challenges. And you had to be prepared to put down what was coming up. We feared no one. I will remain mum on some things, Mr. Lee. I'm glad you came to the source . . . Malcolm was converted in prison by his brother Reginald, who wrote to him and visited him. He said Malcolm couldn't believe the white man was the devil. He said at least the Jews were all right.

"Reginald says, 'If your friend is making $1,000 and you're making $100 doing the same thing, is he your friend?' That one even stumped Malcolm. Malcolm wore double-breasted suits. The Stacy Adams shoe was his favorite. After he saw Mr. Muhammad with hats on, he started wearing hats. I first heard him speak at 1474 Frederick in Detroit, Temple No. 1, way back. He had on a rust-colored suit, with a red tie. He could be devious . . .''

"Let's back up.''

"It was building up between them, Malcolm as Minister of No. 7 and John Ali as Secretary of No. 7. The straw that broke the camel's back was this: Wallace D. Muhammad, one of Elijah's sons, had started going around speaking, lecturing. Malcolm was in California. So John Ali brought in Wallace to speak and rented the Park Place at 110th Street and Fifth Avenue. Mr.

Muhammad's son spoke, and it was a success. When Malcolm got back, he got John and me together and said, 'How come you couldn't have the meeting in the temple?' John said he saw it was going to require a larger space than usual, so we just raised some money and got the place. Malcolm said, 'You never got any Park Place for me. You never raised no money to get no place for me.' John looked at him and said, 'Well, this is the Messenger's son; we just thought we were doing the right thing, we just got a place for him, we didn't think you'd have a problem with that.' Malcolm said, 'Well I have a problem with it.' That was the start of the demise of John Ali and Malcolm X. John eventually went to Chicago and became National Secretary. So it was nip and tuck from then on for Malcolm.''

I had to get from Yusuf Shah confirmation on certain facts about the assassination of Malcolm. I started with the bone of contention—Malcolm's finding out about the secretaries.

''Yeah, he knew those women. Malcolm liked Evelyn, yes. In fact, he was once supposed to marry her, but he—''

''Marry her?''

''Yes. And also Lucille.''

Both of them?

''Yeah. Evelyn was too light, and he was light, and that would make their babies too light. He said that. He said, number two, she was a foot stomper, and if she didn't get her way she would just go into frenzies. Lucille, he said that she was too dark, they'd have a dark baby and a light one, plus she was short. So the sister he really wanted to marry was a young one named Betty Sue. Then he settled on Betty Shabazz because she was a medical student, a nutritionist, which went along with his program of betterment. She was pretty near the complexion he wanted, and she was the right height and carriage. So when he did get married, he called me from Lansing and told me he wanted me to go before the body and announce that he was married. It was a Wednesday night. I made that announcement and, man, Evelyn jumped up screaming, hollering, and ran out of the temple, from the mosque.''

''So Malcolm was kinda crushed that he had recommended his two former girlfriends for jobs as secretaries in Chicago and they ended up getting pregnant by the Honorable Elijah Muhammad?''

''Yeah, that's how he knew. He said when one of them got pregnant, 'Where's the husband?' The other one got pregnant and he said, 'Where's the husband?' And then the next thing you

know, they're out of the Nation . . . And that was the first inkling.
I remember one day Malcolm said, 'Brother Captain, have you
ever heard anything about the Messenger and some children, you
know, his secretaries? I said no. He didn't say another word.

"Yeah, he knew them. He had recommended them."

I asked Yusuf, "Can you tell us about when Malcolm asked
you to leave the Nation with him?"

"It was at the newspaper office. He told me he wanted to
speak with me. So I met him down at the Cuban Embassy building. He wanted to talk in private. He said, 'Brother Captain, I've
got something I want to tell you about the Messenger. You know
he has fathered children by Lucille, Evelyn, Ola, June, and Ver-
nick.' "

"What did Sister Clara, Mr. Muhammad's wife, say?"

"Oh, she was very upset."

"She knew?"

"She found out about it because these women were there in
the houses in Chicago, many of them."

Since he had brought up Chicago, I said, "I met with Minister Farrakhan. The way he explained it was, in most religious
prophecy, all of the old prophets had more than one wife . . ."

"Oh no, no, no, that's not true," said Yusuf Shah. "That's
not what the Holy Koran says . . . Here's what the Holy Koran
says: You are allowed four wives, but one is better for you, if you
only knew. That's what the Holy Koran says. Remember that.

"Malcolm told me this toward the end. He didn't tell me
toward the beginning. And, oh yes, I believed him because I knew
what kind of person he was. See, Malcolm was the kind of person
that anytime he had something, he had it cold. If he came to you,
you knew he had the goods. You don't even have to worry about
it. And I told him, 'I don't doubt that what you say is true,
Brother Minister; in fact I know what you're saying is true because I know you. However, don't you think that we can work
this thing out?' "

I guessed not.

"The two secretaries pressed charges, you know, because of
Malcolm," said Yusuf Shah. "He told them they should. Yeah.
He told them that. His heart had hardened."

And then Yusuf Shah's heart had hardened toward Malcolm.

"Now, Captain, there were a couple of times when some
brothers were waiting for him in the bushes outside his house?"

"They were. The cat was running for his life, brother."

"There's no way that could happen without you knowing."

"What now? Say that again?"

"So, Captain . . . who bombed Malcolm's house in Queens?"

"Now if I tell you—see how you are. It was bombed."

"I know. That wasn't the Nation's work?"

"What do you want me to say? . . . that was the parsonage. Malcolm didn't think so, but John Ali and I had the deeds—the decision was made. It was the parsonage. As long as you're the Minister, you get to stay there. The Nation bought it. Percy Sutton was his lawyer, but we beat it in court because we were right. Malcolm thought he had the deed, and that's why he said it was his house. But it never was, and this was proved in court."

"The house got bombed."

"By some mysterious people."

"Who bombed his house, though, with a Molotov cocktail?"

"Huh?"

"The Molotov cocktail?"

"Well, I just don't want to tell you, Mr. Lee."

"But it was done by the Nation, right?"

"It was done by zealots."

"This is what I got into with Brother Minister Farrakhan. When I went to Chicago, he said he apologized for whatever happened between—you know. He said Black people were a lot worse off, not better off with Malcolm being dead, Malcolm assassinated. At the same time I pulled out documents I had from *Muhammad Speaks,* editorials he had written saying Malcolm is a traitor, is a Judas, his tongue should be . . ."

"Yes," said Captain Yusuf, "he said all of that . . ."

". . . cut off, delivered to the doorstep of the Messenger. Even if Elijah Muhammad didn't say this directly, when a brother reads this in the paper, and they see cartoons with Malcolm's head rolling down the steps, it means . . ."

"You're right, Mr. Lee."

"Were you ever given orders to kill Malcolm X?"

"I won't answer that question."

"Who was making that climate though? Chicago?"

"It was on both sides. The climate was on both sides because Malcolm decided to just go spread that."

"Spread what?"

"Spread about the women and different things."

"In my research, the reason he did that is because he wanted a buffer, he wanted to tell them first so they wouldn't have to hear about it through the newspapers . . ."

"Mr. Lee, Mr. Muhammad called Malcolm out there and

challenged it, told him if he was starting fires to go back and put out the fires . . . to pour water on the fires.''

''Think the FBI and CIA had anything to do with the climate?''

''No. Not that they weren't active. Everybody knew we might be infiltrated. That's just what everybody wants it to be.''

''The FBI or CIA had nothing to do with it?''

''No.''

''It was strictly between Malcolm and . . .''

''Zealots.''

''Did you know any of those guys?''

''I knew all of them.''

''Did you know what was going to happen that day?''

''Huh? You're something, Mr. Lee.''

''What about Norman Butler and Thomas Johnson?''

''They were logical . . . After they went to prison, Mr. Muhammad tried to get them out. Bennie Williams, you ever heard of him? Edward Bennett Williams. He argued that case. He's passed on now, but that's who argued the case in Albany. Kunstler came in later. Kunstler was a ninety-day wonder. Never trusted him . . .''

I named the names connected with the assassination. William Bradley, also known as William X. Very good with guns. Leon Davis. Wilbert McKinney. Robert Benjamin Thomas, the Secretary of the Newark mosque. And Thomas Hayer, who had done time with the two unjustly jailed men, Norman Butler and Thomas Johnson.

''That's about all of them,'' said Yusuf Shah, kind of laughing to himself. ''You're something, Mr. Lee.''

''If you've ever talked to any of these brothers, did they have any remorse . . . or none whatsoever?''

''They say Hayer did. Tell me what Minister Farrakhan said.''

''He said it was zealots.''

''That's what it was.''

''I still think they were recruited, though.''

''Recruited by who, Mr. Lee?''

''Who did you think bombed Temple No. 7 after Malcolm was assassinated?''

''His people did. I know that.

''Mr. Lee, here's one thing I have to say to you, and I'm saying it on tape. Always be cognizant of the fact that what you're doing is going to affect a lot of people. So you want to be as near to the truth as possible. But this thing is bigger than what is the correct word, celebrities. You see what we're doing now with the Caucasian, we're fighting the psychological war. They give you so much money to make the film. Now what you have to understand in your mind, you have to say, what does this man want out of it? Talking about the Caucasian. Does he want money or does he want—what does he want? Why does he want me? Because nobody else could do it. The Caucasian wanted to do it, but he wasn't going to do it because first of all he couldn't even get close. But you can because you're one of us and then you're all right with us. What you have to ask yourself is, how do I handle this? How am I going to put this before the people?

"Malcolm was a brilliant man, a very brilliant man. Smart beyond belief. Quick thinker, could think on his feet, wasn't at a loss for words, could talk. And he wasn't a man to use words out of his character. He could go to Harvard on you or he could come right down to the street, and most people can't do that. So he was a brilliant man, the most brilliant I've seen. That's why I took notice of him long ago, because I could see what he had going for him . . .

"The Honorable Elijah Muhammad was a fine man, best man I ever met. Never met a man as straightforward and honest. I didn't have any fault with him. He would back you up if you were right; if you were wrong then you had a problem. He didn't try to scheme and connive. Whatever it was, it was. Even Farrakhan put me out. Said I stole a million dollars. We aren't all Farrakhan now, and that's all right."

"Captain, are you in good standing with Mr. Farrakhan?"

"I go where I want to go, Mr. Lee."

I think, looking back on the interviews, I was helped most by Malcolm's sister and brothers and by Captain Joseph, Yusuf Shah. But I can't really say that. Everybody was good. Everybody gave me a little bit more than I had before. Wilfred, being the eldest in the family, knowing Malcolm, bailing him out of jail—all that stuff. 'Course, Yusuf Shah was good, because Yusuf was Malcolm's captain and the head of the Fruit of Islam. Everyone had been good, tried to be helpful. I had been warned in so many words by many people during the course of these interviews. Minister Farrakhan's threats weren't even veiled. But I think it would be too risky for them to try some shit with me. Yet they all, even Farrakhan, owned up to everything I asked, just about. I could tell the real truth would be important here. It had to be entertainment, but it had to be on the truth. When it came down between choosing between Malcolm and the Messenger, Yusuf wanted to be down with the Messenger, just like Minister Farrakhan. It appeared to me that maybe Yusuf was asked to assassinate Malcolm out of his own Temple, No. 7, but couldn't do it. That's why they went to Temple No. 25 in Jersey. That Temple was notorious for being a Temple of crooks and all kinds of stuff. And all five of the assassins were from Temple No. 25. Two of them have since passed, and only one of the five real assassins ever went to jail—that was Thomas Hayer. The two other guys who went to jail with him, Norman Butler and Thomas Johnson, were innocent, at least of that particular crime, although I believe they would have killed Malcolm if they'd had the opportunity. But they were not at the Audubon Ballroom that day.

The passing of time only helped me. We know who the assassins are. We would try and go with the facts and re-create the assassination, show how it happened, and what caused the split between Malcolm and Elijah Muhammad. Go into the thing with Elijah and his secretaries; go into Malcolm being under heavy surveillance, being watched by the FBI. We know the FBI and the police had infiltrated the Nation, so if the Nation was acting independently it could have been stopped, if the other two had wanted it stopped. But there were a lot of people and camps who wanted to see Malcolm X dead. To those who wanted it, it was to everybody's benefit to cooperate with each other. There were just too many things happening. The Nation of Islam could not use its influence to deny Malcolm entry into France, but that happened a week before he was assassinated. So there was a concerted effort. And that's the way I really started to see it, and believe it.

I think one of the most telling statements Malcolm made in his last days was: "I can't turn the corner." You know, one group wants me to go this way, another one wants me to go that way. Either way, I can't turn the corner. I think Alex Haley wrote that to the so-called moderates. Malcolm was too militant, and to the so-called militants, he had become too moderate. Malcolm's exact words were: "They won't let me turn the corner. I'm caught in a trap." After doing my research, I really feel Malcolm X knew he was going to die. I feel he knew this and I think he resigned himself to the fact. As long as nobody else—his family—got hurt, I believe he was reconciled to it. However, they didn't care if his family got it; they would have killed them too.

There is no written or taped record of what actually happened in the conversations between Malcolm and Elijah. We have to try and get the essence. A lot of characters will be combined, and we'll change a lot of names. Minister Farrakhan and Yusuf Shah are not in the script; neither is Muhammad Ali. The film won't end with the assassination. It has to be that way for many reasons—number one is that it would defeat the legacy of Malcolm X. Malcolm X lives today; the film will end in the present.

September 1991. Shari Carpenter, the script supervisor, Wynn Thomas, the art department head, Paul Lee, the consultant—everybody is telling me to wait. Paul Lee talked with me and asked me to wait another week. Wynn wanted to get a different location to replace the Audubon, or wait until the Audubon is ready, but that would take too long, as much as I'd love to wait. Shari pleaded with me, ''No, Spike, don't start now, we're not ready yet,'' she said. ''We want it right, perfect.'' She wasn't just talking about the script; she was talking about locations—stuff wasn't ready.

We can't wait. I know that. I think we are ready enough to go. Let's not postpone it any more. Let's go right now before these motherfuckers at Warner Brothers change their minds. Do it now. We've been waiting twenty years already for this film.

I try to do nothing halfway thought-out. As director, I feel we are ready to shoot. It's not just an emotional thing. I'm not going to say we are 100 percent ready. But we have to go *now*. We have to go, and keep preparing as we shoot. We have the momentum. And who knows what might happen if we postpone it—we might not ever be able to recapture that momentum. The same way a coach can have his team going, have the other team on the run, and then blow it by going into a defensive posture. Before you know it, you're fighting for your life in that game again, and the offense can't get it back up for you. They've lost it, and sometimes you can't recapture that magic. So you've got to keep it going—stay with it. Keep the roll going. Then, that shit is sweet.

But this enthusiasm is mostly mine, I must admit.

All the preparation has taken nine months, and some people are already dragging and doubting and complaining. So I decide we need a boost. The night before we shoot, we have a kickoff dinner. We rent out the Two Steps Down Restaurant and Grill in Fort Greene, Brooklyn, around the corner. We fly in Wilfred,

Philbert, and Yvonne, Malcolm's siblings, and his other brother, Bob Little. Bobby Seale comes up from Philadelphia. Charles Kenyatta—all these people are at the project kickoff dinner. And all these people, after we finish dinner, get up and talk about Malcolm. I had wanted them to talk to us. The cast and crew are there as well. I wanted them to hear this. I want them to be inspired, fired up, right now, the night before we start shooting *Malcolm X*. We film it. It's festive, but at the same time a lot of people are crying. When the people who knew Malcolm are talking about him, there is a *hush.* Then Benjamin Karim speaks and tells me, ''Spike, you'd better not have Malcolm in bed with no white women or there's gonna be some problems,'' I think about that.

We already know it's in the script, along with some other things that people might not like. And you know about Salman Rushdie—people can get killed over this kind of stuff. Everybody looks at me when he says this, and a lot of people get scared as shit right there, because they know it's in the script, too.

Too late to turn back now.

I want our people to be all fired up for this. To get inspired by it. This is not just some regular bullshit Hollywood movie. This is life and death we're dealing with, this is a mindset, this is what Black people in America have come through. And we told our people that from the very beginning. If you're not feeling this is going to be one of the most important films in the history of cinema, then keep your dead ass at home!

And for the most part, the cast and crew are with us. There were people who were fighting against us as well—I'm sure they will show up when we shoot—but the people who need to be down, they are down. Nobody will get rich off this film. This is purely an act of love. This is a film that is needed on several levels, and for the most part people realize what's at stake. We're dedicated to making sure that this is the greatest film they have ever been associated with, the best film it could be. That's all I ask. WE HAVE TO TURN THIS MOTHER OUT.

''Roll sound . . .''

JON KILIK
Line Producer

February 21, 1991, was about twenty-six years to the day after Malcolm X was assassinated. It was just about three years ago to the day, when *School Daze* was released, that I first ran into Spike. He had just finished writing the first draft of *Do The Right Thing*, and he was looking for somebody who was based in New York to be his line producer on that project, because his plan was to shoot in New York, and he needed someone who could take the script, budget it, schedule it, and, working with him and Monty, come up with a plan on how to put that presentation together with the script and place it before a studio in order to get the financing. He also needed someone who was based in New York City, someone who had some contacts with the unions.

Spike knew that shooting in New York for *Do The Right Thing*, a major production, would be a lot different from shooting *She's Gotta Have It.* I had a lot of experience with all the unions here, and this would be his first union picture. By the time *Malcolm X* is over, I will have worked in New York for around thirteen years in the film business. I moved here from my hometown, Melbourne, New Jersey, in 1979.

Spike and I were introduced by a mutual friend, producer David Picker, who had worked with Spike on *School Daze.* When David called and asked about my availability, it was to see if I could do a budget for Spike. David Putnam was head of Columbia Pictures, and David Picker was an executive vice-president who helped bring Spike in over there and helped find financing. They were the reasons Columbia made that movie. David is also based in New York, and knows a lot of production people. So Spike and Monty and I met, and they told me how they wanted to shoot with certain crew members and a certain production schedule and the plan for it, all the information I needed to go ahead and start a preliminary budget. And that was my introduction to Spike Lee. We all hit it off.

Spike asked me stay with that project. Initially I had just come on to prepare a first budget, but it's an ongoing struggle. You prepare a budget, you present it to one studio, they reject it—that's what happened with *Do The Right Thing.* We presented Paramount with a $10 million budget, and they passed on it, so we had to regroup and rethink and presented Universal with a $7.5 million budget, and they were very interested but didn't want to spend $7.5 million. So we went back again, cut some corners, and got down to $6.5 million, which was what Universal was willing to spend. And by the time all those changes to the budget happened, Spike and Monty and I had gotten to know each other pretty well.

Spike was the way he is now when I first met him—direct.

Spike has his own way. Concise. To the point. Straightforward. We'd also see each other occasionally at Knicks games. So that's how he came to know me. I had started at the lower levels: production assistant, second assistant director, location scout, location manager, first assistant director, production manager, production supervisor, then finally producer. When I met Spike, it also happened that the first project I had produced was out, something a friend of mine wrote and directed called *The Beat,* which starred John Savage. That movie had been made about a year prior to my meeting Spike. When it finally came out, that's when I met him. So, Spike had opened up the newspaper and saw that I had produced a film. And I knew some of the studio executives, and I knew Spike's lawyer, and I was at Knicks games. None of that hurt. I finally knew Spike.

Spike and I had a few things in common—we were both admirers of John Turturro, the actor. We both laughed when he threw his mother out of the window in the movie *Five Corners.* It just became an easy fit, through *Mo' Better Blues* and *Jungle Fever.* As a line producer, my responsibilities wouldn't by definition go into postproduction, but I just really enjoyed working with Spike and Monty and the whole family. So during post I stayed on it. As a producer, I knew from beginning to end what had happened, and I just said if there was anything else I could add and help out with, I was willing to do that. And I stayed.

We had just finished shooting *Jungle Fever* in December of 1990, when we had a meeting with Warner Brothers. Right from the beginning, Spike was very clear on how he wanted to do the film, what his approach was going to be, and how he saw the movie. He had Monty and me with him at that first meeting. He had obviously been talking to Marvin Worth and Lucy Fisher and everybody at Warners before this particular meeting, but this was the first formal discussion. Then we really started in February of 1991. He finished his version of the screenplay, and that's when I started writing up the budgets. The first one I did was for nearly $40 million. Of course they threw that back at me. Then we came in at between 33 and 35, and I thought, this is really as low as it can go. And then we fought for a long time with that budget, with that number and that plan in mind.

Finally, one night, my answering machine had a message on it. It was from Spike, and it was a long message, which is unusual for him. It said: ''Jon, it's been a hard fight and we have been trying to get the thirty-three or thirty-five million budget, but they are just really serious about it being twenty-seven, twenty-eight total, max, with everything counted in. We got to keep on trying to figure a way to bring it down. But the most important thing is to get the movie made.''

So then we started to talk about cutting the shooting schedule, which is the best way to cut dollars, big dollars. We talked about cutting locations, trying to figure out ways to make the movie for less money without hurting it. We will end up getting all the locations in. We will end up spending the same amount of money as originally planned, going with the original schedule and budget, because there is no way to do it right any cheaper.

We'll go over the smaller budget because Spike won't compromise. The idea was to stay on budget exactly, but we ended up with the same budget and schedule we originally presented to everybody. The film is bonded by Completion Bond Co. The bond company, typically, is the guarantor to make sure the film will be completed and that the script the producer, director, and studio all signed off on is going to be shot completely and then edited and then presented with all of the elements and with the high quality that studios demand. Typically, now, there have been a lot of bonded pictures. I would say a third of pictures go over budget these days. Maybe more. And direct studio productions like *Batman* and *Lethal Weapon* also go way over budget. In our project, Warner was very budget-sensitive. We'll see what happens.

Because this is such a big picture, by the time we finish we will have worked on it for two years from beginning to end. We're talking about forty years of history, tens of thousands of extras, shooting on three continents, with over two hundred speaking parts. Remember the block we created on *Do The Right Thing?* We have to create a dozen blocks with *Malcolm X,* so it was really much more difficult than any film I've ever done. I think the kind of production value we're being able to achieve reflects a much higher budget, a $50 million style of production value. To do the film in New York for $28 million is difficult enough; it makes it even more difficult to bring in overseas locations and so much cast. It is a very big job. We have over four hundred crew members and a cast of two hundred principals. You can just imagine. *Home Alone II* will be shooting in New York soon. I hear the budget for that is $47 million. I'm not sure how big this one is, but the original *Home Alone* was just three people and a house. We're getting our bang out of the buck in *Malcolm X.*

It is just the highest quality all the way around. We'll shoot in super 35 with the plan to blow it up to 70 millimeter. The music, the songs that are going to be on the soundtrack, will not only tell the history of Malcolm X from 1925 until 1965, but much history of Black music during that forty-year period.

Personally I'd love to see it in a thousand theaters, but sometimes movies like *Gandhi* and *JFK,* when they come out, don't get into as many theaters as, say, *The Addams Family.* It doesn't always work that the best-quality pictures get into the most theaters, but I still think there are so many people who want to see the film that it should get substantial release. From seven hundred to a thousand theaters. The most we've had in the past was just under seven hundred, for *Jungle Fever.* Just under six hundred on *Do The Right Thing,* and maybe just about five hundred on *Mo' Better Blues.* The length might hurt us, but there are pictures that didn't do as well when they were cut as they did when they were released in their complete form. There are plenty of three-hour movies like *Dances with Wolves* that do very well at the box office, so if the movie is good and it keeps people's interest and they talk about it with their friends, then obviously it will do well regardless. I've seen a lot of ninety-minute movies that are boring and some three-hour movies that wouldn't let me blink.

I think this is Spike's best work. The whole team is really rising a notch again on this one. The thing I love about each one of the films is that they continue to get better, but I think with *Malcolm X* there is an extra intensity, at a much higher level. There was so much at stake, so much time invested, it was something that we all had looked forward to for a long time. I think everybody came ready and is working as hard as they can. The last three of Spike's films I've worked in were just a great time for all of us to kind of bond as a team, to get us ready for . . . the heavyweight championship. Exactly.

To me, Spike is a very inspiring person to be around. It is something that I just responded to right away. It's the way he thinks, always looking ahead, always preparing. On *Do The Right Thing,* during editing, he started thinking about *Mo' Better Blues,* and then the same thing on *Mo' Better* editing, thinking about *Jungle Fever,* and *Jungle Fever* while thinking about *Malcolm X.* He is always involved with more than you think he is. He seems to want to take on a lot of challenges at once, and looks forward to being ready for them, and being ready for many more to come in the future. He's tireless that way. And that kind of man can be contagious. There are a lot of great stories to tell and a lot of great issues to deal with. Being around Spike has inspired me to look ahead to many more projects we can produce.

I already know *Malcolm X* will be great.

WYNN THOMAS
Production Designer

When I first met Spike, I was art directing a movie called *Beat Street* that was produced by David Picker and Harry Belafonte. It was a break-dance film. Spike came into the office to interview for the coffee-fetching position of assistant to the director. There was also a female classmate of his working in the art department as a production assistant, a PA. So Spike came into the art department to talk to her, and then he saw me there and said, "I didn't realize there were any Black people who were working as art directors." At that point, I might have been the only one. We struck up a relationship at that point and kept in touch throughout that year, I believe it was '84.

He would call me occasionally to see what I was doing.

The next summer, we worked together on a film he called *The Messenger,* only the film never happened. We did the preparation necessary, but I think due to financing it collapsed the Friday before the Monday we were supposed to start shooting. The money was pulled away, and we folded. But Spike stayed in touch with me anyway and the following summer, he got one off the ground: *She's Gotta Have It.*

The job you do as art director is about the same job for every director. The difference with Spike is that he is very easy about letting people do their work. He's already made up his mind on you when you're hired. He has studied your work, your potential. So he's not one of those directors who feels he has to control every single thought, dominate every creative thought you have. He is very good about letting people work, and leaving them alone so they can do their job. A lot of directors don't work that way. Usually the director wants to present you with his concept, his point of view, and you spend hours and hours discussing his point of view. But when you work with Spike, I think the difference is that because he was written the script and poured his heart and soul into that, he then allows us to interpret it, as opposed to saying, "This is my concept." You never have a meeting with Spike where he will sit down and say, "This is my concept." There is freedom of exchange.

The middle-man is gone with Spike. He is not someone taking another writer's work and saying, "This is my point of view on it." It is very rare for Spike to come and say this. He did that once, on *School Daze*. And I think he did that because he felt that was what a director had to do. But I think after *School Daze*, we all knew how to work with each other. A vocabulary had been established. It sort of eliminated the pretense of him having to play the director. He just directed.

I don't know how other people have approached this picture. My relationship to the film didn't really shift on *Malcolm X*. Only because I know that I worked very hard not to make a change; not to make *Malcolm X* into a special project. I think when you are aware that you are working on something important, it can actually hurt the work, so I knew I worked very hard with Spike just to maintain an atmosphere as if we were still doing *School Daze* or one of the films after that. Because I believe you can ruin the work process if you are aware you are doing something important. I don't know how it is for the others. For me, this had to be just another film we were working on. This allowed my creative juices to flow, instead of being restricted.

The thing that is different about *Malcolm X* is that this is the first film where Spike actually rejected some of my locations. He doesn't normally reject the locations I choose. And I think that happened because the project was so big, and he needed to be a little more specific, with more details, as opposed to the other films, where he'd been a little bit looser.

Another difficulty about this job is the size. I feel we didn't have enough preparation time for a project of this size. We had essentially six months' prep time in my department. We really needed nine months. When you have a film with so many locations, it's going to take at least a month just to scout them all, and the director is usually part of that process, part of the tech scout group. The director, cinematographer, and I talk about what is to happen with each particular location. With Spike on *Malcolm X*, we would be running out of time because Spike had to be in rehearsal for dance numbers, deal with fittings and what-not because he was acting as well as directing. We really need another month or two before the cameras start to roll.

The art department was at a disadvantage from day one because I felt we were not really as prepared as we should have been. More time would have made me comfortable. This film is a logistical nightmare, because we are shooting on a different set almost every day, and that is very uncommon in this business.

So, as a result, multiple teams have to work, not the absolute best team working 100 percent of the sets. That's from a design point of view.

I think from a directing point of view, it doesn't really allow you to come in and get comfortable with a set before you start shooting. You have to come in and start shooting right away, and you might not be coming back to that location tomorrow, or ever, in the course of the shoot. Which means you have to be a little bit more prepared. I felt none of us had enough preparation time for the whole film. But once the elephants started to move, there was nothing we could do about it.

It would have been difficult, if not impossible, to shoot the Mecca scenes or the Egyptian scenes in this country. The primary reason for that is we wouldn't have been able to get the extras to have the appropriate look. But we are also trying to be realistic, trying to capture the correct atmosphere, and it would not have been appropriate to shoot here. The Arizona desert would not have been appropriate to the Sahara. Those places are okay for cowboy films, but there is a different look entirely. It feels different, too. There is a psychological difference, and I believe that psychology will end up on the screen. So it was good we got to get that stuff in North Africa. Excellent stuff.

Generally Spike accepts the locations I find, and they usually work. The problem we had on this film was the Audubon Ballroom in Harlem, the site of the assassination. It created a whole situation that was beyond everyone's control, in a way.

The ironic thing is that the Audubon Ballroom was the first place we scouted when we started working on this. The very first place. And we thought things were fine. There ended up being a series of problems. There was an asbestos problem, and by the time we wind up, there'll be an expense problem. Because it would be expensive to clean up the asbestos problem and to reconstruct the Audubon. It would be quite expensive. It would cost almost a million dollars just to reconstruct. Restricting the shots, we might be able to get that cost down to half a million. That still isn't good enough. Money is tight, and we're rushing. I don't like it. So we get it down to $300,000 by restricting shots even further, but by then the art department was so busy setting up the rest of the picture, we didn't start construction work until much later than originally planned. And when we went in there, we found asbestos. As a result, we had to stop work, and lost several weeks of work besides, production time, waiting for asbestos reports to come in. By the time those reports come in,

we'll be behind the budget and it'll never happen. The unfortunate part about that is that there is nothing like the Audubon
Ballroom in all the boroughs of New York.

At the top of the schedule we looked for alternatives, and
Spike rejected all of them. He was very passionate about shooting there, at the Audubon. So what happened was, when we lost
it the second time, I had to present him with a series of alternatives, none of which were satisfactory to him. And I think that
was the very first time we actually clashed head-on. That's when
I saw how much the Audubon Ballroom location meant to him. I
had suggested an Elks lodge over in Queens. We could go right
into that space and shoot there and make it very convincing. All
of the other alternatives needed a great deal of work and were
not quite appropriate. When I saw them I knew they were not
quite right, not quite very correct, but we were running out of
time.

In terms of calendar time, we're literally less than ten days
away from shooting the Audubon, without a set.

In the end, Spike insisted we go back to the Diplomat Ballroom in mid-Manhattan. I didn't want to go back because that
was where we would open the picture. We were using the Diplomat as the Roseland Ballroom in Boston, which we'll see near the
top of the film. And I am going to resist going back there because,
frankly, I didn't see how I'm going to make it work. But it is the
very first time in all my years of working with Spike that he
insisted. The problem is, we ran out of time. I literally have four
days in which to alter, re-alter the look of the Diplomat Ballroom
so it won't look the way it looks when we first see it. We'll have
a crew working twenty-four hours a day for four days putting in
a stage. There is no stage there for Malcolm to be assassinated.
We'll try our best to cover up old details and introduce new ones,
details to give the space its character.

We have to completely forget what the Audubon Ballroom
looked like. We have to approach it as though no one had ever
seen it. I think more than 99 percent of people never have, so
maybe they'll accept our solution. The Diplomat Ballroom
doesn't have the physical scale of the Audubon. My other problem with the Diplomat is that it might rob the movie of a visual
climax—unless Spike can come up with something else. When
you design a film, you are moving toward a climax, just as the
script is, and the Audubon would have given the appropriate
feeling, it would have been spectacular enough. The film will still
have a great deal of power—I know all the locations—but for my

money, it won't have that sheer physical visual power it should have at the end. The story will still work, but the visual climax I'd hoped for and that I'm sure Spike had hoped for—maybe it won't be there.

I think *Malcolm X* is essentially divided into three parts. Youth and the Boston and New York years; the jail years; the development of the civil activist years. Each section has its own visual feeling. And each sequence has something wonderful, I think. We have lots of period streets, streets where we spent lots of money restoring sections of New York to look as they would have in the forties.

The opening shot of the film will cost between $750,000 and $1 million. The bulk of that went to art direction. The effects, the coordination—a train we modified pulls across, pan down, a bustling street, not just a street, a wide intersection, parts of four streets. It takes a great deal of effort, coordination, time, and money. I don't know if this is the same for Spike, but I think when you are doing a film of this scale, sometimes you have to go for the broad picture, you go for the big details, and then if you have time, you come in for the little details. You don't have time to give every little thing as much attention as it deserves, but we try. In some cases we succeeded. In some cases we went for that broad look, and hopefully the broad stuff will be special enough to carry us home. But I know we didn't give up any important details. We got all those right.

This is a group of people who have been working together now for many years, and I think we all kind of know subconsciously what is important. It isn't something Spike has to specify with us all the time. We all work on the same wavelength.

The reward for this will be that we have been able to do a movie like this, and people, especially Black folks, who are not accustomed to having the opportunity to do a film of this size, will have the satisfaction of seeing the completed job. The reward is being able to do other movies like this one in the future. That in the future some movie executive will not say, ''Oh no, these folks cannot . . . We won't let them do that.'' Perhaps it will allow all of us, whether it be Spike or other people working with different directors, to have the opportunities to do motion pictures of this size again.

If I had one regret, I'd like to either make the Audubon work, or to build it in a studio somewhere. To have the time and the money and the luxury of doing it properly. I really think that will be the only thing we might miss. We've got everything else. I

think the most remarkable thing about this movie in the end will
be that it's the culmination of the same talented people working
together year after year after year, honing skills, then finally
working on something very big, very difficult, very challenging,
and succeeding—all without killing each other.

RUTH CARTER
Costume Design

I first met Spike in Los Angeles, where I still live. I guess it was
something like early '86, and he hadn't released *She's Gotta
Have It* yet. He came out to see Otis Sallid's *A Night for Dancing*
troupe performance. He was with Robi Reed, who was my friend.
I was in the lobby, talking to my friend Kathy Perkins. It was in
a little rinky-dink dance theater, Washington's, on Adams and
LaBrea. I had designed the costumes for Otis. I was a design
assistant at the L.A. Theater Center here and making no money—
struggling. I had been an intern at some other places. Had my
little rinky-dink car, just trying to make it—to design.

Spike was sitting in the lobby waiting for the performance to
start when I first noticed him. He was sitting next to Kathy, and
I was telling Robi and Kathy my problems at the time. Kathy
worked for a time at L.A. Theater Center, too. I was trying to beef
up my portfolio, and I had compiled some things—really some
spec things because I hadn't worked as an independent designer
yet. I was reading plays and designing clothes for them and
entering them into my book, just so I'd have some entries. So
Kathy and Robi were like, well, do you have your portfolio here
with you? I was like, well, yeah, I do, but, da-dah, da-dah, I just
gave them excuses why I didn't think it looked so good.

Robi said she wanted to see it, that maybe she could give me
some pointers. So intermission came around and she came out
and Spike was with her. I was introduced to him by Robi, so I
knew who he was, knew his name, but he wasn't Spike Lee then
as we know him today. I went through my portfolio page by page
saying, oh, don't look at those shoes, or, oh, look over the hands
here. Finally all of us together came up with some good criti-
cisms of the portfolio. Then Robi, Spike, and I hung out. We
drove around, with Robi behind the wheel. Spike was giving me
pointers about how to get film experience. Telling me to go to
USC and UCLA and do costume design for student thesis films
and that kind of thing. I was listening to him, but I guess I was

looking out of the window or something. For some reason he thought I wasn't hearing him, and he was like, wow, you're not even listening to me! I said, I'm listening, I hear you. I can't quit my job and go right now, Spike. Okay? Spike didn't think it was okay. All night long he kind of grilled me about it, told me I should go for it. I didn't know why he was so interested.

Days went on. Occasionally Robi and I would run into each other and we would talk about how *She's Gotta Have It* was going to do. We went to a screening here and enjoyed it. *She's Gotta Have It* hadn't gone to Cannes yet. We were like, yeah, it's a nice movie, a real nice movie, I liked it, so what? Who am I? It was that kind of thing. Then I got a card in the mail from Spike saying you missed it, you missed the screening! Actually, I was supposed to go to an earlier screening than the one I saw. Spike writes as he speaks. You can almost hear his voice when you read his writing. He wrote, ''Yo, you missed the screening, wha'sup?''

So *She's Gotta Have It* went to Cannes and it was a major hit, and Spike was suddenly like way up there and on top. I was saying to myself, oh my God, I didn't write him back, I didn't write him back, why didn't I write him back? Being a career-minded person, of course. Then I said to myself, well, you know, that's great for him, but you can't start writing and inundating him with interest now. That would be too shallow. But luckily he continued to pursue me and my work because he'd seen something he'd liked in my portfolio, and that's the way Spike is.

Soon enough I was ready to quit my job at the L.A. Theater Center. This was April of '87 or so. I decided just to quit flat out, with no prospects of a job. I was going nowhere there, and I was tired of it. I quit on a Wednesday and had a bad Thursday following it. At seven o'clock that Friday morning, Spike called me and said, ''Ruth, this is the man of your dreams.''

I said, ''Who is this?''—I knew it was his voice—''Is this Billy Dee Williams or somebody?'' He said, ''No, this is Spike. I want you to do my next film.'' So I said, ''I'm ready.'' He called and told Robi the same thing. Robi and I were ecstatic. Our first movie credit. I was ready to strap it up, having quit my job, and she was working someplace where she was hardly getting paid anything, much less what she was worth. We started to scrape together money to go to the movies because Spike kept telling us we had to go see all these movies. Spike wanted me to start illustrating right away. He said we were going to go in August.

August came and he said we would go in September. Septem-

ber came and he said we would go in October. All the while I'm
freelancing here and there for designers around L.A. I was aging
clothes, dyeing them, whatever, at my home. Dyeing them in
my bathtub if I had to do that. I decided I needed to minimize my
expenses and concentrate on the movie full-time, so I sublet my
apartment and I moved to New Hampshire. My brother is an
artist and has a studio there. I stayed with him for a month or
two and illustrated from the script for *School Daze.* I moved to
New York in December and went on payroll in January. We
sacrificed eight months of waiting, but in the end it was well
worth it.

I think since that was my first movie, Spike really made me
think about it early, spend time with it, and research it, and all
that prepared me for the really, really difficult job, the experience of being a department head for the first time. Spike has been
that way from the beginning, and he's still that way now in terms
of prep—in terms of knowing what his people need to do to
prepare. Now I feel Spike really knows me as an artist because
we grew together from back then. If I go to New York and say,
"Spike, they put me in this crazy room with leaking pipes and
dust everywhere, and that's not a creative environment," he
understands that immediately. He knows me. In fact, he gets
mad, he gets very angry because not only is it obvious that an
artist needs a suitable environment to work in, but because we,
he and I, have a relationship which evolved from pure artistic
collaboration. Usually, when I get to New York, the first thing we
do is have lunch, and he says, this is the person I want for this,
and that person for that. You can call this person at home,
whatever—so that I can begin to do my job. He knows what the
casting director needs, what the production designer needs,
what I need—everybody. He's amazing in that way. I love him
for that. I love that overwhelming competence and confidence he
has.

So many people don't understand people like Spike does.
They might hire you and then every question you ask, they say,
"We don't know yet—can you give me some ideas?" They don't
realize the components you need in order to fulfill your job.

We're costuming five decades in *Malcolm X,* if you count the
contemporary one, and three continents, really. Little things.
The Egyptian galabia, the white robe they wear, for example, is
quite different from the Saudi galabia. And the American period
clothes required much research.

I'm from Massachusetts. I knew Malcolm had been in Boston in his early life. I knew people in the Nation of Islam. I was in the Nation of Islam for a very short period of time myself. I felt very comfortable starting out on my own to do some research. My mother and I went to Boston to take care of some business for her and myself. We're from Springfield. While my mother was conducting her business, I went down to the city department of records. I had spoken several times to a person who worked there before I went. I went in there and that woman was ready for me. She gave me Malcolm X's prison file—which was two inches thick. I couldn't believe she just let me alone with it. I went into a cubicle. There were original pictures, letters, all sorts of documents, names of the people who were convicted with him. Somebody had obviously kept the file up pretty well. They had Malcolm's booking picture, his release photos—what a difference there!—his medical history, his interviews, what the cops said when they arrested him, what he had on when he was arrested, the real name of the guy who is named Shorty in the film and in the autobiography. His real name was Malcolm Jarvis. And there was a Sonny Brown. And the woman who is Sophia in the film was really named Cora. There were Cora, Beatrice, and a third woman. But the third girl was never mentioned in the book.

I was so excited. I didn't realize that other people had read that record long before I had found it. They let me Xerox anything in the file. I Xeroxed a package and sent it to Spike. Spike left me a message on my machine: "Ruth, this is great!" And in conclusion he said, "Ruth, I love you." And I was like, what? Not that I ever doubted it, but for him, Spike, to say it, I must have done something really great for him.

I had just come off a film called *House Party II*. But the whole time, even while I was working on that, I had set up an *X* desk at home, researching periods, compiling design books. I started with learning the history of the times. I knew from the book that Malcolm's father was a Garveyite. So I started to read about him, and to check old newspapers and magazines, anything to show me the dress of that period in time. I felt Malcolm X was such a political being, it was important to look at him in that sort of political context. It was kind of nice at the fittings to dress Tommy Hollis, who plays Malcolm's father, and when you're done you turn him and say, yes, this man is a Garveyite. I looked at Black people in Harlem and Black people in the South at that time. During that period in Harlem, you could tell it was Sunday even if you didn't know what day of the week it was just by looking at the clothes. If you saw a lot of white, it was Sunday.

People have told me the first blue zoot suit that Denzel will wear as Malcolm in the movie really captures what they had imagined that first blue zoot suit was like from the book. We designed that suit. Everyone was so excited about the zoot suits. It was like a hoodlum fashion. You know about the Zoot Suit Riots in L.A. I wanted the entire suit to be powder blue. Spike and Denzel had their fittings together in New York, and Spike was screaming with laughter when he was putting on his clothes, and you know he can laugh. He's got a laugh on him.

Denzel put on his own and Spike said, "No Ruth, no, no no, come on, baby, you can do better than this. It's got to be loud! It's got to be loud!" And I kept saying—to myself—no it doesn't. The zoot suit itself, the cut of it is very loud. But it threw me when he said it. I thought, Oh my God, here we go. We painstakingly cut another jacket for Denzel that was much louder and still went with the powder blue pants. But after the tailor finished with that suit and I had Denzel come back for his third fitting, he put that blue zoot suit on and said, "Ruth, this don't need nothing." It was beautiful. It looked beautiful on him and he said it felt beautiful. It was perfect. Sharp as a tack.

We tried to repeat the blue outfit, but Denzel also threw me for a loop, because he said he thought Malcolm's character should wear one zoot suit for the entire forties period. I had had six of them made up. I wasn't planning to use all six, but Spike had sat down earlier and mapped it all out. Repeat this one here, a new one there. We didn't want it to seem like—where's he getting all these clothes from? But if you remember from the book, Malcolm got credit, he got credit from that Jewish tailor. But something came over Denzel, I don't know what it was. He said let's just use one. I nearly had a heart attack. Those suits are $2,500 apiece. Eventually, they decided only one suit would not show the transition of time well enough. We could change his clothes.

I'll have as many as fourteen people working for me at a time on this film, and on big days like the monster rally and the Joe Louis parade, I'll have I don't know how many.

Really, I want to help give an accurate portrayal of Black history on film. Dramatized history, but history all the same. We've had such a compact, truncated view of Black history. Little things. Like the earrings Angela Bassett will wear as Betty Shabazz. Really distinctive. I went and talked to Betty Shabazz because I felt I couldn't do this portrayal without talking to her.

I wouldn't want anybody to try and portray me without at least having a conversation with me. And she gave me insights, like her eye for earrings. Or that her kids wore footie pajamas. Little things. It is still the story of Malcolm X, though. I know I'll end up picking people for crowd scenes here and in Egypt. Part of costume design in crowd scenes are the people themselves. You want to get a good mix of looks. I felt going in that I had really nailed my end of things. I really felt that strongly. I was ready.

PART THREE

THE SHOOT

September 1991

*A*ction!

It starts off with a sign: a giant billboard from the 1940s, advertising Coca-Cola. We're panning down past it to a subway train going through the Roxbury station in Boston. It's supposed to be Roxbury station, but it's Brooklyn, New York. We had subway cars from NYC Transit painted to exactly match the Boston trains of the forties. As the train rolls by, we're shooting with a Steadicam on a Titan crane. The shot continues down to a very busy intersection of Roxbury—the Black section of Boston, made to appear exactly as it was back then, the war years. The camera comes down, tighter, until it holds on my feet. I'm Shorty, Malcolm's best friend from teenage years, getting my two-toned shoes shined on the street. Then I bop from the shoeshine stand across the street into a barbershop. Life is bustling, jostling, happening around me, all the way into the barbershop. The shot cost about one million dollars. We felt it was important *from the jump, from the git-go* to let people know this is a *big* movie, no skimpy fake-ass wannabe shit; show them what the dimensions of the film will be for the next three hours or so.

It is true that my stories have always been small. Well, the stories have not been as small as the scope necessary for me to tell them. I'm not talking about small subject matter—just a small scope. But this joint spans four decades and will be shot on different continents. When I had decided to do this film, I thought of the films of David Lean like *Lawrence of Arabia* or *The Bridge on the River Kwai.* So in order to set the tone right away in the audience's collective head, we had to establish scope from the beginning. Why okey-doke around? It's like football: We're going to run the first play right up top, the bomb, for fifty yards, and then up the middle for twenty yards, and it's going to be like that all day, baby. We're going to be doing that to you for the rest of the game. Until you prove you can stop us. And you can't.

The first day we shot was Monday, September 16, 1991. The location was the barbershop interiors where Shorty is giving Malcolm his first conk. I could tell right away I was going to have a lot of fun playing Shorty, except for getting my hair conked, which was not any fun at all. We stayed on schedule for the next five days, waiting until Sunday to get that big opening shot. I think film is one of the toughest of human endeavors to coordinate and accomplish correctly, and one major reason is big shots like this. There is so much involved. This was such a big shot we had to wait until Sunday so we wouldn't be tangling up commuter traffic as we blocked shots. I'm telling you, we were becoming a traffic jam all by ourselves out there.

The first week looked like this:

Malcolm X

Oneline Schedule

Shoot Day #1–2—Mon., Sept. 16, 1991–Tue. Sept. 17, 1991

Scs. 6	INT BARBER SHOP Malcolm has his hair straightened. Cast: 1,4,29,30,31,120,153	DAY 4 pgs.
Scs. 64F	INT BARBER SHOP, HARLEM Barber gets number from Ching Chow. Cast: 120	DAY 1/8 pgs.
Scs. 9	INT CLOTHING STORE Malcolm tries on a zoot suit. Cast: 1,4	DAY 4/8 pgs.

Shoot Day #3—Wed., Sept. 18, 1991

Scs. 101	INT COURTROOM Malcolm & company get sentenced. Cast: 1,2,4,14,88	DAY 6/8 pgs.
Scs. 125	INT PRISON, ANOTHER ONE Shorty waves letter he received from Malcolm. Cast: 4	DAY 1/8 pgs.
Scs. 33	INT DRUGSTORE Malcolm's "Not for Sale" line. Cast: 1,10	EVE 2/8 pgs.
Scs. 36	INT DRUGSTORE Laura is simply watching Malcolm. Cast: 1,10	DAY 1/8 pgs.
Scs. 36B	INT DRUGSTORE Laura suggests it's not the end of the world. Cast: 1,10	DAY 1/8 pgs.

Shoot Day #4—Thur., Sept. 19, 1991

Scs. 94	INT HARVARD SQUARE APARTMENT Malcolm suggests Peg turn out for him. Cast: 1,2,4,14	DAY 7/8 pgs.
Scs. 95	INT HARVARD SQUARE APARTMENT Peg suggests Rudy as a driver for them. Cast: 1,2,4,14	DAY 4/8 pgs.
Scs. 99	INT HARVARD SQUARE APARTMENT Shorty conks Malcolm's hair, no water. Cast: 1,4	DAY 7/8 pgs.
Scs. 100	INT HARVARD SQUARE APARTMENT Cops get the draw on Malcolm and Shorty. Cast: 1,4,134	DAY 5/8 pgs.

Shoot Day #5—Fri., Sept. 20, 1991

| Scs. 95a | INT HARVARD SQUARE APARTMENT
Malcolm meets Rudy.
Cast: 1,2,4,14,26 | DAY 3 5/8 pgs. |
| Scs. 95b | INT HARVARD SQUARE APARTMENT
Malcolm shows Shorty the bullet chamber.
Cast: 1,4,26 | DAY 3/8 pgs. |

End of Week #1

Shoot Day #6—Sun., Sept. 22, 1991

| Scs. 1 | EXT ROXBURY STREET
Shorty bops down the street.
Cast: 4 | DAY 2/8 pgs. |
| Scs. 5 | EXT ROXBURY STREET
Shorty w/packages on way down street.
Cast: 4 | DAY 1/8 pgs. |

Scs. 10   EXT ROXBURY STREET   DAY 3/8 pgs.
                 Malcolm and Shorty strut
                   down the street.
                 Cast: 1,4

                                              End Day #6

I knew right away this was special because of Denzel Washington as Malcolm Little and Malcolm X. Denzel had done Malcolm in the play *When Chickens Come Home to Roost,* around ten or twelve years before this, so nobody, least of all me, should have been surprised he could bring so much likeness. For me it was more than a likeness. It wasn't superficial, it seemed to come from inside out. Malcolm X was radiating from him. I'm sure some other actors would have loved to have tried to do the role, but I can't think of anybody else who could have brought it off like Denzel. I don't know. I wasn't speculating, because Denzel already had the role. He was attached to the project before me—I'd talked to him while I had been making the deal to do this picture.

Denzel had come to New York that summer, and we spent time together really going over the script. He had made a lot of suggestions, and together with consultant Paul Lee and myself, we were able to come up with the final script, which is what we are shooting. I wasn't worried about Denzel's acting. We were just trying to get the script into shape. We were still working on that last third, trying to find the right speeches, because the speeches that Baldwin had in the script weren't necessarily Malcolm's best. That was where Paul could help us. He was able to give us the necessary material so we could pick and choose Malcolm's lines, the necessary themes so we could show the different transitions Malcolm came upon in his political thought, even though Paul wasn't ready for us to start when we did. That is why good brother Paul is the consultant and I'm the filmmaker.

But Denzel was ready. He was chomping on the bit. He had done all his research, he had done his fasting, and once he got made up, he was young Detroit Red, he was a God-abandoned Satan of the prison, he evolved into Malcolm X. Between takes we'd talk and he'd laugh and say, "Spike, me and you gotta be ready to get the next jet out of the country when this comes out." We're both pumped and ready to roll—and not out of the country, but through shooting the film.

We are shooting the film for the most part in chronological order, because of Denzel's conk. That was a big thing, you know.

We'd had meetings for months where the only subject was the best order in which to shoot the film according to the conk, what was most feasible. Really the whole shooting schedule of the movie is predicated on when Denzel's hair is conked and when it's not. Larry Cherry, our ace hair stylist, is going to take care of it. It's a hard job, and I will say I haven't been understanding about it all the time—the hair got fucked up a couple of times, frankly. But Larry has worked with Denzel before and knows the texture of his hair. After we finally cut Denzel's processed hair, there were still one or two scenes to shoot from his earlier days. We're going to come up with a wig—Larry calls them "hair-pieces"—so it doesn't look fake. Maybe we'll use a hat.

Denzel is in the whole film. He's scheduled to have only a couple of days off. He has to be in shape. And he is. You might say he went through a personal hajj, a pilgrimage of his own, for himself. He went on a strict diet with periodic fasting, no alcohol, reading the Koran, going to bed early, going through a cleansing. He felt—and I felt along with him—that he had to come to this subject right. If you weren't righteous, if you weren't trying to reach a level of high spirituality—that might show up on the screen.

Denzel makes suggestions all the time. I can hear him now, off in a corner, whispering in my ear before a take: "My question is this, why . . . ?" Or it would be: "What I'm saying is this, Spike. Why don't we try . . . ?" I think it is really good in this case that *Malcolm X* is not the first time Denzel and I have worked together. That really helps this film, in that we had really gotten to know each other's moves on *Mo' Better*. On that film there were some things I did that he probably didn't like, and there were some things that he did that I didn't think were so hot. And because of that our working relationship is a lot better on this one. I'm listening to him, he's listening to me. But, already, we're in concert on the scope, the viewpoint, and the methodology.

I think Denzel is underrated as an actor (even though he won an Oscar for Best Supporting Actor as Trip in *Glory*), mostly because he's handsome. I think a lot of times people take his good looks for granted—I mean that since he looks so good, that automatically means he can't act. That's the thinking in the case of women more than men, but that also applies in D's case. Denzel is a fine, trained stage actor, and I believe that on the whole that matinee idol stuff obscures his craft. I think that was one of the reasons he wanted to do *Mo' Better*, so he wouldn't have to play another saint. In my eyes, he has largely chosen to play a lot of the Sidney Poitier–type roles. His characters never really had flaws. On *X,* Denzel ended up giving a Herculean effort. He was amazing. Every single day, he was just amazing. He had the full range of the Malcolm character in four different stages. He played beautifully with three different female leads at different times, sometimes on concurrent days—the Laura character, the Sophia character, and the Betty Shabazz character—and was totally successful. He could regurgitate Malcolm's speeches verbatim, and then change them around for effect. He had those looks and those mannerisms down pat. He *became* Malcolm X. And, you know, we never talked about the importance of the role for him or the picture for me. We knew what it meant. I don't think there was anything to discuss about it on that level. It was understood.

Shoot Day #22—Wed., Oct. 16, 1991

Scs. 104	INT PRISON SOLITARY CELL Water can spout comes into Malcolm's cell. Cast: 1,15	NIGHT 2/8 pgs.
Scs. 106 Prt	INT PRISON SOLITARY CELL Malcolm tells Chaplain to shove symbols. Cast: 1	DAY 1/8 pgs.
Scs. 107	INT PRISON SOLITARY CELL Malcolm is at low point in his life. Cast: 1	NIGHT 2/8 pgs.
Scs. 108	INT PRISON SOLITARY CELL Malcolm is beaten and says his number. Cast: 1,89	NIGHT 3/8 pgs.
Scs. 109 Prt	INT PRISON SHOWER ROOM Bembry gives Malcolm nutmeg. Cast: 1,3	DAY 3/8 pgs.

End Day #22

It was hard casting the film because we have so many speaking roles in it. Robi Reed and I spent a lot of time together casting every single role down to a T, and then having to do a lot of casting even while we were shooting. Usually, once we start shooting, we've casted everything, but there were so many roles in this picture, that wasn't the case. I knew we'd have to do a lot of this kind of work on the fly when we started this.

We had a lot of talented actors come through with us in cameos. A lot of times their egos won't allow them to do that. That wasn't the case on *Malcolm X*. Christopher Plummer is exceptionally good. He really came through as Chaplain Gill, the prison religious instructor from Malcolm's days in prison. We shot some of those scenes at Rahway State Penitentiary in Rahway, New Jersey. Ruthie Carter, our costume designer, had an older suit jacket for him to wear, and she was concerned about a stain on it, but Christopher brushed it off, said it was properly in character or something like that, and gave us one great scene, performing with Denzel. All cameo performers were outstanding in this film: Karen Allen, Peter Boyle, John Sayles, Craig Wasson, David Patrick Kelly, who rocked as Mr. Ostrowski. We had cameos from political figures, or people who had known Malcolm: Bobby Seale, Al Sharpton, William Kunstler.

Speaking of casting, I am very quietly, you-have-to-drag-it-out-of-me proud of the people who have acted in my films and gone on to do bigger things, better things—from my sister Joie to Annabella Sciorra to Wesley Snipes to Rosie Perez to Sam Jackson to John Turturro to his brother Nick to Martin Lawrence, to whoever comes out smoking from *Malcolm X,* and some of this talent will.

Albert Hall has the right blank somber tone as Baines, the character who converts Malcolm in prison, then undermines him later on as one of Elijah Muhammad's right-hand men. And Angela Bassett is doing a fantastic job of portraying Betty Shabazz. I mean fantastic. It matters to me, what people have said in the past about my depictions of women in my films. The first thing I think they have to understand is, I'm not a woman, so I can't see women as women see women. But I can understand women saying there should have been more or better-developed female characters in my films.

Looking strictly at this one, women were told to step into the background and walk behind the men in the Nation of Islam, so all I'm really doing is showing that the way it was. You can't really come down on me for the second-class status the Nation of

Islam gave women, because the brothers in the Nation always made the sisters ride in the backseat. Having said all that, I think Angela Bassett brings off one of the best female performances, in terms of characterization, that I've gotten from anyone in any of my films—although the credit has to be shared with Baldwin in this case, I think. Betty Shabazz herself should really thank Angela Bassett after this.

But the man who really rocked the set from roof to floor is Delroy Lindo as West Indian Archie, who was Malcolm's numbers-running mentor in the streets of Harlem. Delroy is throwing down so hard, it's hard for me to believe now that he wasn't my first choice. My first choice had been Sam Jackson, who played Wesley Snipes's crackhead brother, Gator, in *Jungle Fever*. But Sam chose to do a movie called *White Sands*. He got a lot of critical acclaim for *Jungle Fever*, including a special award at Cannes, so I could understand—he had gotten a much-better-paying role. Then after Sam, we were going to try and work it out with Roc Dutton, but we couldn't get our schedule together with his television show, *Roc*. Then we thought Avery Brooks, the Rutgers professor of drama. He'd played Paul Robeson on the stage, and Hawk on TV. Couldn't get it together with him, though. So, we ended up getting Delroy Lindo. He turned out to *be* West Indian Archie! You never know. I think even Denzel is blown away by him—he's always commenting about how strong Delroy's performance is.

The cast has come to play! I likes, I likes.

What's more, Al Freeman, Jr., the Howard university drama instructor and veteran stage and film actor, is nothing less than extraordinary as the Honorable Elijah Muhammad. He has my man's halting speech, inflections, and physical presence down cold. Kate Vernon is an actress we brought in to read with Denzel, and she turned out be a great Sophia—I couldn't picture anybody else in the role after her first few readings and rehearsals. She really had a good understanding of what we needed there. In one scene, where Malcolm is playing Russian roulette to impress his gang, her look at him afterward—slightly trembling hand pulling on a cigarette, and a fearful but star-gazing dazed look, then she whispers, "I love you"—is just ripping! Great cinema. I laughed out loud when we finished that take. We're getting it.

Details are important because they show up on 70 mm film, so we have to be very meticulous with our period stuff, and the set dressers and production designers have done well. We even found the old brother who made Malcolm's original star and crescent gold ring. Kevin Ladson, our prop master, found him up in Harlem. The brother used the original ring molds and made up another gold one from the original and two others as backups. Denzel will keep the gold one after we shoot. Authenticity is very important in any film. If you see a pack of cigarettes, we had to find old Chesterfields, or old whatever you might see in a shot. When there's a press conference in the film, those are the actual old cameras you see. Period cameras. Period guns. Period cigarettes, period silverware, games, period whatever. As I said, this is one of the most difficult endeavors known to humankind, filmmaking, so it's good to give somebody like Kevin his props—a prop master needs his own propers, his own good notices, and his own respect—from time to time. So there it is. It takes people like him to make a film work. Kevin and his people have left nothing to chance. I've insisted on this. No shorts.

Same goes with the locations. We used a little town just upstate, Peekskill, New York, which stands in for Omaha, Nebraska, and East Lansing, Michigan, for the scenes of Malcolm's childhood in the Little family household and for the attack of the nightriders, and it's coming off good. Later on we'll shoot some interiors at a house on Park Avenue in Manhattan for the burglary stuff that was supposed to take place in the ritzy Beacon Hill section of Boston.

Problems. Big problems. I will admit it is hard, with the problems we had early in the shoot. Big problems. I think we're being tested. I know I am. Hurdles are being thrown in our path—personal and otherwise—and we have to overcome them. And we will. I know it. I know it 'cause I have to know it. First, before the shoot, there was the whole so-called controversy with the writer Amiri Baraka, who didn't want me directing this film, said I was too middle class. Then my girlfriend, my ex-girlfriend, Veronica Webb, who was playing one of the Muslim secretaries that Elijah Muhammad got pregnant, axed me. Two weeks into the movie, this happened. I was reeling. I wouldn't recover from that until the next spring.

Then my father was busted for heroin possession in a cab in Brooklyn. Then a young woman who was going to be an extra for us in one of the Harlem crowd scenes was raped and murdered on 135th Street. Then we had security problems. We didn't know whether or not we were going to have any problems with any factions from the Nation of Islam—some of their forces gave us security on both *Do The Right Thing* and *Jungle Fever.* Mysteriously, one day while were setting up to shoot exteriors for a Harlem rally scene, a car came screaming down the block, crashing to the curb. Somebody had tied a brick to the accelerator, and gunned it in our direction.

It was, you know, little things like that.

The young woman who got murdered—that really affected me. She had not even worked on the film. She was supposed to work in one of the large crowd scenes, where we'd have many hundreds of extras. This was to be later in the next week. She was raped and murdered, and the cops found her date book, and she had a date down there for one day the next week when she was supposed to be an extra on *X.* So all of a sudden the newspapers are calling the office at Forty Acres, as though I was responsible. Part of me knows I'm not responsible, the film's not responsible, but, still, that was a human being that someone killed on 135th Street, and the tabloids want to appeal to that part of it, any lurid interests, and they don't care who might get hurt in the process. And it sure made headlines in New York, almost like I had set her up to be killed by making a film about somebody like Malcolm X, who was dangerous. I had put her life in danger. These newspaper editors know *exactly* what they're doing. They choose what is news based on their own personal agendas and prejudices. Sometimes it was hard to concentrate on directing during this time. But I had to do it because nobody is going to sit out in the audience and say, ''Well, cousin, it's a fucked-up movie true enough, but the brother was going through some hard times, his woman left him, his father is in rehab, and we should cut him some slack. We understand.''

Don't hold your breath waiting for those sentiments. Bet on this: Your average motherfuckers don't want to hear no fucking excuses. ''Look,'' they'll say, ''we don't care if your whole family died during the full moon and left you with a limp dick, when we come to the theater we want to see the shit up on the screen! *X* better be slammin'. Period. End of story. There *is* no excuse. I don't want to hear that shit about how you had a fight with your girlfriend. We don't give two motherfucks about that. Only the work counts.''

They are absolutely correct, but then I woke up and my father was in jail on a heroin charge, I was crushed. And when that shit hit the front page of every tabloid in town—I was too through.

My father has been using heroin on and off, like many of the jazz musicians of that era. He never shot up, that I know of. He just snorted the garbage. I'd told him many times, "Daddy, later for that." I had told him he needed to go to the rehab or detox. He's been arrested for it two or three other times, but it just never got out. But after this particular arrest, while we're shooting the film, he squealed, "Spike Lee's my son. I'm Spike Lee's father!" He was trying to get favorable treatment. Well, it didn't take too long from there. In a frenzy, Desiree Jellerette, my assistant, called me up on the set and said, "Spike, the newspapers are calling and saying something about your father!"

So my father sacrificed me to try and save his own ass. He told me later he hadn't wanted to spend the night in jail. My head was spinning, so I don't even remember where we were supposed to be shooting the next day. He said he couldn't get to a phone to call me to let me know. He gave me up not even thinking about the consequences to me or the film. So I was talking to my brothers and sisters and to my grandmother and my uncle, trying to piece it together at the time. But there was nothing I could do about the papers. That shit was out. I mean, they were running that shit on television the same night, Thursday. I mean running a scrawl on the bottom of the TV—like it was a hurricane coming, or an earthquake had hit, or the president had been shot. Spike Lee's father arrested. Details at 11:00. That was some very cold shit.

I really dreaded going in for the next morning's shoot. It was on a Friday. Ironically, that was the same day Veronica was supposed to work, I still loved her and I was grieving on the inside. That was the first and last day of the entire shoot where I didn't see a single newspaper. There wasn't one newspaper on the entire set. At least I never saw one. Understand me clearly. I don't know what they were saying behind my back—plenty, probably, because people are people—but it seemed to me the cast and crew made a conscious effort to keep the papers away from me and not to mention the situation. That was the roughest day of the entire shoot for me psychologically. So that's Daddy and Veronica right there in one day, then with the young woman getting murdered later, it was just hard. Hard. Hard. A motherfucker. That whole day was a blur—me going through the motions.

I was like, "Damn, what else can happen?" I shouldn't have asked. Here comes that runaway car crashing down the street with a brick tied to the accelerator. Nobody got hurt, but if there was one thing I didn't need was any more distractions. We still don't know what that was about.

We had three or four security groups working with us during the shooting schedule. While we were shooting, the construction crew would be at one site, getting another location ready for us, and all those places needed security. A Nation of Islam chapter here in New York called the X-Men has done security for our films since *Do The Right Thing.* That movie was shot in one block of Bed-Stuy, and before we began to shoot there were three crack houses on that block. The Nation closed them up—without violence. They just did it, let the people know they were not welcome and would be paid attention to by the Nation of Islam if they stayed. And that was enough to get them out of there. The same thing happened in Washington, D.C., at the Mayfair Mansions project. The Muslims cleaned it up. But you don't read that in the tabloids. So we had a very good relationship with them. We'd had X-Men security on other movies, and I'd like to thank brothers Anthony and Wayne for providing it. But during the middle of the shoot for *X,* they got word from Chicago, national headquarters, to step back from us. Brothers Wayne and Anthony flew to Chicago and smoothed everything over, because some of their guys had pulled out when Minister Farrakhan sent the word down. But everything was worked out in the end. We hope. We gotta wait to see what happens when the film opens in the late fall of next year.

This feeling that everything had been worked out with security didn't come before more problems occurred. By losing regular security for a while, and due to the size and different locations, we had another security force from another group—so while we were shooting one day, this group was at the construction site of the next location. Somebody said something wrong, and a brother with the security force pushed a white boy through a plate-glass window and fucked him up. The whole crew left and said they weren't coming back until adequate security was provided.

Little, petty bullshit like this—it can make you crazy.

Shoot Day #35—Mon., Nov. 4, 1991

Scs. 152   INT HOSPITAL WARD   DAY 2/8 pgs.
                  Betty gets call from
                     Malcolm.
                  Cast: 6

Scs. 133B   INT MENTAL WARD   NIGHT 2/8 pgs.
              Cadillac is old and
                  wet-brained.
              Cast: 25

Scs. 147   EXT HARLEM HOSPITAL   NIGHT 3/8 pgs.
              Malcolm and crowd arrive
                  at hospital.
              Cast: 1,7,8,9

Scs. 148   EXT HARLEM HOSPITAL   NIGHT 3/8 pgs.
              Malcolm confronts Captain
                  Green.
              Cast: 1,7,8,9,85

Scs. 149   EXT HARLEM HOSPITAL   NIGHT 6/8 pgs.
              Malcolm disperses Fruit of
                  Islam and crowd.
              Cast: 1,7,8,9,85,98

Scs. 141   EXT HARLEM HOSPITAL   DUSK 6/8 pgs.
              Malcolm prodded to action
                  over Bro. Johnson.
              Cast: 1,7,8,9,102,141

                                          End Day #35

Betty Shabazz has been asking and asking for a script, and finally I let her see it. And my instincts were right. She hated the script—hated it. She said it was the worst piece of shit she'd ever read in her life. She came and told me she and Malcolm never fought. Now what married couple in the history of the world has never had an argument? There was never any tension about money, about their financial status? Ever? Was this some kind of Disney, Merrie Melodies, Archie and Betty life they led? Myself, I don't think so. I just—I'll have to handle it. We're trying to approximate the truth. How are we going to tell a realistic story about Malcolm X if we have it so that he and Betty never fought, never had words? What kind of film is this supposed to be?

I wish we had gotten a lot more input from Betty, but at the same time I realize that it must be painful for her still. She sat there and saw her husband killed in front of her eyes, with their four children at her feet and two babies in her belly. So no matter what I feel, you can't get around that—so when she would go and curse me out, which was often, I'd have to sit there and take it. She had raised six daughters by herself. It's not like she had a lot of help, either. She has gone through a lot, so no matter what she had said to me, that was always at the forefront in my mind. I had to understand that she was married to Malcolm; this was her husband that we were talking about, making a film about. But I have to admit, I did have my moments.

Betty's dislike of the script might have been in part what set Amiri Baraka off, but then again he was going off before she ever saw it, so there had to be some other motivation behind his attacking me, although by now I oughta be used to it. Something in me just won't let me take that shit without saying something back; it's not my personality to just persevere. I know Baraka. I used to go out with one of his two daughters, Lisa Jones (Baraka's name used to be LeRoi Jones), and she collaborated on three books with me. But out of nowhere, even before we began principal photography, here comes Baraka on a blitzkrieg, attacking me, saying that the masses of Black people didn't want Spike Lee directing this film, that I was a petit bourgeois Negro who had no claim to the legacy of Malcolm—some serious blathering.

What really hurt me about the whole thing with Baraka was that you never heard a peep out of him as long as Norman Jewison was directing the film. Not one peep out of him. He didn't say shit then, but now he's going to take me on? What kinda shit . . .

But Yusuf Shah had dimed on Baraka, too. He said that back in the day, when he was LeRoi Jones and was "down in the village, in those little tea shops, reading poetry," Baraka had come up to Harlem one day and given a little speech to Malcolm and the people in Temple No. 7. I got the feeling Yusuf Shah didn't remember it as a good speech, like they were being taken to task, criticized by Baraka, talking about Africa and the Black man this and the Black man that. Like Baraka has always tried to make up the rules for Black people all by himself. Who elected him? But the most interesting part of that story is that Yusuf Shah said Malcolm had gotten up, sighed, looked at Baraka, then looked away from him and told the audience, "Imiri Baraka has nothing to say to us. And until he gets rid of that white woman he is married to or that he is living with, he can't say nothing. What does he look like, coming out and telling *us* about blackness . . . ?"

Now this is what Yusuf Shah said Malcolm had said. I wasn't there. But I used that when Baraka attacked me in the press. Deep down I was sad, because what do Baraka and I have to fight about? Nothing. I asked people why he would've started attacking me, and there were many theories—maybe he was jealous, maybe he wanted to work on the project with me himself, maybe he was taking Betty Shabazz's side for some reason, maybe this, maybe that.

Denzel told me to just forget it and not even respond, but that's not my makeup, to let that kind of shit go. I fired back about me being just a little kid when Malcolm came along, while Baraka was down in the Village, being a beatnik, running around with Allen Ginsberg, not Malcolm, and living with a white woman. *Newsweek* asked me to write a piece about the "controversy."

Who was he to talk? Then somehow he got a script. In some mysterious fashion, he got an early draft of the script. And for quite some time Baraka was the one cheerleading the whole Spike Should Not Be Doing This Film parade. He was trying to convince the masses. Maybe that's what he was jealous of. I think jealousy has to come into play a little there. You know, we're *doing* what these guys were just talking about in the sixties. Not to negate what anybody did in the past, what they did, what Baraka did, but he has never had access to the people that we have access to through film, or been able to take it to the next level, *and* we're getting paid. Baraka has been around a lot longer than I have, to put it mildly, but how many people are going to see a play, now, really? Even a hit Broadway play is only, what, four or five hundred seats a night? With a movie you're talking about reaching millions and millions and millions of people. So because of film, I have far greater access to the masses than he does, or ever will. And with the access comes the influence, comes the power, and comes the money.

There were several attempts by co-producer Preston Holmes and filmmaker St. Claire Bourne to get me together with Baraka to talk during preproduction. When we started to shoot, I didn't have time, nor was I going to try and go out of my way to meet with Baraka. My feelings were simple—fuck it. I still feel he should have come correct from the git-go.

During this time, in the summer before we shot, we had a big celebration for the first anniversary of the opening of Spike's Joint, our retail outlet just up DeKalb Avenue from our production offices in Brooklyn. Big celebration, people happy, gala affair, all that kind of shit. Baraka shows up with some thirty protestors, chanting, and gives me a letter saying and he and the other people who had signed the letter had big problems, big problems with me directing this film about the life of Malcolm X. This had happened in July. And there's more to it as well.

I had wanted Baraka to be one of the essayists in my book

Five for Five, which was scheduled to come out after *Jungle Fever* in 1991. I had wanted him to write about *Mo' Better Blues.* And he wrote something that was, to me, horrible and ineffectual. He didn't have one positive thing to say for any of my films. Not one good thing. So I said, "I'm not going to use this." He said, "Look at those other essays and you'll see that all the people had some problems with your work." I told him that's fine. Most people do have some problems with my work. That was fine. But he had a total disregard for my work. I can read. He flatly condemned everything I had done, and wanted me to publish it. I didn't use it, which is my prerogative—it's my motherfucking book. I gave him the $500 kill fee, then said I'm not using it. And I didn't.

So Baraka ended up on the soap box against me directing *Malcolm X.* And that's when he got the script. Somebody on the crew had a brother who knew Baraka and had seen him with the script. And in the end, that bothered me as much as anything, that he could have gotten a copy of the script. His legitimate concern might explain some of his reaction concerning *Malcolm X,* but not all of it. They had a couple of more weak rallies, and then it sort of died down. Maybe Baraka and I will get together and talk about it soon, so I can find out what his difficulty with my directing the film could be without seeing the result first. He's an artist, and to me he ought to know better. Right now, I've got to get this picture shot. Like I said, nobody cares about your troubles.

Because of the budget crunch, we had decided not to shoot in Boston. There were several locations there that we had in mind that would have been great, but we had to scrap them due to economic infeasibility. Like, we knew we couldn't use the inside of the Audubon Ballroom, but that didn't keep us from being able to use the outside of it for some shots. The assassination shoot during the week of December 9 through 13 was the most difficult, technically and emotionally. We were shooting so many different, difficult-to-reproduce elements in that one scene, and shooting them until we got them right. As I said, film is a motherfucker to get right. The brothers who were performing as the assassins, including Giancarlo Esposito as Thomas Hayer, had to really get into their roles, which drained them emotionally. Choreographing chaos is difficult. A tough, intense, five-day week for what undoubtedly will be the most charged moment of the film.

I felt we had it. I likes, I likes!

Sometimes the weather can play havoc with you. The week after the assassination scene, we were shooting Malcolm's father, Earl, dying on the trolley tracks in Lansing, Michigan. Only we were at the port of Brooklyn at midnight. We had the rain towers going full blast, and it was cold out there. Frigid. This will be maybe only ten seconds in the film, the shot of the trolley closing in on Earl Little's battered head lying on the tracks. But every shot had to be as near to perfect as we could get it. So it was Cut! Let's go again! Tommy Hollis, who plays Earl Little, was game. He was game until about 2:00 A.M. Then he finally looked up, wet from the constant dousing from the rain towers, freezing, shivering, and he said, "Spike, I can't go anymore. I don't care if we can get it or not, or whether I'm in it or not. I'm whipped. I can't go anymore, man."

That was the first time an actor ever quit on me. We had it. We'd finished shooting principal photography in North America, and we broke for the Christmas holidays.

The Completion Bond Co. was never going to be Santa Claus to us, and I was determined not to give them anything either. They stuck their noses in trying to snuff out our foreign locations in Africa. We were in late December by now, and getting to the bottom of the original budget. The money was getting funny. There weren't even any bones left.

The Completion Bond Co. didn't want us to go to Egypt. They said we should shoot the Mecca section at the New Jersey shore. Now, how are you going to shoot fucking Cairo or the Sahara desert and Mecca in fucking January at the fucking New Jersey shore? These people don't know how to make films. Then they said, "Let's shoot in Arizona!" Oh yeah? Where are you going to get the extras from? How many Arabs are there in Arizona? How many Black people? They don't even celebrate Dr. King's birthday in Arizona. I'm not spending a red nickel in that state. And the Sahara doesn't have any Western pitchfork cactus or tumbleweeds anyway. Hey people, you ignorant motherfuckers, this ain't no John Ford Western. Wake the fuck up!

How can you have 160 minutes of Malcolm saying white people are blue-eyed devils and then not go spend the time or money to shoot the pivotal moments that caused him to turn around on that line of thinking, which occurred in Africa and in Saudi Arabia? We had them by the nuts on that one. We *had* to go to Africa. And our second unit was the first American film crew that I know about to be allowed into Mecca for the sacred rite of hajj. Had to go. Just like Malcolm had to go.

When the bond company came in at the beginning of December, I went through the script to see if and where we could compress the remaining scenes, or cut some stuff out that would save some money. Cut the cost of the film. But it's not like we were spending money out of control in the first place. It's not like that money was going into anybody's pocket. All that $33 million and then some was on the screen. It's not rare for a film to go over budget these days, you know.

The Completion Bond Co. is presided over by a Black woman named Bette Smith, and her emissary to us was a guy named Mack Harding. I'd heard he was walking around with his chest stuck out, trying to take over my film. He never said any of this shit while I was around. But the crew quickly began calling him Indy, short for Indiana Jones, for the felt hats he wore. Then, the Terminator. He came in trying to take over. In December, when we had our first meeting with him, his attitude was such that I got up and walked out the minute he opened his mouth. But I heard what he had been saying when I wasn't around to the crew: "This is my movie, this is my set! Mine!" He never said that shit to me. I knew I was going to have a series of confrontations with him.

Juice opened while we were in Cairo. We got there on January 15, 1992, in the middle of the week, and left a week later. I was really hoping Ernest had a success with it. He's had to do a lot this year, his directorial debut, shooting *X*. And then we heard somebody had been killed at a theater where *Juice* was showing. People think this genre of Black film, the b-boy shoot 'em up, fosters this sort of violence. Ernest was trying to show how futile this is, this violence, but a lot of times if the audience isn't sophisticated enough, when you're trying to slam something, they don't see it that way. They see glorification. They don't think through: "Oh shit, look at that gun." When I went to a showing of John Singleton's *Boyz in the Hood,* a lot of kids were cheering and applauding Ice Cube when he blows the guys away in the end, saying, "Kill the nigger!" A lot of young people missed the point entirely. And, yes, maybe you could avoid that by preaching in a film—"guns are bad," or "we have to stop killing ourselves"—but that would make it not the best movie you could make. It would be infantile. Rather than be a fool for fools, you hope the audience gains intelligence. But yeah, it's depressing.

I know Ernest had to be depressed about it. I'd be depressed
if I made a movie and somebody got killed the first day it opened,
just for coming to see it. But the moviemaker has a responsibility. Hopefully, you're not just doing this to make exploitation,
make a quick dollar, play to the lowest common denominator.
You know what the media is gonna do, it's gonna say all Black
films will draw violence in the same way.

Cairo was wild. I saw an old photo of King Faisal of Saudi
Arabia, and I hollered out "Alec Guinness!" Another reference to
old *Lawrence.* But the power of the land and the depth of the
history was there, in the pyramids, the Sphinx, the old mosques,
the Nile, the very air, the morning and evening calls to prayer by
the muezzins. We're authentic. New Jersey shore my Black ass.

Associate producer Fernando Sulachin had done a great job
setting things up for us in Egypt, and also with the second unit
stuff in Mecca. And an Egyptian director named Samir helped me
out for the crowd scenes we set up on the streets of Cairo. He
kind of cracked me up in a way. When his bullhorn didn't work
to instruct the extras on movement, he waded in and started
slinging and pushing people around. I was like, Damn! I'd never
try that on the streets of Brooklyn. The people themselves were
beautiful, and they made us feel right at home. Later, I was
interviewed on *Good Morning America,* and I was asked about
going to Egypt and Africa. So I just said, "Egypt is in Africa."
Divide and conquer.

The bond company didn't want us to go to Cairo, and then
not to South Africa, even with just a skeleton crew, unless we
had a signed agreement beforehand from Nelson Mandela, saying he would appear in the film. So I just thought, "Fuck it, we're
going anyway." I told Preston, "Book the tickets."

On our way from Cairo to South Africa, we had a bomb
threat. We stayed on the ground at the Nairobi Airport while all
the luggage was searched. Somebody knew we were on this
plane.

In Johannesburg, we were met by the Welcome Wagon,
mostly the African National Congress representatives. We never
really came in contact with emissaries from the white-controlled
South African government at all. I don't feel like we were kept
away from anything we wanted to see, though. We went into
Soweto, and other places. I can't compare anything I've ever
seen to Soweto, or some of the other Black townships. We only
met up with whites at the airport, or in customs. They were away

somewhere behind their barricades, taking the best of everything.

South Africa is beautiful, great topography, prettiest place on earth. If it isn't, I know it's the richest. That's why they ain't giving that shit up. It's all about what they can pull out of the ground over there. The mines, man, the mines—there were great piles and hills of earth all around; you could see them, like small mountains, in so many places. They're digging feverishly over there, man, and the trip of it is, they haven't found the bottom of all those riches in the bowels of Mother Africa yet. Not after greedily digging, nonstop, all these years, digging at a fever pitch, hauling out all those diamonds and sticking the name DeBeers on them, or digging out all that gold and calling it the Krugerrand, digging out all that uranium so they can make that fucking plutonium. All that digging, all that oppression, all that death and social nightmare—and they can't find the bottom of it. That should humble them, right there.

Mandela had his reservations, though. He didn't want to say the line "by any means necessary" at the end of the film. Because of the political situation in South Africa, he didn't want to say those words. When that point comes, we'll cut from Mandela and go back to Malcolm X, and we'll use actual footage. Mandela's trying to accomplish what Malcolm is saying, peacefully. But after going there, I believe the only way that shit in South Africa is ever going to change is through something that simply ain't no tea-and-crumpets negotiations. Frederick Douglass said it: "Power surrenders nothing without a demand." One man, one woman vote, that ain't gonna happen as long as those mines are so profitable.

The best move the South African government ever made was letting Nelson out. In a way, the people would have been better off if they had kept him in isolation, in jail, because now everybody thinks South Africa is on the road to social recovery. Now that I've been there, I can tell you that this isn't so, by no means is this true. If you compare the outcry against apartheid before Nelson was released to that sound you don't hear nobody making now—well it's obvious to me. Not a squeak from the world court of opinion. Black people still cannot vote there, Black people are still pitted against each other in these murderous confrontations there, all the fucking time, used like pawns, less than pawns, like dogs. Black people are still living in what amounts to concentration camps over there. And all that talent, all that love, all that beauty, all those lives are being wasted, all that human potential down the drain. That was the first time in my life that I wanted to pick up something—anything—and start killing people, when I went there to South Africa and saw what was happening to my sisters and brothers. It would be just like God to have the woman who could cure cancer or the man who could cure AIDS be there in one of the hellhole South African townships, flirting with government-induced disaster, maybe even already dead. You can't fool the Maker with this bullshit.

We shot a lot of documentary footage, ten-year-olds doing this dance, singing "one bullet, one settler." Ten-year-olds singing this. It's come to that in South Africa. But South Africa could not exist if it was not being propped up by American and British big businesses.

It was an education for me. All these factions, not just the ANC, but SWAPO and that government stooge Buthelezi and his Zulus and all these different groups. Divide and conquer. Oh, there was one other thing. We made no news reports while we were there that I know about. There was a whiteout of our activities, like we were never there, according to the news organizations of South Africa. They think they can remain frozen in time, while they rape land, rape those people, just so they can sit in their tennis whites on a veranda and tell some Black person to bend down and pick that up and change their babies' shitty diapers. But time doesn't stand still—not even on film. We had what we needed, so we got the hell out of there. The filming of *Malcolm X* had been completed. Usually, when you finish a shoot, especially one as important as this, you get all kinds of congratulations from the studio—if not a bottle of champagne, at least a telegram. What did we get from Warner Brothers? Jack-shit. Nada. Not a thing.

So now we move on to the postproduction phase. We have to edit, and we have more film to look at than I've ever shot before, by far. But it's a pleasure to edit if you have something there worth editing in the first place, which we do, big time. The looping, everything, will be a big job. For example, my brother David shot over nine hundred rolls of film doing still photography during the shoot. Over nine hundred rolls. I know we still have to make so many decisions about how the film is going to end up. We started principal photography back in September, and as I sat in the international airport in Johannesburg, whipped, all I could think of was this: There are still a million decisions to be made before we have a final outcome on film. And all the time I'm knowing . . .

ERNEST DICKERSON
Cinematographer

I went to Howard University as an undergrad, while Spike went to Morehouse. We hooked up at NYU's film school, and we've been doing films together ever since. I've shot each one of his six films to date, and I just directed *Juice,* which is my first feature. Of course I looked forward to *X.* Also, *Juice* came out while we were in Egypt, and before that, while we were shooting in New York, I had a son, Ernest III. It was a hectic time, a hectic year. I was all over the place.

What we wanted to do was use color and light to express the different moods of Malcolm's life, the four parts of the film. Take color and make statements with it. We wanted the first part of the film to be warmer, more idealized. Then when Malcolm goes to prison, we shot that very monochromatically, very blue, very cold. Then very stark as he becomes Malcolm X. In Mecca and in Africa, the clarity is softened by the awareness of knowledge.

We got any number of great end frames during the course of the shoot, and I know a great end frame when I see one.

Spike trusts my judgment in lighting, photographically, but that was only after years and years of working together. For me going to the Sahara to shoot some scenes was exhilarating. I am a big fan of David Lean's *Lawrence of Arabia,* so when we arrived at the location in the Sahara and began setting up, I was screaming ''No prisoners! No prisoners!'' This was in my best Peter O'Toole British accent. *Juice,* which I directed, opened while we were over there in Egypt, and it did well the first weekend. This has been one long year for me.

We went to the Egyptian Museum in Cairo, which was a good way to relax. There was so much to see, so much history . . . and none of the statuary of the many queens in those rooms looked like Elizabeth Taylor, either.

PRESTON HOLMES
Co-Producer

Well, it's interesting, isn't it? The first time I met Spike, we were introduced by a mutual friend on the street one day, informally. This was before *She's Gotta Have It* broke. I am sure he wouldn't remember that, but our first official meeting was probably in the early stages of *Do The Right Thing*. After the success of *She's Gotta Have It*, I took note of that, as did everyone else in the country, pretty much, but from my own perspective within the industry I thought, "This is somebody I want to hook up with, and work with in the future." I had been in this business for some time, and at that point I was looking for Black directors and project personnel to team up with on the same staff. Spike was like the new guy on the scene, and he came onto the scene with a big bang. I wanted to hook up. Why not?

I knew some people who had been working with him, and they all would say to me that we should hook up and I said, "Well, I'm down." So while I was working on a television movie down in Louisiana based on a story by Ernest Gaines, I got wind of Spike's preparation for *School Daze*. I sent him a résumé, and somebody else that I knew who was working with him sent him a résumé for me as well, and then I sort of waited to hear. I also tried to call him, but that didn't quite work.

Eventually, a young woman got back to me and said she had gotten the résumé and, yes, they were going to do another film, but they had all the positions filled. Then she proceeded to pick my brain about how computers could readily be used in production management. So I said, "I still want to do this thing." She said, "OK, I'll keep you in mind for something else." That was the end of that. I didn't make any other attempts to get to Spike.

I remember getting a call from Monty Ross some time later. He said they were about to do a third film, and Spike wanted to meet with me about the possibility of my working with them. I said, "Great." Went to Brooklyn and met with Spike and Monty, and they told me about this project called *Do The Right Thing*. We talked a little about me and what I had been doing and all that, and they asked me if I'd be interested. And I said, "Absolutely! When do we start?" They said they'd get back to me. They did. He asked me to work with him, and I did from then on. This was 1988.

Do The Right Thing was Spike's third film. But it was sort of another step for him, in a way, because he was coming back to New York as THE Spike Lee, back to Brooklyn as a highly visible director who couldn't make another film the way he'd made *She's Gotta Have It*—nor would he want to do that, I suspect, or even the way he made *School Daze*, totally non-union, down in Atlanta. The fact that he was going to be working in New York forced him to deal with some of the realities of working in this town—namely, the unions. But once that fact was faced, Spike didn't try to fight it. What he did was try to make sure of two things: one, that he could still use the people that he wanted to continue to use, and, two, to use his position as the director and producer to do something about getting other people into the unions—African-Americans, specifically, but by no means exclusively.

If Black people were not being shut out entirely, they were certainly facing incredible odds in terms of getting into the various unions. At that time there were the two main unions, which were NABET and IASTE, the latter being the larger, older one that did most of the movies. NABET was an alternative that had the image of being younger and more progressive, etc., etc., and was also less expensive to work with. At any rate, at that time there were a mere handful of African-Americans in any of the craft unions, and most of those, I would guess, were people like myself who had been around for some time and who also had gotten in fifteen or so years prior to Spike's coming on the scene. Usually we had gotten in through programs. I got in through a program run by a group called Third World Cinema. Then there was this gap. Third World Cinema came into existence during the time of the last era of a significant number of Black films, what's called the blaxploitation era. But I can say that then there was at least significant pressure to do something about putting Blacks behind the camera and training and all of that. But, anyway, the gap in between lasted fifteen years.

I think Spike saw me as a facilitator in this area. I was in one of the unions; I still am. Spike is not. He has chosen to steer clear of joining any unions for his own reasons, although, frankly, I'd like to see him join the Directors Guild of America so he can have the kind of impact on the DGA that he has had on NABET and the Teamsters and some of these other unions.

NABET is the National Association of Broadcast and Electrical Technicians. IASTE is the International Association of Stage and Theatrical Engineers. When we started on *Do The Right Thing*, Spike was aware I had been around working on union pictures for a number of years, and therefore I had experiences along those lines that would be useful to him. But I think also from the beginning he was looking to reach out to as many experienced African-Americans as possible. It was sort of a two-pronged thing for him—use the people who were out there, and bring along a newer, younger group. And it's worked phenomenally well for him, and for us. Work generates work. Oh yes, yes, yes, no question about it, for me and for everyone else. Before

Do The Right Thing, I had been around a while and managed to be involved in a number of films. But there is no question in my mind that my association with Spike and *Do The Right Thing,* because of the high-visibility factor with Spike in everything he does, led to increased work opportunities for me and everyone else associated with that film.

When we were wrapping *Jungle Fever,* that's when I first starting hearing these rumors about *Malcolm X.* Spike wasn't saying anything about it at the time, but I'm sure that was because he was deep into negotiations with Warners and with Marvin Worth. Probably the first time I heard anything I would deem official was when I saw Spike on a morning talk show. He was lighting into Warner Brothers for even thinking about letting someone like Norman Jewison, who is a fine director, do *Malcolm X.* Shortly after that, I heard another rumor that Spike had it. My immediate reaction was to think, "Spike is right." Anybody other than an African-American director taking this on would've been crazy. It's a minefield for anybody, for a number of reasons. But it would have been downright stupid for Warners to complicate matters further by having a white person direct it. All they had to do was look at what happened with *The Color Purple,* even being directed by Steve Spielberg.

Anyway, somebody at Warners recognized this. And I'm sure they saw something else, too. Spike is very controversial. He is probably one of the most recognizable personalities in the world these days. I'm sure they saw the benefit that would bring to the project. Then I started thinking, who else could do it? Who else should do it? Who else? Which is not to say there are not other talented and creative Black directors. There most certainly are. But it just seemed to me Spike should be the one. And then, you know, to be practical if not selfish about it, I assumed and hoped that if he was doing it, then I would be doing it. I came into this business because I thought media was the way we change the world. I had visions of doing something and being involved in something significant from the beginning. And over the years there have been things I've done that I feel very good about, that I thought were very good, that I'm proud of, and that I thought were very significant, but they all obviously pale next to the significance of doing something like *Malcolm X.*

The next thing I thought was that Spike, aside from the fact that he is Black, is probably the preeminent Black director on the scene, or of all time. There have certainly been other directors, as I've said, but I can't think of any offhand who've had the kind of impact, the kind of run Spike's had.

From the beginning this was obvious to me: that Spike hit a chord with people, all people, he connected with the audience. Spike's creativity reminds me in some ways of Melvin Van Peebles. They are very different and all that, but there are similarities. They are both extremely career-oriented, very creative.

Spike will continue branching out because he has to—it's his nature. He is a kind of maverick, and at the same time he has made peace with the Hollywood Establishment. I think that's what he wanted to do. I think he succeeded. I think of someone like P. T. Barnum when I think of Spike, because he's so successful at putting on a show you can't resist, and making it seem as though he's doing it in this effortless fashion, full of flair.

I don't know how much he thinks about the way he markets himself and his films, but knowing Spike, he probably thinks about it quite a lot. It started back with *She's Gotta Have It,* when people were saying who is Spike Lee? He was already selling T-shirts and what not. Of course that has to do with income, but that seems to me to be almost secondary. The main thing he does is increase public awareness of himself and everything he does.

I was never ambivalent about doing *Malcolm X* with Spike, and I knew the only way to do it was on the scale Spike had in mind. It was the only scale that could have done justice to this story. It would have been (I almost hate to say this) a tragedy to have Malcolm's story relegated to the level of a TV miniseries or a TV movie of the week. *Malcolm X* will be the first American Black man whose story has been told on this scale.

I had read *The Autobiography of Malcolm X* a long time ago, back when I was in college, and I hadn't read it cover to cover since then. The first thing I did was go back and read it and read the script. I saw a lot I hadn't seen back then. I had a different perspective, that of an older man, and that of a filmmaker. So I knew what we had was even better than what I first thought. After *Jungle Fever* wrapped, the next thing I did was *Juice,* starting in February of 1991. On the weekends we had a couple of meetings out at Forty Acres about *X.* Spike was working on the script, but the first order of business was to get to work on the budget, which ended up being the first and last order of business. It's still going on now, and will continue to go on until Spike delivers the final print of the film.

At first it didn't occur to me that Warner Brothers would expect the film to be done cheap. I think we all assumed early on that they weren't going to low-ball us. It never occurred to me that the film would cost less than 30 million. I had some input on the initial budget we made up—John Kilik, Monty, Spike, and me. I was in the middle of *Juice* at the time, but I had conversations with Kilik about it. I think we came up initially with around 36 or 38 million. And at that point, after it was done, Jon and I looked up at each other and said, Shit. Wait a minute. This is a movie about Malcolm X! We knew it wasn't gonna come cheap, but do you really think they are going to come up with that kind of money? They didn't. They said, "Not a chance." And so Spike told us to go back to the drawing board and come up with another budget. They were only going to come up with 17 or 18 million, and the foreign distributor would come up with around eight more, and that was it. No discussion. End of story. Take it or leave it. And we all knew that the script we had could not be made for that. Put it another way: To some extent you can do anything for just about any amount. But you get what you pay for, and Spike was not going to skimp on the quality of this film. He never does, but especially not on this film. The other thing about Spike is that he has never been one to waste money. Generally speaking, he's more budget-conscious than anybody I know. And he's usually a step ahead when it comes to this. When the cost report comes to Spike and says X-Y-Z, he's generally already given some thought to what he is going to do to make it all fit.

To some extent that is the nature of the business, but let me put it to you this way: I think the studio bitches and moans when Oliver Stone comes in for money as well. But they end up writing a check. The only difference here is that we knew that this was a negative pickup, as all Spike's films are, and not a studio picture. And there was a completion bond in place for a fixed amount. Once that was done, Warners could just sit back and see what happened. They are in a no-lose situation. They got the film; they have it, no matter what happens. And they don't have to put up any more money than they did initially. You can ask them to do it, but they don't have to hear you. Actually, they did put up a little more near the end, to cover the Africa trip.

The bond company was really kind of comic at the end, at least from my own perspective. I'm sure Completion Bond Co. didn't see anything funny in it. The bond company sent in their guy, Mack Harding, and he was with us from Thanksgiving on. He's still with us. He is to some extent calling some shots. He was there living in the office at the end of the shoot, looking at everything, saying that we must do this and we can't do that, etc., etc. Meanwhile, Spike was saying, we will do this and you won't do that. And what Spike said was the end of it.

I got caught in the middle of this all the time, but then that is my job. I'm a facilitator. But what was funny—maybe I should say ironic—to me was that Mack was doing what he had to do, what his job called for him to do. He's a filmmaker, he knows, and his job was to save the bond company's money. But I think he knew, even while he was going off, that the bottom line for us was that we were going to do what was best for the film itself, and what Spike wanted, because, after all, Completion Bond Co. and Mack Harding are not who I'm likely to get my next job with, eh? I really shouldn't be saying that because bond companies can have a certain say about personnel on a film before they decide to bond it or not. But, at any rate, this kind of thing happens all the time in film. It got so much publicity this time because it was Spike Lee. Anything he does is going to draw attention.

Once we had a evening shoot at this particular location, and Spike was there. I was on the talkie telling him that at nine we had to break, or we'd be into overtime and all that entails, which is a lot in this industry. Believe me, you don't want to know. It's complicated working with unions. Anyway, Spike said, "We'll be here until we get the shot." That's all he said. And Mack was around and went down to the location with me, and started to give Randy Fletcher, the first assistant director, all kinds of hell. Spike came in and told everybody to keep working. Spike said, "What's he doing on my set? Get off my set." I took Mack downstairs and tried to calm him down, distract him, make him less conscious of time—while I was checking my watch. Just when the second hand was about to sweep past, making us late, Spike ordered the break for the day. It was like that a lot.

The Africa trip was a classic example. Mack Harding came to town first talking about, we don't know if we are going to be able to let you do that. Spike laughed at that. He laughed. And he knew he was right because Warner Brothers was going to insist on him being able to go because they had to be delivered a film that was true to the script that everyone had signed off on. And the script had Africa in it. Period. Warner Brothers even sent a memo to that effect. So now the shoot is over, and I believe we got what we needed. I'm also sure the bond company will be there all during the postproduction. When the bond company came in, it really kind of put a damper on the spirit of things and it upset Spike, but I don't really know how much. I do know Mack—who is not a bad guy, who is a filmmaker—would rant and rave at me or at Randy Fletcher, or at Monty or Jon, but he never raved at Spike. He would cool down when Spike was around. As for Spike, he probably knew exactly how it would go down all the way, that it would be touch and go at the end of the shoot. Spike can be hard to read. I remember when I first starting working with him I was told, don't wait for Spike to call you and hang out with you and be your friend. Spike is about business. Do your work, and you'll be fine with him. So I did.

DENZEL WASHINGTON
Actor

I think when I first met Spike it was a combination of a social and a professional situation, and Spike coming on with it. I was performing in *Checkmates,* a stage play, on Broadway, and he came backstage one night and said hello and mentioned that he had a project that he wanted me to do, something at the time that was called *A Love Supreme,* but ending up as *Mo' Better Blues.* Or we might have first met backstage up in Oakland at the Black Filmmaker's Foundation awards dinner. Anyway, we did *Mo' Better Blues,* and I'm glad we got to do that movie together because we learned about each other and felt each other out and—you know, got all those petty kinds of things, both good and bad things, out of the way. So I think by the time we got to *X,* we both had come to feel that everything in our lives had prepared us for this film, basically. It was quite simple.

I can't think of anyone more qualified, or more prepared, to do this movie than Spike Lee. He lived that man's life over again. He retraced his steps. He loved—*loves*—that man. And, you know, it could be argued that he *is* that man, in his own way.

Malcolm always lived what I call a concentrated dose of life. I think he had a sense, and he always said it, that he wasn't going to be here long. I fasted for the role, and researched, researched fully, royally, and did a lot of stuff, but by no means was I able to discipline myself to the degree that he did. But, you know, I didn't have to live the life he led, either. He—again, I'm going back to broad strokes here—he, Malcolm X, to put it simply, had a concentrated dose of life.

I mean, the whole thing with his father, his parents, their thinking he was a special child because he was the seventh child. Traveling with his father, the color thing with his mother being fair-skinned, him being the only fair-skinned one, really, out of his siblings. Obviously that was something I couldn't accomplish in the film, but I try to make sure this concentrated dose of reality was accomplished. One of his brothers told me that even when they lived near white families and the kids would play together, Malcolm would always be Robin Hood, or whoever the boss was. He had natural leadership abilities. Even when he was a soda jerk, he was in there inventing new flavors and different dishes, taking over. It seems he would take over anything he was around because he had to get out of it what he had to get out of it, because he wasn't going to be here long. Like he lived his life knowing it. One brother also told me that when Malcolm got out of prison, he knew he had to go get him, because with the personality Malcolm had, he would have ended up back in Boston or New York, running some Black syndicate, whatever the Black mafia might have been then.

Spike was good about getting my input. Take the speeches. You know, it has to be fresh for the audience, even an audience of extras, to react. They really weren't seasoned extras, for the most part, they were just going with what they felt. If they didn't feel like it, you know, I doubt they would've reacted.

This was the easiest role I've ever played in this sense—I didn't want it to end. I learned so much doing this, portraying Malcolm X. I'm a research fanatic, but this—this went on and on and on. I got very calm once I realized I couldn't *be* Malcolm X. There was something more important than Malcolm X here, much more important than any of us, and that is the betterment of all of us.

I remember when we were shooting in Rahway Prison, I spoke to what you might call the graduating class, and I told them I could feel some of the brothers out there, I could see how they were looking at me—so I told them straight out I wasn't Malcolm X and could never be Malcolm X. But I did also tell them that if for a second I tried to make myself bigger than that same spirit that made him, then all would be lost.

But if I don't do that, if I am humble and straightforward and honest, then that presence, that same God that moved through him can move through me. And they might or might not have liked hearing that from me at Rahway. But that has allowed me to keep the peace with myself. It's like I always say, I have faith in God, but I have hope in man. And on this one, if I had only hope in man, I would have been a nervous wreck, because man was coming at me with all different angles and threats.

I got flak in New York for taking the role, subtle flak. But I had done a play about the man ten or eleven years ago, so people felt I could handle it. It wasn't too long before that play that I had

first heard of Malcolm X, believe it or not. I grew up in Mount
Vernon, New York, and my father, Denzel, was a minister, too.
COGIC—The Church of God in Christ. I was in my twenties
before I'd heard of Malcolm X. That play went over quite well,
but, like I said, that was ten or eleven years ago. More importantly for me, I knew I could handle it in the sense of an actor
portraying a role. I wasn't coming into it blind or cold, I knew I
could handle it, so whatever people said, I wasn't afraid it was
true.

Malcolm was a martyr. In some ways that makes the job
more difficult. He is legendary in one way or another, like it or
don't, to everybody who ever heard of him. In that way martyrs
are. You look at Nelson Mandela. Nelson Mandela was a huge
political figure, unbelievably huge, and still is, but even more so,
perhaps much more so, when he was in prison. Martyred. And
now people can take snips and pokes and bites and chomps out
of him, and he becomes just a human being again. You know, in
death, Malcolm and Martin Luther King and the Kennedys, they
became much much bigger than in life. Malcolm was not that
well known when he was alive—at least nowhere near as well
known as he is now.

So that's why I didn't worry about trying to imitate Malcolm
X, necessarily. Because imitation is what it would be. There were
moments when I felt that was happening and I said, "Let's cut."
Because I'd find myself imitating, trying to go to the source. And
then there were other times . . . well . . . we had it.

I believe that the universal stems from the specific. I do
things based on what I think and feel. Not based on how I think
they'll affect everybody. I think in order to have any kind of
universal effect, you have to be specific. You know, you have to
be very honest. As an actor, I work on that probably more than
anything else. I say, be honest, be honest, be honest. Come to it
with the truth, don't lie. And that's from within, because it's all
lying, in a way. Acting is lying, because we're not in 1963 at a
rally but in 1991 at a staged set, but there is area within the
acting itself that is honesty. Within that given world that you
have re-created, you have to try to be honest and truthful.

My desire, my prayer is for this film to show how a man or
a woman can evolve even when the worse things happen to you,
even when you've been taught to hate. When everything in your
life has taught you to hate. You can still evolve, you know. That's
my desire, to reflect that in this role. To show the spiritual,

political, and philosophical evolution of a man who happens to be named Malcolm X. But I don't want it to just stop there—oh, that's him, that's Malcolm X, and that's what he did. That's why I felt it was important to show the lower part of his life, so these young boys out here can say—well, whatever they'll say, but maybe they will follow that curve he followed or a similar curve, and uplift themselves. The universal from the specific. Maybe they won't do that. Maybe they'll say, aw, fuck dat, and not understand, but that is my desire.

I started in the theater. I come to the work from a different perspective and tradition than Hollywood movie stars who didn't come from the theater. I was fortunate enough to be taught as a young actor that it's about the art. It's about the work. The play's the thing. To interpret the work. To service the play. Not to force the play to my will, not to bend it to make it a Denzel Washington vehicle, but to somewhat lose—and hopefully find—myself in the character and in the work. I did a production of *Othello* in college. Joseph Papp asked me to do a production of it with Meryl Streep on Broadway before he died. Perhaps I decline into the vale of years. That's part of a line where Othello is saying perhaps he is too old, but it could be argued that he was too young. That he was a young genius of war, but when he got to the court and the courtyard with all that intrigue, he couldn't hang. So, do I find a correlation there between Othello and Malcolm X? Perhaps there could be.

It was extremely liberating doing some of those speeches, saying some of Malcolm X's words. Because it was kind of like psychotherapy, the kind where you hit each other with Styrofoam bats or pillows. You get a lot of aggression and anger out. At the same time you take a heck of a lot on, too. Because you're going, Damn, God damn, this is true. Not all of it is true, but the majority of it is true. And you get caught up in it. Like that thing outside Temple No. 7, where I was calling up the women to the front. I just kept going on and on when we were shooting, on and on past what was scripted. And it was like, I meant it. I was going on and on, man, it was just coming, and I meant it, and it was true. It was honest. Then it got to a strange place. Because Malcolm had said something about the government being a bunch of crooks like Frank James, Jesse James, and the Whatyamacallit brothers. And then I came out there and talked about the false promises and realities of those on the *Nina,* the *Pinta,* and the Whatyamacallit. I mean I was already flying so I didn't stop and listen to myself. You don't have time to decipher it, you're doing a speech, you're acting. You might catch it, but it's just a fleeting moment because you are not you. Then you are quickly on to the next lines, the next movements, the next expressions. But it was just something that happened that I remembered. Often when I gave speeches I would just keep going when the crowd was with me, and they were usually with me. Damn, God damn, this is true!

You get moments like that as an actor anyway, if you're lucky. I had some moments like that in *Glory.* The reason I was given an Academy Award for that performance was basically about two scenes, I feel: the whipping scene and the scene around the fire at the end. You know, my character in that movie, Trip, was not so far removed from Malcolm X, either. And both those scenes were, again, improvised. No dialogue. In the whipping scene they were supposed to bring me in chained up. They were supposed to forcefully tie me to that big wagon wheel and whip me. But I had connected with all these spirits. (I'll interrupt myself to tell you what I mean: When I was doing research for *Glory,* I came across these slave narratives. I wanted to read the actual words they had said. There was one quote I read, I remember it said, ''Ol' Masser threw a biscuit out there in the yard to the dog—I beat him to it, though.'' And that was a victory. You had to take your victories where you could get them in that man's life. Then I read about slaves who were beaten to death because they refused to give in to their masters, or were forced to work with dead men tied to their backs, and when the dead man began to rot, the worker's flesh began to rot too. And on their last breath they still refused to give in to their masters. So I took those kinds of people and said, maybe, in some small way, I can represent them, I asked them to be with me in my attempt to do so.)

In that scene, I connected with all those spirits. I remembered everything they said and did. I said, with my actions, you don't need to tie my hands up. I'd already asked for the heavy scarring makeup on my back. Now I knew why. This was not new to me, these whippings. And I looked at Matthew Broderick, who was playing the officer, Robert Gould Shaw, who ordered the whipping, and I said with my eyes, this has nothing to do with the man who is whipping me, since you told him to do it. You did it. It's between me and you, so come on with it. You don't have to tie my hands. Bring it. There is a famous picture of a slave whose back is so heavily scarred from such beatings it was nearly unbelievable. And I wanted to be that guy. When I take off my shirt, I want that officer to realize it's got nothing to do with the whipping. You can't change me with whippings, because I've been whipped before. And I'm still here.

I can move easily in the public still. I consider myself an actor, not a movie star. I do move easily in the public—at least in New York. I think you can do that when you don't run around with thirty bodyguards and twenty limousines. If I throw on some jeans and a T-shirt, I'm just out there. I can blend in with the best of them and the worst of them because I've got my hat or my cap on, especially in New York, I'd say, because ain't nobody looking at you anyway. It's harder to do that in other places. But I can go to the Schomberg Center and get work done, get research done. I can still do that. Go to the libraries. Or sit a little lower in the car seat watching somebody on 120th Street, you know, just checking it out, human observation, whatever.

Let me tell you, man, it all comes down to the same thing, whatever you do. If you have faith in your God—and I'm not saying I've lived a godly life or the best life one can possibly live by any means, because I swear and I've done things wrong—but if somewhere in your life you keep God in there, and when you understand that you are not the reason the sun comes up in the morning, then all these other things you can keep in line. You can remain humble. You see, if you start saying I, Me, I'm The Only One, it's not going to turn out well for you. It's not. It's like that old saying about the guy who says to God, I thought you were walking alongside me, God, and now I see only one set of footprints. And God said, yeah, they were Mine. I was carrying you all along. I was carrying your butt all along, while you thought you were doing such a great job of walking alongside Me!

I know I've been carried a lot. So I don't trip. I don't look at it as though I'm doing all this wonderful stuff and that I'm the baddest nigger on earth and all this stuff. I look at it like, if I can just do some small part of God's work . . . I'm not on any kind of religious trip or anything, but I'm finding it increasingly important to voice that. Because we're in warfare, man. On the ultimate level, in my opinion. And it's all coming down front right now. I mean, look at what's going on. You look at what's going on. You look at what we see in the movies. You look at what's going on in the world. They're eating folks—and making movies about it, too! You know what I mean—killing people, crazily. You've got AIDS. You've got disease. You've got all this unreasoning hate. I think it's got to get better, but I think things do have to bottom out before they can get better, and I believe they're going to get better. But at the same time, the situation now makes you say, whoa—how am I going to fight it?

I'm having a difficult time accepting another role right now. You can imagine. What do I do, as an actor, after this?

This man, Malcolm X, was the role of a lifetime.

PART FOUR

POSTPRODUCTION

January 1992

This thing is set up so we're not supposed to win. I know it. I'm not bitching and moaning. That's just the way it is. But we will be vindicated in the end.

We're back stateside. I know we've got the material. But it's not over. It is a long, long way from being over. The film has to be molded and sculpted, formed into the final product. But all of the raw material is there. We put the money we had on the screen. Denzel took a huge cut in pay. I took a huge cut in pay.

Two million of my $3 million salary went into this film. It's not like we were trying to pull a fast one on the Completion Bond Co., either. But their attitude over there has been: "Look, you're over budget here, Spike. We don't care about the plot and the look of the film anymore. What we want is to finish the process in the quickest and preferably the cheapest way possible, and we're not going for anything else. Period."

All of this could have been avoided if Warner Brothers would've come in and helped the bond company. Usually, when these kinds of occasions arise, the film studio rarely if ever lets the bond company take the full hit on a film that goes over budget. The film studio will come in and say, "Look, here's an extra million or two for you." They'll offer assistance. Something. But in this case, Warner Brothers was letting the Completion Bond Co. take the full hit, and the bond company's president, Bette Smith, was hopping-up-and-down mad about it, and, I must say, rather rightfully so. We simply got caught in the middle. The money we have budgeted isn't enough to finish the editing process. Warner Brothers and Largo, which has the foreign rights, have to come in and help—they don't *have* to come in and help, but I damn well wish they would—because I refuse to finish this in a way that I feel is incorrect, in a way it's not supposed to be done.

Now these idiots at the bond company are even trying to say that I had promised to remainder my entire salary. I never had that conversation with Bette. We'll shut it all down if they try to float that one by me. And they'll have no movie because I have the work print. I have the quarter-inch tapes. Earlier, we had to close down shop a few days before they would give me my remaining salary, which was due. This was in February, less than two weeks after we finished shooting. At the same time, I found out the bond company—that guy Mack Harding again—is trying to say we'll have a rough cut by the end of February. And they're saying my people are the ones who authorized the dates!

Well, how about this option: You can FORGET it!

On February 22, Jon Kilik, Monty Ross, and I had a brief postproduction update meeting concerning this along with some other bullshit, and to go over the new postproduction budget and schedule to see if there was any place we could cut back without hurting the film. Like we don't already know this. We'd be cutting bone.

JON: 29.6 million spent, in total, net, by today, Spike. Estimated 32.4 million to complete the entire project. Completion

Bond Company has spent . . . about three million so far.

SPIKE: I don't want that goddamn Mack Harding in my editing room, do you understand? I don't want him in the building!

MONTY: He did come out to talk to Barry Brown and me. He went back and said a director's cut would be ready on February 29.

SPIKE: February 29? February 29? February 29 is a week from today. February 29 is way out of the question. Who told him in December we'd have a cut by the end of February?

MONTY: Well . . .

SPIKE: . . . no . . .

JON: The music. We're looking at five days, two sessions a day, with a seventy-piece orchestra. Looks like total post costs are around three million. At this moment we have seventy thousand dollars for looping.

MONTY: The bond company is hoping Warner comes in with at least another million.

SPIKE: Warner Brothers is not going to kick in a million until they see a rough cut . . . Listen, Mack Harding is barred. That guy tricked you and Barry into half-agreeing . . .

MONTY: I didn't agree . . .

SPIKE: You didn't disagree, which is all he needs. He comes up with an unreasonable-assed screening date, now he's trying to make it stick. It'll never happen. That assassination scene is huge, and tricky to cut. Africa will take time. We may not even make April 6 . . .

JON: Spike . . . put a great deal of his salary into the film. Today is February 22, and he hasn't been paid. This kind of stuff has been going on for almost a year now . . . no one believed it would happen, but Spike always did . . .

Alex Haley stopped by the office. I could understand his curiosity. I think he, and especially Malcolm, knew exactly what they were doing twenty-eight years ago when they did the autobiography. In my research, people—like Malcolm's brothers and sisters—said they knew the autobiography was not 100 percent accurate, and from my research I'm sure it wasn't, with assumed names, and some hyperbole here and there. He might not have been a big-time gangster, just a small-time hustler, and he wasn't a pimp, but a steerer, but he knew the more degraded he became in the book, the greater his triumph would seem for having overcome such hardships. I still think it is a great book, because it tells a greater story. And meeting Malcolm had turned Alex onto his own African history. The last conversation they

had, on the phone on a Saturday, the day before he was murdered, Malcolm had told Alex (after telling him the government
was working in concert with the Muslims on his death), "You
know, I'm glad I've been the first to establish official ties between Afro-Americans and our blood brothers in Africa." Those
were the last words Malcolm X spoke to Alex Haley in this life.
And after Malcolm was killed, Alex started remembering all
those things his grandmother and great aunts had told him on
their porches in Henning, Tennessee, when he was a boy, all that
lore about their ancestor, the old African, and a *ko* being a string
instrument, and the river being called Kamby Bolongo. So Alex
went on to research and discover that the African's name was
Kunta Kinte. He wrote *Roots,* and the rest is history. I was glad
to show Alex footage. He looked at me and smiled and seemed
pretty happy about it, all in all. Physically he looked kind of
bloated. I didn't think about it much. Later, I found out he was
telling people what he'd seen was "very powerful." But within
two weeks of coming by, he was dead. He died in Seattle. Alex
Haley never got to see the finished product, the complete *Malcolm X.*

On the twenty-seventh "anniversary" of Malcolm's assassination, February 21, 1992, I went to a memorial service at the
Abyssinian Baptist Church in Harlem. It was quiet. Not that
many people turned out—less than three hundred. Baraka was
there. In honor of the memory of the man, Malcolm X, we shook
hands, we spoke to each other with respect, and we were civil.
Maybe we'll sit down again in the future. Right now I have to find
the way to finish the film.

As far as investors coming in, you would think some Black
people would invest, but, really, there is nothing there to offer
them. Warner Brothers isn't going to give up any of its share,
neither is Largo, and I'm not going to ante up *all* my share, which
I believe is what they'd like, because then it really would be the
plantation. So it's still to be decided. Somebody may come in at
the eleventh hour. But I can't worry about how the film will be
paid for now. I have to worry about the film itself.

Oliver Stone and I remain good friends. Warner Brothers
was telling me, "Oh, Oliver's cutting pages out of his script," and
he was telling me the straight deal in the other ear. At the Show
West distributors' convention in Las Vegas in late January, I saw
him. He signed a copy of the script of *JFK* for me. He confirmed
to me that he was going to let me use some footage, some of the
stuff they did of the Dallas Kennedy motorcade. We will make
use of it.

As far as the differences between *JFK* and *Malcolm X* go, there are many, starting with this premise: It's a much bigger revelation that the American government would kill its own president. I think most people who know anything about the situation with Malcolm know the assassination was carried out by "zealots" within the Nation of Islam—and that government agencies knew it was coming and let it happen and/or were involved directly themselves. So that is one fundamental difference. When I finally saw *JFK*, I loved it. The one problem I have with Oliver's film is this: I don't think JFK was killed because he was trying to withdraw from South Vietnam. I don't believe that at all. I think it was for other reasons. But I go along with Oliver in believing there was a conspiracy. When you think of all those things that matched the theory, how they lost the brain, how those witnesses died mysteriously. Car accidents. Cancer. Really, it's a joke.

Great film; a result of great filmmaking. Wonder if it was test-screened? Ha!

Using test screenings and "focus groups" on *Malcolm X* has always been in the air from Warner Brothers, and I don't like the smell of it. I knew they were going to want to do that all along. That's when they'll bring in people for screenings and give them questionnaire cards with questions like, Was the ending good for you? Was it as good for you as it was for us? Did this character have too many bad traits? Was this other character good enough? All that shit. Which is fine for them. But this is not that type of film, by no means, where a focus group sits down and tells us something we can take seriously.

Warner Brothers would strictly go by what those cards would tell them—if we were stupid enough to let them do that. That's the importance of creative control, which I always make sure I have in my film contracts. When they have those screenings, they don't care about what they see on the screen for themselves. It is those cards that tell them whether or not the movie is working. If the test audience fills out the cards and they say don't change anything, it's perfect, then the studio says fine, don't change anything. If the test audience majority says we don't like the ending, the studio runs with it and says gotta change the ending. If the cards have problems, they want you to change the film. This is what they believe in. *Goodfellas* tested horribly, and the studio was worried, but long ago Martin Scorsese had already threatened to shoot somebody, if not everybody, and in the head, too, if they didn't leave his films alone, starting with *Taxi Driver*. Why? Well, *Strictly Business* got one of the highest ratings ever from a test screening—and that movie was a piece of shit. You can't make your film off statistics that say, "39 percent of the people think Edna Jean was all wrong, while 20 percent . . ." No way you can do that and live with yourself if you're an honest filmmaker with the kind of material that I knew we had in *Malcolm X.*

I've had test screenings, but it wasn't for the research cards. What I get out of a research screening is this: I can tell what works and what doesn't work when I sit amongst an audience. The other problem with having a test screening of *X* is that there is so much hype about this film, there is no way possible to have a screening without somebody sneaking in and then letting people know Mandela's in the film, for example, or some other fact gets leaked, whatever. Malcolm in the film is doing drugs—it would be terrible, out of context of the entire picture. We're going to hold our shit as close to the vest as long as possible on this. But there's too much to do to worry about it.

On March 13, while en route to Boston to teach my class at Harvard, I'm reading the papers and magazines. I go through them like popcorn. The headlines of the articles being written across the country—*Time* magazine: The Battle to Film *Malcolm X.* They're writing about the ongoing battle between us, Warner Brothers, and the bond company. A few days ago, Bette Smith had a meeting with me, Monty, and Jon in her suite at a midtown Manhattan hotel.

Bette had opened the festivities: "Who's going to start first?"

I said, "You go ahead."

"I'd hoped you would have said something, Spike. When are you going to have a first cut?"

"Our first cut's April 6."

"Well, I can't wait that long, Spike. We need a cut now. You know, if you were in the editing room, instead of teaching classes at Harvard, and doing Prince videos, and flying all over the country for speaking engagements, maybe you'd have time to do your job."

I had shot a Prince video for his song, "Money Don't Matter," right around the corner from my house in Brooklyn. Every Friday, I lectured a class on contemporary African-American film at Harvard U., and I had done some speaking engagements. Invariably, whenever I did a speaking engagement, there would be an impromptu press conference. All of this stuff comes with the territory. I wasn't about to apologize to Bette Smith for it.

"Look, lady. First of all, I've never been a director to sit in the editing room every single minute. That's why I hired Barry Brown. He cuts a scene, I look at it, comment, he makes the changes. So I do not have to be in the editing room twenty-four-seven, because Barry is the editor and it's his job to cut the movie. My job is to direct and produce and write, oversee the editing."

She said, "Well then, I'll start again. It doesn't take ten weeks to edit any goddamn film! If you were in the Directors Guild of America, they would have taken it from you by now!"

Well, I'm not just going to sit there and take this. I jumped up. "Oh, you're gonna take my film from me now? Is that what you're gonna do? Huh? Are you gonna come into my office and take it? How are you gonna find it? Are you gonna find the quarter-inch tapes? Are you gonna find the work print? Without the tapes, you got no film, lady!"

Then she got kind of calm and said, "Spike, remember who your enemies are."

I'm looking at one now.

Bette said, "You've got enough time, you've had enough time, you finished shooting the film in December."

I said, "Look, we did not finish shooting in December. What we did in Cairo and Johannesburg, we considered that first-unit stuff. There was no film without that stuff. If the lead actor is working and the director is shooting, then that is the definition of first unit. That ain't second-unit stuff."

But her whole thing is wanting the film to be finished. Mack Harding had already tricked Barry and Monty into saying that I would have a cut in February, or at least not saying otherwise, which I never agreed to do. So we sent them a revised schedule.

BY ANY MEANS NECESSARY CINEMA, INC.
MEMORANDUM
RE: MALCOLM X POST PRODUCTION SCHEDULE
2/25/92

Below is revised postproduction schedule:

April 6th —First cut

May 15th —Locking picture for sound editing

July 13th —Start mix

Sept 18th —Finish mix

Oct 9th   —Deliver answer print
Nov 1st   —Contractual delivery date

I looked at Betty and knew she didn't care about the outcome
of the film. She doesn't give a shit about *Malcolm X* at this point.
It really comes down to economics. Her company is out $5 mil-
lion, and they want to get this thing over with so they can get out.
So I told her that. I said, "You know, you're an Uncle Tom, you
don't give a shit. You don't even care about the film's quality."
Then she threatened to pull the plug on everything.

Two nights before this I'd spoken at Gustavus Adolphus
College in Minnesota, and an article about my presentation appeared in the Minneapolis newspaper the next day. I didn't think
much of it. I'd been giving basically the same presentation everywhere I spoke, from the campus of the University of California at
Berkeley to WLIB radio in New York.

Here's the plan: I had to make sure a lot of people knew the
situation with this film, the background, how we were being held
to this double standard. But, for some reason, it was after I spoke
at little Gustavus Adolphus that Warner Brothers got suddenly
mad about it. Terry Semel had a hissy. It got back to me eventually, and it came flying back, from all fronts—from Marvin
Worth, from Charlotte Gee, from Jim Miller . . . I don't know
why. All I did was call Warner Brothers what it is. The plantation.

All I did was emphatically say that in Hollywood there are
two realities, one black and one white. I said in my heart of
hearts, I knew the way Warner Brothers looks at Spike Lee and
Denzel Washington and *Malcolm X* is simply not the same way
they look at Oliver Stone and Kevin Costner and *JFK*. It's not the
same reality. So the shit supposedly hit the fan with Terry Semel
after the Associated Press ran a wire story. I'd been using the
same technique in the last four or five speeches I'd given. I don't
know what made this one different. Maybe it was just time. The
last time we flew to L.A., we presented Warner Brothers with the
budget to finish the film the way we need to finish it. That was
1.3 million. They ain't budged. I'm tired. It's still touch and go.
They say they're waiting—waiting to see the first cut before they
even begin to think about committing something else. Maybe this
was just a method to get an earlier screening date.

We should have something to show them on April 6 that will
be worth their while. But, if not, it'll be a week later. What are

they going to do? Shoot me? And Betty Smith can't pull the plug, because the only way she's going to get any money back is to turn in the complete film. Warner Brothers might throw something at her then. But nobody's obligated. No, they won't do shit for her, on second thought. In some ways I empathize with Betty. But not at the expense of the picture. This has not been Warner Brothers' stance on this, that they would help. Plus, the Completion Bond Co. has two other films that are over budget, right there at the Warner Brothers lot. One is an animated film, and the other, I don't know what it is, only that it's over budget big time. So she had three films she had to take over—but mine was the only one in the papers. We had to scrimp to make this film, yet studios would spend $45 million for *Radio Flyer,* over $50 for *Bonfire.* Motherfucking Dan Ackroyd got $45 mil for *Nothing But Trouble.* You see what I mean? I know I'm repeating myself, but it happens over and over, so I talk about it or it'll drive me crazy.

I got a call from Charlotte Gee, who's a v.p. at Warner Brothers. Nice lady. She called very disturbed the other day saying she understood my problems with Terry, but that the film was getting the moniker of "troubled film," and that I couldn't kick Warner Brothers in the teeth every time I gave a public speech because it was putting a negative spin on everything. I can understand what she's saying. Just Monday, this—I would say asshole, but I won't—reporter from *New York* magazine calls me and says, "Ahem, well, Spike, we heard that you've made some serious statements against Warner Brothers. In fact, a reliable source has said that you called Warner Brothers and told Terry Semel to his face that you believed Warner Brothers was just a bunch of white Jew boys. So. Did you say that, Spike?"

Now, how am I supposed to carry on a conversation with somebody like this? I said, "Of course not, number one, and, number two, this is bullshit. You would never call up Martin Scorsese or Steven Spielberg or Oliver Stone or Barry Levinson with this kind of shit, now would you? And, number three, this ain't no news. Why don't you cover something important? Why aren't you covering the United States turning away some Haitian refugees on a sinking boat, a real affront to human rights? Instead, talking about some nothing rumor about what I said, which has no effect except maybe to inflame bullshit emotions."

Then I called the editor of *New York* magazine and cursed him out too. They've really done a job on me. When *Do The Right Thing* came out, they are the ones, Joe Klein and David Denby,

who said I was a racist—imagine this: *I'm* the racist, now—and
that the film was going to cause race riots across the country.
They also printed a story saying that I stole the idea for *Jungle
Fever* from Charles Lane. They're into rubbish. They're supposed to be *New York* magazine, they're supposed to publish
what happens in New York, not what they wish had happened in
New York. But they're more interested in whether or not I'm
trying to tell off Joel and Ethan Coen, or Steven Soderberg. So I
told the editor that in six years of my making films, *New York*
magazine has done one feature story and about a hundred neck-
lacing jobs on me. I'm not talking about the press as a whole,
because *Vanity Fair, Esquire,* the *Village Voice, Rolling Stone,*
they've all come through and done stories, but *New York* magazine seems to have a vendetta against me, or maybe I should say
an agenda, although I have to admit two things.

There are several Black writers who despise my ass, too.
Stanley Crouch (or Stanley Crotch, as I'm forced to call him at
times) wrote about me and criticized me because I'm short, and
then compared me to a middle-aged white pedophile mass murderer from Chicago named John Wayne Gacy (who, by the way,
they recently made a TV movie about called *To Catch a Killer,*
starring Brian Dennehy, and Stanley Crouch didn't write a mum-
bling motherfucking word about that). Yet I'm supposed to be
the bad guy. I'm supposed to have the mental problem. The lady
up at the *Amsterdam News,* Aviola Sinclear, doesn't care for my
work too much either. And the mighty *New York Times,* not to let
them off the hook, printed a story that noted I was teaching at
Harvard, and I didn't even have a college degree. They were
trying affirmative action backlash shit on me. That shows you
how some white people think, and how they try and position you.
I guess whoever wrote that actually thought I was Mookie in *Do
The Right Thing.* I had to make another call, curse out another
editor, but this time I cursed out an answering machine. Here's
that message: "This is Spike Lee. How you doing? Look, how in
the hell are you going to write some bullshit that I don't have a
fucking college degree. I got a fucking master's from NYU and an
undergraduate degree from Morehouse College. How's the fucking *New York Times* gonna write some bullshit that I don't have
a fucking college degree. You know you motherfuckers ought to
do some fucking research or whatever you call that shit before
you write some fucking bullshit, all right. I got a fucking master
of fine arts from fucking NYU. I want a motherfucking retraction.
All right, motherfucker." Who is checking for accuracy, Mickey

Mouse, Yosemite Sam, and fucking Goofy? I take it back. Mickey wouldn't be so sloppy.

People know what they're doing when they play with your rep like this. The *New York Times* later printed a retraction. Three or four people might've even seen this retraction.

Okay, in the face of all that I can understand Charlotte Gee's point about talking in the press. But my strategy is that whatever's being done with this film cannot be conducted behind the closed doors of some boardroom somewhere. This thing has to be played out in full view of the public, specifically African-Americans, with Warner Brothers knowing there are a lot of people watching how they treat this film. And especially where there are a lot of Black people who are concerned and watching, you have to be careful if you are an American manufacturer and retailer of goods of any sort, because, as quiet as it's kept, Black people run the engine of commerce and consumerism in America. It is Black people who do the buying. We've almost gotten to the point where the old saying is not, "All I can do is stay Black and die," to "All I can do is stay Black and *buy*." Black people spend their dollars more readily than white people because white people make enough money to save; Black people only make enough to buy. And Black people could very easily stop putting their money into the vast Warner Brothers–Time Inc., conglomerate. So that's why I'm doing it. It's been too long. Black people are tired of a knife in our backs. And this film is too important for that to happen.

There are going to be times when it looks like I'm making daily reports to the press of how this thing is going. I have to, because if I don't say shit . . . not to say Warner Brothers will not market well. As far as selling and marketing, I think they're going to be great. So my problem is not with that department. I know they will spend the money then. I know they're going to sell the film hard. They know how to sell a movie. If they sold the shit out of *Batman* . . . and that movie *still* stinks to me. Rob Friedman, Barry Reardon, Joel Wayne—I don't have any problems with those guys. My problems are with Terry Semel and Bob Daly. I can remember what Bob Daly said, what seems like long ago: *Oh, oh, this is a prestigious film, an event film, an Academy Award film*—all that might be good and true. I just have to be given the leeway to make all those words worthwhile, prophetic, instead of Hollywood bullshit. I have to make it come true, make the product as great as the campaign in front of it. If I don't, it won't reflect on Warner Brothers. It'll reflect on Spike Lee. It will be my skinny Black ass in a sling is what it will be.

Marvin Worth called yesterday and said, "Spike, Terry Semel went crazy. You know, I think it's starting to backfire. You just can't go blasting Warner Brothers all the time in the press! I don't know if it's going to get us what we want. They said they might give us some money to complete the project." I told Marvin I didn't know what he'd heard, but I hadn't heard from Jim Miller, I hadn't heard from Terry Semel, and I hadn't heard from Bob Daly. I had some doubts about them extending the budget out of the milk of human kindness in their hearts. It's been more than a month since we last flew to L.A. We're getting to the point where we need the additional funds because the bond company ain't spending a dime over what's in the budget, and there's a lot of stuff we still need. It's peanuts, really. One point three million. I know Oliver Stone would have gotten that 1.3 million, ASAP, no problemo, just sign here. This isn't the first film that's gone over budget. And it's not like it's way over budget.

In the middle of all this I still have to fulfill other obligations. Like checking out the Knicks. I went to a Knicks practice, up in Purchase, New York, at the State University of New York and interviewed coach Pat Riley about that Kentucky–Texas Western NCAA championship game he played in way back in 1966, the all-white Kentucky vs. the all-black Texas Western squad. Riley was on Adolph Rupp's Kentucky team at the time. I was speaking to Pat for an article I was doing for *Interview* magazine. I asked Pat Riley about Adolph, the coach, the man in the brown suit, who was a hardline, lemon-sucking segregationist. I didn't press Riley on it, though. Later on I went to a Kentucky home game in Lexington. And Rick Pitino, who is the coach there now, was great to me. He let me come in before the game to the locker room, had me speak to the players, and sit on the bench. So even I can't say at least one thing hasn't changed in America.

I went to see the Knicks and Lakers at the Garden, and the Lakers won, somehow, when Sedale Threatt went off on us for like forty-two points, had the game of his life. It was a great game though. I sat next to Magic Johnson and his agent Lon Rosen. It was fun, although I was a little reflective about it. Magic had been diagnosed HIV positive back in November, the seventh of November, but you would have never known by his demeanor. He is a happy, brave man to be that way.

We could've won the game at the end. Xavier McDaniel, the X-Man, let fly a wing jumper to win it at the buzzer. Yes! It went in! I jumped up and I guess I was so happy, before I knew it, I was in the middle of the court, saying to myself, "Oh shit, let me get out of here." Turned out the shot was released after the buzzer went off. It didn't count. Knicks lose.

I was being honored in Boston by the Morehouse Alumni. The famous Morehouse Glee Club was to perform at Old South Church on March 13, but it wasn't a relaxing day and evening. I had class that afternoon at Harvard. I've been showing a different film to the class every week, from *Blue Collar* to *Daughters of the Dust* to *Sounder* to *She's Gotta Have It* to . . . hey, it's no gimme class. On March 13, the film of the week happened to be *Superfly.* After I let them kick around their own conjectures for a while, I explained that the music soundtrack by Curtis Mayfield had been released before the film and was such a hit the producer knew what he had; how this producer was a gangster type named Sig Shore, who then added a montage which glorified and glamorized cocaine use, and the movie, as bad as it was as a movie, which was really rotten, was all the more reprehensible because it was responsible in a lot of ways for the explosion of cocaine use, especially in many Black communities. It was the epitome of what people meant when they labeled an entire genre "blaxploitation."

Of course, Harvard students, being contrary, made their points. One of them even tried to compare *Superfly* to *Goodfellas,* although I told him a first-time director like Gordon Parks, Jr., from twenty years ago might not hold up well under that kind of comparison, and it wasn't even fair to do a comparison in the first place. I have an interesting time at Harvard, although I get upset when these kids try to soft-pedal racism or tell me it's a thing of the past or that I can't blame stuff on it. They are so naive. This one white girl, from Alabama I think, got me so mad at her today after she said something to the effect that some of these racist depictions and decisions about *Superfly* might not have been based on racism. So I got a little louder and said, "You can say that? You can say that and you're from Tuscaloosa, Alabama? The home of motherfucking Bear Bryant and Roll Tide?" Then I thought about the white girl who a long time ago asked Malcolm what she could do to help the situation, and he told her, "Nothing." I was reminded of that. Him being sorry later. In *Malcolm X,* we have a scene which gives him the opportunity to heal his regret. Class at Harvard will make you think, one way or another. Some Black people want to know why I'm not teaching my film class at Hampton University, Howard U.,

Morehouse, or another historically Black college, and all I can say back is, none of them asked. Harvard did.

Big development, even as we speak. Semel and Daly are going to Japan the first week in April, and we've been told we have to show them the first cut before they leave. We have to show it to them on the day of April 1. I've decided we have to work around the clock. The editors are going to be working twelve hours a day, seven days a week, so we can finish a cut in time. We just found out tonight, the same night of the Glee Club concert in Boston. We've got to show it to them then because they'll be gone a week to ten days. This is what Jim Miller told me when I spoke to him. Betty Smith says if we don't show it then, her company is going to start pulling the plugs—stop the payroll to the editors, lay them off. She might do it anyway. So I've got no time for her, or especially for Mack Harding. Him, I will bury. His claim to fame is that film *Weekend at Bernies.*

Really, I may have brought this earlier deadline on myself. They didn't call me. I called. What I found out was that Warner Brothers had already told Bette they might give her some additional money. But nobody told me. So Jim Miller called, and that's when I found out that Terry and Bob were leaving, that Terry didn't like the press I'd been giving him (like I hadn't heard that before), and they wanted to see a cut. So it's gonna be tough. Get a cut ready. Screen it for our people, including Denzel. Present an Academy Award for Best Documentary with John Singleton in Hollywood on the night of the thirtieth of March, hang out a minute, fly back to New York for the Bulls vs. Knicks game at the Garden on the night of the thirty-first to see Jordan—I am not missing that game!—and then fly back to L.A. and screen the film at the Plantation, the Warner Brothers lot, the next day, April 1. Piece of cake.

Warner Brothers is saying they can't pledge any additional money until they see the film, and until they see the film they can't even say it's a three-hour film—which is bullshit because it's going to be a three-hour film anyway, no matter what they say. The bond company is saying, well, since it's in the contract as a two-hour-and-fifteen-minute film, they should get a refund from Warner Brothers for everything—for all additional footage we shot that is over two hours and fifteen minutes. But how would they know what that footage might be? Everything we shot was in the script. They signed off on the script. And that script is what we shot. I'm telling Warner Brothers from the jump, I don't want no eight million motherfuckers in this screening, trying to act like they're determining how long this film should be.

I told Barry, "Well, you and the guys work twelve hours a day, seven days a week, until you get it done." I'd met Barry years ago in Atlanta. He was there doing research on a script that he wanted to do about the civil rights movement, and he came to the Haynes Center down in Atlanta to show a film, and he saw one of my student films called *The Answer,* and we became friends. When I came back to New York and NYU, I needed a job, preferably in film. He was one of the co-owners of a small, independent distribution company called First Run Features, and he needed someone to work there part-time to clean film and keep up with the inventory and shipments. So he gave me that job. So when I took off and did *She's Gotta Have It,* Barry came over and helped with the sound editing. After that, he cut *School Daze,* and then *Do The Right Thing.* Then he cut *Salaam Bombay.* He wasn't available to cut *Jungle Fever* for me because he was cutting Madonna's *Truth or Dare* at the time. He then directed a film of his own called *Lonely in America* when I made *Mo' Better Blues.* Sam Pollard cut that for us, and did a good job. Originally my idea was to have Sam and Barry work on *Malcolm X* together. Sam was supposed to come on the project, but he was doing a documentary and just felt he couldn't give his all to both projects. I said, "OK, Sam, thanks for telling us."

Again, it is not a rare occurrence for a film to go over budget. That's why I was amazed that we are on the front pages. No, I wasn't amazed.

Barry had a rough cut ready before I left for Europe. I had to see it before I could okay a rough mix of the sound. When I come back, I'll screen what they've mixed, and then we'll have another week to make some changes, then remix Monday and Tuesday, and go out to L.A. with both barrels blazing.

It's time to put up or shut up.

A week from tomorrow, I have to go to Paris and Rome. Just some vacation and business. Wait'll Bette Smith hears about it. She's gonna flip.

I'm looking forward to seeing the whole film projected for the first time myself. I thought about nothing else on the way over to Paris, and then Rome. In Rome, I spoke at a big film conference and met with Lina Wertmüller and Federico Fellini, the great directors, and both of them made me feel welcome, and

were interested, if not anxious, to see what I would do with
Malcolm X. But it wasn't much of a vacation in the end, because
there is no time to relax. It seems I'd barely taken off from Rome
when, boom, it's a few days later and I'm on my way to Los
Angeles in the friendly skies. Oh, shit. All of a sudden, it's April
Fools' Day. I'd forgotten about it being the Day of All Fools.
We're screening the film on April Fools' Day. I don't know if
that's good or bad.

But I do know we've been working hard. Barry and the other
editors have been working like Georgia mules, from cain't see in
da mornin' till cain't see at night, until the bond company ordered the editors to stop work this weekend, on the twenty-
seventh of March, to be precise. Warner and the bond company
have been dead on our ass to have the screening before Semel
and Daley leave for Japan. They thought we'd have a cut on
February 29, which was completely crazy. That would've looked
like a cartoon. They've been coming up with these arbitrary
dates which we hadn't agreed upon all along. So finally, last
Friday, boom, the bond company forced the layoff of all editors.
Just laid off all the editors "until further notice." So now we're
going to have to pay ourselves, for everything. We're going to
have to somehow come up with additional funds, because I can't
afford to lay people off. We've had the momentum all the way,
we have to keep going. Have to keep going . . . Fuck you Betty
Smith, you ain't stopping history.

This past Saturday, we screened the film for the first time,
in New York. Denzel flew in, so at the screening were Denzel,
myself, Jon Kilik, Monty Ross; associate producer Fernando
Sulachin, the Argentinian who had done such a great job on the
South African and Saudi locations; the editors; Arthur Klein, my
lawyer; and Terence Blanchard, the composer. We had the
screening at Magno on Seventh Avenue in Manhattan, where we
usually go. The picture was 3 hours and 50 minutes long. Afterward, people were subdued, hopefully because it was a four-
hour cut, but I could see they were moved deeply by it. And
Denzel was very pleased. I couldn't see his face during the
screening because he was sitting directly in front of me. He told
me it was the first time he'd seen a film this early in its stages
of production. There were one or two things that bothered him,
but overall he liked it.

That next Monday, at the Academy Awards, he presented an
award and read the TelePrompTer, which had him saying that
JFK was "the most controversial film of the nineties." Denzel

ad-libbed, ''. . . so far.'' A lot of people got what he meant by that. Also that night, John Singleton and I talked, after we'd given out the award for Best Documentary. I had a screaming toothache because I'd just had a root canal done earlier in the day. But even though my mouth was throbbing, I was excited, not because I was at the Academy Awards, but because I think we've got a great film here. A great film. And I think Denzel's going to be up there next year, and NOT reading no TelePrompter, either. When you see his total performance for the first time as we did at the end of March on Seventh Avenue, it is completely magnificent. I really think he captured the complexity of Malcolm X. The real man. Not bullshit myth like throwing a dollar across the Potomac or chopping down a cherry tree. Making heroes larger than life. We want to do that, but realistically. That is needed for our people. Our people need and deserve it.

After watching dailies for months, and then putting the segments and elements together, you can end up working on a film for a long time and you've never seen it as a complete work. You're as interested as anybody else might be. I really couldn't enjoy it at that first screening because I was trying to analyze the picture and, at the same time, I was being somewhat overwhelmed by seeing it projected for the first time. What I want is there, but there was some stuff I saw that I definitely didn't like, and that was the first ten minutes, to come out later.

Now, our job sounds simple, but is actually hard. We've got to cut around another fifty minutes out of the movie. And when you're in this position, right away scenes stick out—oh yeah, that one has to go—but other scenes won't reveal themselves until later, until I've thought about and listened to people and seen it again. Now comes the process we talked about, the molding and shaping and sculpting, trying to be concise, to avoid repetition. And a lot of it is not taking whole scenes out, but a sentence here, a sentence there, starting some scenes in the middle instead of at the beginning. I still can't see us taking out more than fifty minutes—if we can get it down that much. It's still a three-hour film, just like I said all along. It's not going be two hours and twenty minutes, which is what they were looking for. I think we've got the material, the stuff of a great film, it just has to be treated properly. It's something totally different when you've got to make something and you don't have anything there to work with in the first place. But when all the goods are there, on film, then it's a pleasure to create with that.

When the lights came up in the screening room on March 28,

we came back to the office and made changes and cut those ten minutes out right away. The cut we are showing to Warner Brothers today is 3:50, and choppy. I don't feel any pins and needles. I just know it's going to be a battle until the end. I'm in the limo on the way over to Warner Brothers now. Afterward we're gonna meet for a couple of minutes with them, probably in Lucy Fisher's office. They're going to like it, but they'll come back to us about the length, and that's where the war starts up again.

I had to get on the phone because we still have work to do, and it will cost money. The bond company has bailed out on me. They let my editors go. Warner Brothers *been* bailed out of here a long time ago. So things are getting really tense, moneywise. The work must be done. I called Bill Cosby on Monday, Oprah Winfrey on Tuesday, and Magic Johnson this morning. I saw Rocket Ismail at the basketball game and hit on him. I've got to call Reginald Lewis, Michael Jordan, Janet Jackson. Like I said before, it's a drag, begging, but we need help. I'm going down the line. It's come down to this, and I need help to make the film, just as I knew I would. No different, really, than with *She's Gotta Have It,* a long time ago. Self-help.

"Hello, Michael . . . ?"

So now, going into this screening in building D at the Warner Brothers lot, I don't really feel like I'm on my own here. Faces are running through my head. Malcolm. Alex Haley. Denzel. Angela Bassett, so great as Betty Shabazz. Delroy Lindo. Betty Smith. The bond company's not legally done with their financial obligations either. They're just a bunch of jerks trying to make me knuckle under. There were not many people in the screening—fifteen or twenty at most. Semel and Daly, Rob Friedman and Lucy Fisher, that Mack Harding guy, and Jim Miller; a few other suits, and for the home team Barry Brown, Monty, Jon, Preston Holmes, Marvin Worth, Art Sims, who designs posters for my films; Dede Allen, a Warner Brothers consultant who was the editor of *Reds* and *Bonnie and Clyde;* a couple of other people. I didn't know them all. But I knew what we had.

I got up slowly. I was calm. Pretty calm.

"Thanks for coming. I don't know how many of you have ever been to this kind of screening before. I want to apologize for the bad sound and the roughness . . . Lights."

I wasn't concentrating on how people were reacting. I was looking at scenes to see where they could be cut out or down without affecting the film overall. I sat with Barry and we took

notes. But later on, Monty told me that Terry Semel watched
intently for the entire four hours, with his jaw in his hand most
of the time. He also said it looked like Bob Daly went to sleep
. . . *event film, awards film.* Nobody went to the bathroom
though.

There was some applause when the lights came up. Larry
Gordon, who owns Largo, the foreign distributor, looked pretty
happy, I would say. Some people tried to stop him and talk—I
have a feeling Warner Brothers would love to buy back the foreign rights—but Larry was gone out of there faster than you can
say Jackie Robinson. Terry Semel came over and gave me that
we're-partners-now look. We retired to Lucy Fisher's office. We
talked, and I knew we still had money problems. Even though it
went over very well, it was far from the final version. There is
still much editing to do, and the music, and sound mixing. The
long postproduction phase wasn't over, not by a long shot.

I went to the Château Marmont Hotel on Sunset and put
down my bags and prepared to get back on the phone and wait
for my dinner date. It wasn't over, but something in me felt at
rest. I felt Alex Haley would be proud. I felt James Baldwin
would be proud. I was proud. I hoped Malcolm X was at peace.

BARRY ALEXANDER BROWN
Editor

Wow. There is so much stuff! All these boxes right here, twenty
or so of 'em, twenty thousand feet of film—and this is just
second-unit stuff of Mecca! And out of all this, a few minutes, at
most, make the final cut. A few minutes of time from the actual
hajj, which was shot last summer, and it's up to me to cut the
footage that Spike shot of Denzel playing Malcolm X in Egypt, so
that you never have the feeling he's not there, so you never get
the feeling that there is any difference at all. There is so much
film to look at overall. Big job. Loose, in a way, because sometimes there is some 16mm color and 16mm black and white
throughout, for effect, for time reference, but the cut itself will
be a beautifully pristine 35 millimeter. Beautiful.

Oh yeah. Sorry. Spike? Spike was working for somebody I
had met in Atlanta, a guy named George Folkes. They had gone
to school together at Morehouse. I was in Atlanta, the summer of
1981, to research a screenplay I wanted to do. I'd been in touch
with George, who was doing a project with high school students,

a video project, a really neat project where he was taking kids and going out and actually doing a kind of news show. And Spike was one of the people working with George, as one of the instructors, one of the adult supervisors, even though he looked just like a kid himself. George brought me over to the office one day, and Spike was around. Honestly, my first impression of Spike was . . . hmm . . . well, Spike takes a long time to warm up to people.

I had a little bit of feeling that Spike was asking George with his eyes, "What's up, George? Who is this white guy you're bringing in?" He wasn't hostile or impolite. He was never like that. Very cordial, in fact, but somehow, a standoffishness, kind of an arms-length-away thing. The irony is that now George is in California, he's doing other things, and Spike and Monty and I are the ones working, and I'm considered to be one of the fellas now, on these terms: We've been through a lot of things together.

Back then, George just said, "Spike? He's a student at NYU."

I was living in New York. I had a distribution company, First Run Features, of which I was president. Spike and I didn't really become friends until I hired him to work part-time at First Run Features. I called him up back in New York and asked him if he'd like a job. He said, "Yeah, I'd like a job. Sure." Spike came in as a student, with the kind of job where he had to check the prints that were coming in and out, the 16 millimeter prints, get 'em clean, make sure they were rewound, make sure they were ready to go out fit for the next day's rental, and to preserve them. He was good at it. I thought it was a great job for someone at NYU film school, although we were only two blocks away from NYU and he was the only NYU student I knew. He seemed together.

Over the next year or two is when we really got to know each other, become friends. When we talked about movies, I always caught myself thinking, "Wow, this guy has the same ideas about movies I do. He thinks about movies the way I do. He respects movies. He respects the art of cinematic entertainment."

I had found that a lot of independent filmmakers I knew in New York at the time did not respect it. Many of them, in a funny sort of way, looked down their noses at the art of cinema. So many people I knew at the time had gone into making movies strictly for political reasons—the reason was to use the power of the medium to get your message out. Which is fine and good, but you are never going to be a great filmmaker that way.

Spike would talk about movies, talk about directors and writers and actors and cinematographers in a way that made me say, "This man knows and loves what he is talking about here." It was refreshing to talk to someone who loved movies for movies. I remember telling people about Spike—my wife, for one, whom I had just met at the time. She tells the story about how Spike came alongside us one day in traffic. He was on a bike, we were in a convertible. We had a conversation and Spike rode off. I said, "That guy is going to be a great film director." Marty said, "What?" Very disbelieving look on her face. One-take disbelief. I just said, "No, you watch. This guy is going to be great."

There were a lot of people who looked at Spike back then and wrote him off. I know a lot of them who wouldn't give Spike the time of day. They saw a skinny Black guy who wasn't important enough to take up their time. That's the way it is. You read people. If you don't take time, or you're prejudiced, you lose.

So, anyway, Spike and I became good friends. Whenever Spike was working on a project, he'd ask me to help him. I helped him. And whenever I was working on a project, I'd ask him to help me. And he would. Then it came down to him doing *She's Gotta Have It.* He really didn't want . . . he was embarrassed about not having any money. He didn't have any money to pay anybody. I think that's one of the reasons he cut the movie himself. I don't think he did a bad job. He did a good job. But I also think it is difficult to write, produce, direct, and star in a movie you are editing too! I think that's too much. But he did ask me to do some editing for *She's Gotta Have It.* I cut one scene with Nola and Greer making love, which got halfway cut out the first day of editing. They tell me people still talk about that scene. They would talk about it even more if they'd seen the whole scene. Someday I hope to put it all back together. It was good. But the MPAA being as they are—sexually repressed and racist—it was a bad combination.

During that time, he simply said, "I'm going to have you edit my next picture." And that was *School Daze.* I cut *Do The Right Thing.* I didn't do *Mo' Better Blues* because I directed my own picture, *Lonely in America.* I didn't do *Jungle Fever* because I think Sam Pollard was just going to do that after doing such a good job on *Mo' Better Blues,* and also I was busy cutting *Truth or Dare* for Madonna. But *School Daze* was my first feature.

I just have to cut *Malcolm X* as I feel it should be cut, no matter the length. It's not my job to be concerned with length. Once everything is cut and we look at it as a whole, then we can say, "All right, this is a little long, and we really don't have to spend so much time on this part." Some things you wonder about. Is it better to concentrate more on this early part of his life before he becomes Malcolm X? Is the prison stuff too long? Too short? Is this speech going on too much? Is there enough of this speech? I came to *Malcolm X* with an open mind. I figured that was the least I could do for him, for Spike, and for me.

The assassination scene, I don't know, I'll probably eat my words in a week or two, but I don't see that as a problematic scene to edit. There are a lot of angles, maybe twelve set-ups. Re-cut, re-cut, re-cut. Some of the elements that have to come across are the cold-bloodedness of Malcolm's killers; you've got to see the devastation of his family—know that they are there; you have to see his awareness of what is happening; you have to see all this clearly in the middle of the chaos. It is also the confusion of the crowd, because when the police finally come in, you have to realize that you haven't seen a cop.

However, there are always some scenes you come across that, for whatever reason, don't immediately speak to how they should be cut, and the script is only so much of a guide. You're really going on what you see, not what you read, by the time it comes down to the cut. That's true in every movie, not just *Malcolm X.* The vast size of this picture means there are even more scenes. Sometimes I find it disheartening to be in the middle of a scene and not be absolutely sure of where to go with it. But I just force my way through, cut it one way or another, because I know when Spike and I sit down, it will tell us what's wrong with it. It will speak to us. Often, it will be painfully clear what's wrong. Sometimes it's not as clear to me as it is to Spike. Spike will say, "We gotta do this, and this, and this . . ." Sometimes I'll look at it and say, "Wow, why didn't I see that before?"

Like the scene of the impromptu press conference. Malcolm comes out of the door of Temple No. 7 and the press is there waiting for him, and they are just shooting questions at him and he is responding. Most of it is an improvisation, if not all of it, and one of the angles was shot 16 millimeter, as if it were actual news footage of that time. You can actually see the 16 camera in the shot at times. Good. I want it there. I knew what I was going to do with that, back and forth between the 35 and the 16. Looking at reality and in reality. But then there is also the matter of what are we trying to say here? What is the theme of the scene? How is it helping the story? Is it just that it is an impromptu press conference? Well, that's not enough. Everything has to build.

Spike and I looked at it, and for some reason I didn't think he was sure about keeping it, either, but then I cut it down and we sat down and watched it. And then it hit us. The press was trying to put words in his mouth. They know they need to get a hot story to go anywhere in New York, and they were trying to get him to say it, to give them that story. What they were trying to get him to say was that he was anti-white and pro-violence. That's what they wanted him to say. Yes, people at that time, just as in this time, see famous people through the press, so oftentimes the press decides who a man is. They decide: "This is what you are. You protest, but I'm not going to let you tell me you're not like this. It is my job as a reporter to make you admit it." At one point, Denzel as Malcolm repeats a question: "Has there ever been a white person in history who has helped my people?" A reporter has asked this. Then Denzel says, "What do you mean by that?" So that scene became clear to me and Spike, and then I could really focus on just how the scene should be cut to drive home that theme, that people's images are shaped most often not by the people themselves, but by what the media makes of them at the time.

Stylistically, *Malcolm X* and *JFK* are different, but there are some parallels. I think to some extent *JFK* is having some influence. Anybody who is a filmmaker has got to see that movie because it's a big step in feature films. And I feel the same way with what Spike has done with *Malcolm X.* Both are huge steps, because both break down barriers of what you can feel, what you can do with film, and what you can't do.

I don't know if critics will recognize this or not. Good critics are few and far between. I think we get you close to Malcolm X. I personally hate moments in motion pictures where directors are really milking emotion. I think that in *Malcolm X,* emotion speaks for itself. There is no reason to try to milk it. Unnecessary.

As much as I have liked working on this picture, as proud as I am to do this movie, I still think it is my swan song as an editor. I don't know where my ability to edit came from. I've always thought of myself more as a director. Sometimes I'm sitting here cutting this phenomenal movie and I think, "Man, people must be out of their minds to hire me as an editor, because I didn't come up as an editor, I'm not famous as an editor, I really don't know where it comes from." Not that I didn't learn the craft—I just didn't learn it from somebody else. I want to direct after this, so I'm trying to set things in motion in that direction. I may direct some things with Spike as the executive producer. I love working with Spike, more than I love working with anybody else, that's for sure. I think it's easy for us because we've known each other for so long. I think it goes back to something about the people who knew you and respected you when you didn't have a dime, didn't have credits, didn't have anything but belief in yourself. You've got to think of those people differently somehow.

I'm not saying somebody else can't get close to you and collaborate with you and go and do great things—but you don't have to wonder about your fellas, you know. You know Monty is not here because he wanted to get close to Spike Lee. Same for me. You know we are here because we believed in Spike Lee.

It's a matter of just opening your eyes. But that's a lot of what this film is about. There are a lot of people, especially white people, who had their eyes closed to Malcolm X from the get-go, and still do. I have talked to white people who saw him speak, people who met him, and their response to me working on this film is always very different from the people who don't know much about him. Very different. Because somehow—not somehow, I know how—their eyes got opened, and you can't ever close your eyes again once you see somebody, y'know?

Most people will say, "This is not the person I have been told was Malcolm X," once they see the picture. And there are people who consider themselves friends of the Black man who would like to write him out of history, turn away from the fact that he ever existed in this century. I read the autobiography when I was twenty, and I almost wanted to believe white people were devils myself! Otherwise, how do you explain it? How do you explain people being that mean to other people? Across the board?

Now I didn't grow up anywhere near New York. I grew up down in Mississippi and Florida. I grew up down South in the fifties and sixties, and I know how mean it was down there then. It was a mean, nasty place and I've seen mean, nasty things done to people. All that nastiness has seemed to move geographically since then, you know what I mean? There is nothing else to say about it, other than it is incredibly inhuman to be that cruel. But beyond all that, which is fairly obvious, I found myself inspired by Malcolm X. A human inspiration. Because like Malcolm X, I never went to college. So I could relate to the fact that Malcolm X never went to college. He became an enormous inspiration to me in terms of being able to succeed. I felt, "He could do it, so I should not feel like I cannot get an education simply because I don't go to college. It's there for the taking—all you have to do is take it."

Somebody—white—recently said to me at a party. "Well, I just can't respect Malcolm X. I can't respect someone who was so narrow-minded." I said, "Narrow-minded? Really?" Here is a man who fundamentally changed at the age of thirty-seven, thirty-eight. I can't name a single person I've ever known who fundamentally changed that late in life. So I said to the woman who had said this, "Have you ever stood up and said, 'The people I followed were wrong, the people I believed in I have had to question, and now I don't believe in them, even though you can truthfully say they changed my life, these people who saved me. I must now turn and denounce them because they are wrong, and there is a right and wrong.' " I don't know anyone in my life who could do that. You've got to look at somebody who does that, and you've got to look at yourself, and you have to say, "Can I ever do something that courageous?"

I think that some white people will make this enormous mistake of thinking this is a "Black story." This is a person. This is an American. This is somebody who did phenomenal things with that bit of life God gives all of us. This is a hero.

TERENCE BLANCHARD
Composer

My relationship with Spike goes back to *School Daze*. I performed on that sound track, playing with Branford Marsalis, who, like me, is originally from New Orleans, and with Harold Vick, another tenor sax player. They needed a trumpet solo in the movie, and I ending up performing that. Later, a lot of people thought it was Miles Davis because I used a mute, and it was expressive. Yeah, I know, everybody thought it was Miles. I was at the movie's opening night, and a cat said, "Man, Miles sounds good tonight!" I didn't say anything. That was a compliment.

Spike called me back for *Do The Right Thing,* and I worked on that film as well. Then he called me on *Mo' Better Blues,* which, as you know, was a movie with a jazz motif, so I really had to work with Denzel, who was portraying a jazz trumpet player, Bleek Gilliam. I am a jazz trumpet player and pianist, among other things, but I had never done anything like trying to show someone how to act the part. I didn't even know how to approach doing it. How do you teach someone to act like they're playing an instrument? It was unusual for me. But it turned out well.

One day I was at the piano, and Wynton Marsalis happened to be in the studio with me, and Spike was there, too, I don't know how, Spike has a knack for showing up places. I was recording some stuff with Wynton, writing for my next album. Spike heard the tune I was playing and he liked it and said, "Man, I want to use that!" So we recorded it, a capella trumpet, and we used it in *Mo' Better Blues* as well, in the scene where Denzel as Bleek is playing by himself on the Brooklyn Bridge.

Later Spike said, "Man, I want some strings like that! Can you write for strings?" I said, "Yes." So I did it, Spike listened, and then he looked at me with that Spike look and said, "Terence, you have a future writing for films." And I didn't think about it. I thought he was just complimenting me, the way people do, that it was cool and that was it. Then he gave me a call to score *Jungle Fever.* Then he called for *Malcolm X.*

For me, *Malcolm X* is an intense project. When you say the words "Malcolm X" to me, it brings back childhood memories. One of the first memories I have of Malcolm X stems from an album of his speeches that I heard. We were outside, in New Orleans, during a jazz concert, one day when I was in junior high school. And on a break they played this Malcolm X album on loudspeakers outside the park. He was talking about blue-eyed devils, and that shit scared me to death at the time. But then I found out about the man and his life, and gained an understanding of what he was trying to do with his life. So when Spike called and gave me a shooting script, I started working immediately. Ideas just started popping into my head.

Let me put it to you this way: A lot of people say my writing is very dark in the first place. When I think of Malcolm X, I think of a solitary person in search of a truth all alone. I mean, he constantly ends up going to Elijah Muhammad as a father figure, and he had his own father, Earl, as a father figure, but basically this guy is alone. And he is honest in his search. So I constantly hear singular instruments portraying that kind of emotion. I hear strings, but used in a totally different way, highlighting one particular sound instead of a harmony of sounds, trying to create a mood musically that is kin with a character who is very solitary, even though he was a very public person.

Malcolm's theme. That was one of the hardest things, because I had to see the film before I could commit to an idea. So I kept pressing Spike, saying I had to have a copy of the film, I had to go to the first screening, the very first screening that he had, and I needed a tape. I'd seen dailies, but that isn't the same. Spike didn't want to give me a tape at all. He didn't want any tapes out there, even with his friends and co-workers. He played it close. Spike said, "Can't you just write from the script?" But I didn't want to do that, especially the theme, because I needed the vision of what was going on up on the screen. I have to see the film and live the film in the same way that I lived the script. That's why I needed a videotape of the film. I think Spike only wanted to give me scenes that I'm scoring, but I preferred to have the whole film. I understood security with people copying these films like gangbusters and everything. But what I would really liked to have done was to be able to sit down alone and watch the entire film over and over and over again, so that I am not rushing anything, so that the film can speak to me. Get a feel for the flow of dialogue, where the empty spaces are. All that has to be incorporated into the music because that *is* music in a sense. It's dialogue, but it's still musical. When you see great Shakespearean actors orate, that is very musical. I saw Denzel in the park last summer as Richard III, and I called him later and talked to him for like three hours because it just blew my mind. I'd read Shakespeare before, but it can be hard to read. But to hear it read right—you have to have someone who really knows how to draw the potency and the rhythm of those lines. Film is the same way. And music is the exact same way.

This leads to a hard problem: One of the hardest things is that sometimes Spike and I will use the same terminology, but we work in two different mediums, music and film, and terminology will end up meaning two completely different things. Not a serious problem, but something that must be worked around.

I just played on the soundtrack for *Housesitter,* a movie starring Goldie Hawn and Steve Martin. The man who composed the music and score is named Miles Goodman, and he was going through a similar thing with his director, Frank Oz. I asked Miles about it and he said, "It happens on every film." Which is understandable, because the director's thing is film, and the musician's thing is . . . well, it's obvious, isn't it?

We don't actually go into the studio until June. So I have been trying some different things in the meantime. There are some things I want to check out. Some African melodies. Some Arabian melodies. American melodies. New melodies. My biggest problem is finding musicians. I've been trying to find people who can play disparate music. Because I don't want to use synthesizers or anything like that. I want fine musicians.

At my house I have a synthesizer and a computer and a VCR. Basically you can score a film like that, if you have to. I don't want to do that, though. It's not the best sound for me. I understand how the instruments work, how they work in nature. That's a problem that people who aren't true musicians don't quite understand, don't really get. A lot of people just think, well, it's more economical, therefore go with it; just go the keyboard route for everything you need. Cheaper? Well, that's not necessarily so in the first place, because you wind up spending a lot in studio costs because somebody has to find the proper sound if you can't or tweak the sound just so, or the computer may crash—anything could happen. So I would rather go the other route, and luckily Spike has always been one to want to use a live orchestra, which is great for me. Because when you press that trumpet valve, or that piano key, there is something that happens in nature. The sound vibrates off the walls and there are overtones that you hear. Waves. That is natural. You can re-create that artificially on a keyboard and come close, but there is that human factor that you won't pick up.

This film could be overwhelming to me, for any number of reasons. First of all, I never thought I would actually get a chance to write a score. That's the first thing. I thought I would be in my sixties by the time that happened to me, after I had done two hundred recordings, when I was on my deathbed. So that part is overwhelming. I have one film under my belt with *Jungle Fever*. But this . . . the character himself, Malcolm, is overwhelming. But I am one who has always trusted my instincts. I tell the cats in my band, look man, if the stuff doesn't feel good to you, it's not going to feel good to the people out there. Don't give me that crap about they don't know. Everybody knows. They know what they feel. it's true. You can be playing the slickest shit, or Top 40, or whatever. If it's sincere, people will feel it. If it's not sincere, they can tell. It is that intangible essence that goes through any kind of art form, that we can never quite explain or bottle up or write down. I draw upon that.

I have learned some things about scoring in the meantime. Sitting in on dubbing sessions. Sitting in on a lot of things. Learning. I don't need fifty strings to get a big string sound. I don't have to do that. It's all in the writing, doubling voices, doubling notes between viola and violin and violincello and cello and bass and so forth. It also depends on how you combine voices with the brass and the woodwinds and the strings and metal pieces and drums. Then we have to get into the way it will be recorded. But the primary thing is the essential voice and feeling. For some of these scenes, I don't hear that solitary voice I spoke of before; sometimes I hear a massive orchestration of sound. It's almost like scoring two movies. More than that, really.

The theme is the biggest thing, because the biggest thing about any recipe, no matter how many spices you use, is the main ingredient. Once that's in there, all the trackings will fall into place. I have been sitting in with the editor, Barry Brown, when I have the time. I just sit there with a piece of paper and, as it comes to me, I don't say anything, I just jot down the configuration of notes. I have a tape with me now of three ideas. I have more stuff at home. I take chances because it is unusual. But I think my role as composer with this film is to reflect what Spike is doing, and Spike takes chances. It's like I don't want to come in here and try to write like John Williams writes, those brilliant, booming themes. This score has to reflect the film and the filmmaker to me, and even though the scope is big, the story is right here, tight.

We are going to produce the score, meaning we are going to do all the administrative stuff. I think it is going to be for the Warner Brothers label, because it's their film. Don't know if Quincy Jones will be involved or not, but he has done so many films and he is working with and for Warner Brothers, I think. I usually have a contractor who hires all the musicians for me. I have an assistant as well. I do the score. I print the music with the computer. A lot of people get bent out of shape when I do that, say I am putting them out of business. But I look at it this way: I'm not taking any chances. You might easily read through a typo in a script. If a musician plays a typo note—I don't have to tell you, do I? And he can't guess what you might have had in mind, either. With the computer, I know I won't have one wrong note. Stan Hunt is helping me with all that. James Nichols remixed my last album, as well as *Jungle Fever,* so I'm going to be working with him again. The music editor, Alex Steymarker, will let me know as they make changes in scenes.

Film is an interesting process to me. I was in on *Mo' Better* mostly from beginning to end. It was eye-opening to me because I was there every day on the set, watching these cats work fourteen- and sixteen-hour days. I'd say, "How do they do that shit?" You're on the set twelve or fourteen hours, then you go look at dailies and then go to bed and wake up and right back to the same thing before the crack of dawn the next day. Not a musician's life.

It's funny. I'm not working with my band as much, preparing for this. I'm working on this film all day, but until we go in June, most of the work is theoretical. I took March off and most of April just to prepare myself for this, because when I get that cut I'm going to be in my home studio, late night hours, after hours, just dealing with it. We are talking about doing six-track recording. Everybody is going digital these days, seems like. But I think we are going to go analog. Digital is not a wave form of sound. Analog is a wave form—just like what happens in nature, remember? We want to use sound called SR, which is the best in that it rivals the clarity of digital, but it has the warmth of analog. The *Glory* soundtrack? Analog. James Horner. Sound!

All this is really enlightening to me. After I did the work in *Mo' Better,* I was saying to myself, "Terence, God works in mysterious ways, maybe you were cut out to . . ." You know. I walked out of the studio, and right up the hall somebody was mastering some Stravinsky. I said, "That is some bad shit." I mean, it brought my ego back down to where it should be, you know.

A lot of times people ask me, "How do you write music? How do you come up with these things?" I answer them by telling them there are technical things you can do, anybody can do this who is finely trained, but my best melodies never came to me that way. I can't explain it. There is this one composition I wrote—Wynton loves this tune—called "The Grace of God," and it was the only composition in my life that when I sat down at the piano, I simply free-composed it first note to last, just by sitting down and playing. That really kind of scared me, because I had just seen this television program on the homeless, and I just went to the piano and started playing and this—creation—came out. A couple of friends and I, and the Marsalises too, and some others, sometimes when we play, we know we have to put our egos aside and let the Creator enter. That is true creativity, when you are nothing but a vessel. You've got to let it speak through you. Sometimes when I play, I feel it's not me, somehow, and invariably, those are my best performances. Denzel once told me he felt the same way, when he was portraying Steven Biko in *Cry Freedom,* during the courtroom scene. He said it wasn't him anymore. And when they said cut, nobody called him Denzel for a while. They just looked at him. Somebody called him Steve.

The thing I constantly try to tell people is that yes, you can be technically expert, and you must work constantly at your craft, but all that is merely so that you can be spoken through when you perform. I have noticed there are times on the road when I was extremely tired, and some of those were my best performances because I wasn't really thinking about it. I was feeling, and playing. Sometimes you feel weird taking compliments from people because if you had to do that again, you couldn't, so you know it wasn't you. It dumbfounds you sometimes. I used to play with Art Blakey and the Jazz Messengers. Art used to talk about this state all the time. Whenever we'd do a gig, he'd start off by telling the audience, "This music is the damndest thing, you know. It comes from the Creator, to the artist, right to you. There is no way in the world you can beat that." Art was exactly right.

MONTY ROSS
Co-Producer

The high point to me in all this was Denzel Washington's portrayal of Malcolm X. To hear Denzel's voice in some of his speeches and the way he handled the material, a lot of times he sounded like Malcolm, and I know what Malcolm sounded like, so that to me was the thrill. You know, I was a small boy at the time of Malcolm, and there wasn't a whole lot of evidence of Malcolm being there with the civil rights movement. What we did hear were tapes. To actually see Denzel and to hear those words—that was a highlight not only of the movie, but my life.

These things are all part of history now. Many times, like the brothers who played the assassins in the film, down to the PA's, people just gave you the impossible of themselves: if you were to try to quantify, 200 and 300 percent. You just hope the camera caught it, and most of the time, it did.

I don't think there's anything to fear from the advance marketing and publicity, although it will have been a long haul by the time the movie opens in November. I just think that's a caution. You have to be careful of people's intentions, because you don't want to give away your product beforehand. A lot of information has slipped through the cracks already. Everybody wants some glory. Everybody wants to come and hang out for a minute just to see what's happening, but if you aren't here out of sincerity, or for the long haul, the doors are closed.

Well, what I think needs to happen is, we need to have a national film conference where we can set an agenda. I'm not saying that we shall overcome, either. I am saying Oprah Winfrey, Spike, Bill Cosby, Eddie Murphy, John Singleton, Charles

Lane, Danny Glover, everybody with the talent and the means and the experience in film should come together. Now maybe that's too much talent in one room and knees will start buckling, but somehow I don't think so. I think we can see we need to discuss things, that things aren't right and images have a lot to do with it, because these are people who can control some images. To me that is a big first step. We need to make all kinds of films, from epics to simple films, rich culturally, which speak to a lot of things we need to be dealing with now. Now I'm not necessarily putting anybody else's thing down, but I'm tired of seeing Black men shooting and getting shot and killing each other on screen when there is no morality behind the plot. We have got to expand. And I know that the money thing is always there, but I feel there is enough money that can be made even while dealing with this agenda. Every studio in the country has an agenda. They say, "This is our slate of movies this year," and they invite in exhibitors from all across the country. They bring 'em into Vegas, they party hard, they give them a good time, they show the reel, they bring out the movie stars and say, "Look, we're hoping for a big year." They're hoping to take 17 or 18 percent of box office shares. That's around $5 billion. That will be stock options for them, money for their children's education, positive images, for the most part, of their time on earth.

We went out to Show West, in Vegas, in late January. Warner Brothers showed their reel for 1992. A huge ballroom full of exhibitors were there. The little guys. All the guys who sell the popcorn, the peanuts, the candy, the nachos, the sodas. We're in the ballroom: Danny Glover there with *Lethal Weapon 3*; Morgan Freeman there with *The Power of One*; Spike and Denzel there with *Malcolm X*. A very good year for Warners, if you throw *Batman Returns* in there. Everybody else in the room was white. White and male. Yet there were these four brothers also there, knowing their circumstances, our circumstances as a people. What was interesting was while we were hugging and talking, slowly but surely, the big boys started drifting toward us, seeing what was going on, saying, yeah, er, yo, you know we're in this together now. The four brothers were in the room being catered to. Next year there might not be any Black faces in that room. But if Paramount made a billion dollars off Eddie Murphy movies, how much do you think the distributors made? Another billion. If Eddie Murphy got entertainer of the decade, you know lots of popcorn and peanuts were sold off him, and you know there should always be somebody Black in that room.

It just showed me that if we organize, collectively, in groups large and small, we can create anything we want, because we are together. The talent, the acumen, is there. What is to stop us? Maybe it won't happen in my lifetime. But it will happen, of course. Realistically, all people are going to take their destiny into their own hands, eventually.

We want to create something unfiltered. Uncensored. Real. Maybe we already have.

NTSHAVHENI WA LURULI
Production Assistant

I first heard about Spike six years ago in 1986, when I came to study filmmaking in the U.S. He had just shaken the world with his first feature film, *She's Gotta Have It.*

Three years later, I met him when I was working for Cinecom Entertainment group as a script analyst. A friend of mine, Shelby Stone, the then vice-president of Cinecom who was also Spike's friend, set up an appointment to meet him at Sound One Studio where he was mixing his movie, *Mo' Better Blues.* Contrary to what I had heard of him, read about him, and seen of him on TV, I found Spike to be what we would call at home in South Africa, a *comrade.* A people's man. Down to earth. He wore sneakers, shorts, and an ordinary T-shirt and also a baseball cap. He uses subways and doesn't have a driver's license. He still can't use a computer; he uses long hand to write his scripts.

Since that meeting, I have worked on three of his movies, *Do The Right Thing, Jungle Fever,* and now *Malcolm X.*

On the production of *Malcolm X,* he has given me many opportunities to learn the process of filmmaking; everything from principal photography to postproduction.

Since I have known him, I have found him to be full of surprises and also extremely unpredictable. You just can't figure him out. The most exciting thing that ever happened to me was when he called from Egypt and asked me to go to South Africa for the additional shooting of *Malcolm X.* I had not been home for six years. This, really, was the most wonderful moment of my life. I quickly bundled up my luggage and I was off. That was January 18, 1992.

If anybody had told me that I was going to have a cultural shock when I got back to South Africa, I would have said he was out of his mind. On Monday morning, January 20, as the plane descended onto the tarmac at Johannesburg's Jan Smuts Airport, I thought maybe we were stopping to refuel in some kind of a country airport.

My mind refused to accept what my eyes saw. In those seconds, I flashed back to the "real" Jan Smuts Airport that I knew before I went overseas. That wonderful place where we used to pay a special visit to see the airplanes. That sophisticated place where sophisticated people from all over the world came. The amazing place where we ate the best food in the world. Jan Smuts Airport, the biggest airport in the world, the most beautiful airport in the world. Memories of yesteryear.

As I looked at the scenery through the window, I couldn't help but feel some kind of disappointment . . . even a betrayal. A strange undescribable feeling. You know how you anticipate something and somehow it turns out to be the opposite of what you thought.

But now this feeling was overtaken by another sensational thought. Who was waiting for me out there, my mother? My father? My grandmother? My longtime friend Coralie Trotter?

As I pushed my luggage toward the arrival hall, an excruciating excitement mounted with every step I took.

They saw me first: my father and my uncle. My father rushed toward me and hugged me. The very best moment of my life! You see, my father and I have never hugged before. Not because he is not passionate; no, because of tradition. According to our tradition, a handshake to a son is most appropriate. But that particular moment, tradition flew out of the window. I clung to him for what seemed an eternity. Both of us were fighting back tears. My uncle stood by proudly smiling from ear to ear. I reached for his big hand. We shook hands hard.

Rapitse Montsho, the *Malcolm X* production coordinator in South Africa, came forward to take my luggage. He was the main man I was going to be working with in the shooting of *Malcolm X* in South Africa. We had never met before, although I had heard of him.

We pulled up chairs and had tea to get acquainted. Every now and then I would glance at my father. He had aged. He was frail. A man they once called "Palm Beach" because of the sharp, cool way he dressed, he was now a shadow of himself. My heart wept in silence. My uncle too was turning gray, beaten down.

I asked about my mother. My father told me she could not come to the airport since she was working. That I understood very well. The reality was that she could not come to the airport to see her son whom she had not seen for six years because she feared that if she did, she would lose her job. Her job was very important; after all, she would see me later. The reason my father came to the airport was that he was on a night shift. Otherwise, he would not have come, either. I knew then that I was back in South Africa. To say that I was angry is an understatement.

I had to start working immediately. We were shooting on Saturday and Sunday. Spike and the crew were due on Thursday the twenty-third. The location would be the following day on Friday. That meant we had literally three days to put everything in order—or, to be precise, two days since Monday was already over.

At 8:00 P.M. Thursday, transportation comes to pick up Spike and the crew outside Jan Smuts Airport. The press and TV crews are already there waiting. I look at them and think, these are the people who have been flooding our production office with requests to interview Spike. The place is crowded with people. Banners, including a huge one from AZAPO (Azanian People's Organization) are held, ready to be unfolded.

Suddenly there is an announcement; Spike's plane is delayed and is rescheduled to arrive at Jan Smuts Airport at about 1:30 A.M. The people wait. When he finally arrived everyone was overjoyed. The long wait was worth it . . .

But this joy, this happiness, this spell of jubilation, this hoorah!, could not go on like that. Not in South Africa. A couple of policemen with batons in their hands materialized from nowhere. They had to be there to remind us that this was too good to be true. They put down the banners. The banners that simply honored a brother who had come home to visit. There were no stones, no spears, no A.K. 47's, no nothing. Only love. In South Africa, love seems to be one of those things that is considered to be a threat to national security. Especially when it relates to Black people. But Black people are unstoppable if they really want to do their thing. Spike was mobbed. People wanted to touch him. To talk to him. They helped carry his luggage and those of the crew to their cars. He was pleased. He told me there had been a bomb scare in his plane in Nairobi. The plane had to be grounded and thoroughly searched. He was unruffled, cool as a cucumber.

At the press conference the following morning, he faced another barrage of bombs from the press. They wanted to know how and why his trip to South Africa was cleared and blessed by

AZAPO, ANC, PAC, and their affiliates, whereas Paul Simon's and
Whoopi Goldberg's were controversial; in other words, what
makes him legitimate?

Some people wanted him to allow his movies to be shown in
South Africa. But he made it clear that he would do so once not
one, but all the major Black political organizations give him the
go ahead. It is because of this kind of a stand that Black people
in South Africa have embraced him. They know that he is no
phony. Black people know that Spike Lee knows exactly what
time it is in our struggle, unlike many artists who come to South
Africa as philanthropists and messengers of change.

Spike, like many people, had heard about Soweto. He had
seen it in newspapers and television. On Friday as we went
location scouting in Soweto, I was interested to see his reactions.

As we entered Soweto, he was amazed by the huge size of it.
All he saw were rows and rows of infinite bungalows with asbestos roofs. We stopped by the shanty town next to Klipspruit.
These little homes are nothing more than sheets of corrugated
metal knocked together to make shelters. Others are made of
plastic and cardboards. Piles of garbage and excrement lie in
front of these little shacks. Naked children run around mobbed
by flies. Everybody was quiet. Spike's face was gloomy. We
moved on to the next three shanties, including Mshenguville,
where a lot of people were murdered a year ago. Here we were
shown charred spots where homes once had stood. Spike and the
crew did not want to stay long. We all understood; it was too
painful.

On our way back to the city, we stopped by the hostel (living
places for male migrant workers). There is only one way to
describe these dwellings; they are concentration camps. Here
again, nobody said anything. Their faces reflected what they felt
inside.

Later, during his interview with the press, Spike best
summed up his feelings about Soweto when he said, "You have
to be there to know it . . . you have to smell the place to feel it."
Outraged, he said, "I feel like dropping the bomb in white South
Africa."

Our first shot was the sign WELCOME TO SOWETO, at the entrance of the township. I guess it was important for Spike, because it captured the friendly spirit of Soweto. After shooting a
major scene at a school, we went back to the shanties where
small kids gathered, sang freedom songs, and danced Toyi-Toyi
for Spike and the crew. Spike and the crew were impressed by

their enormous energy, which was a reflection of hope and determination. Everyone felt relaxed and was smiling. Indeed, Spike joined the kids dancing Toyi-Toyi.

We wound up our shoot in Alexander Township. By Sunday afternoon, Spike had everything he needed in the can. The shoot in South Africa was over. The shooting of *Malcolm X* was complete; it was a wrap.

Monday evening as Spike waited in the departure hall, there was a sparkle of triumph in his eyes. You could tell that his long journey from Harlem, to Egypt, to Soweto had finally come to an end, both spiritually and physically. He knew all along that the road was going to be hard and dangerous, but at the same time he knew that it had to be taken . . . by any means necessary.

PART FIVE

REVELATIONS

June 1992

I have a certain instinct, and it's maybe my one and only God-given ability. I sometimes see things that haven't quite materialized, haven't quite happened yet. But, sooner or later, these things become obvious to everybody. I seem to have an eye for these things, and I can take no credit for it.

Two of my favorite touches in *Malcolm X* are the opening, a full-frame of the American flag, which then burns down to an American red-white-and-blue X; and near the end, when Denzel-as-Malcolm is taking that fateful drive from the New York Hilton hotel to the Audubon Ballroom, on February 21, 1965. The music behind him is of Sam Cooke singing "A Change Is Gonna Come." I love that song, love the way Sam Cooke interpreted it. I've always loved it, and knew one day the way to use it would make itself known to me.

Those were two of my favorite moments in *Malcolm X* because they are so evocative of what it truly means to be an African-American in this country today. There's our reality, and then there's the hope inside that reality. The reality was that it was now May 4, and I was screening *X* for the second time to the suits at Warner Brothers in Hollywood. This time what we saw was a three-hour, eighteen-minute version of *X.* South-central L.A. was burning as I got up in front of everybody and said, "This film is needed now, more than ever." And not only South-central was burning, but some of the rest of the City of Angels. It was getting warm on the Left Coast, and it wasn't summer yet. This was on a Thursday, the day after the infamous Rodney King verdict came down from Ventura County, California, north of the L.A. basin. It was a bad day to be an American, and maybe the perfect day to think of and reflect on the man they'd called "Brother Minister." We all sat there watching *Malcolm X* in the dark as the light flickered the image onto the screen and hopefully indelibly into the viewers' minds.

This is what it was like. Outside, the switch had been thrown on chaos, pandemonium. Gunfire, burning, looting, murder—a breakdown on all sides of the "law," and all because a jury from Simi Valley, California, one of those suburban lily white Steven Spielberg communities if there ever was one (*Jaws, Close Encounters, Poltergeist, E.T., Always,* and *Hook*), decided that L.A.'s Gestapo, the police trained and led by Daryl "Sieg Heil" Gates, had not been beating a man, a human being, when they viciously and cowardly beat Rodney King. The jury's verdict of not guilty meant they actually believed the police were beating an animal. Why, that bear, that linebacker, that piece of shit, that "gorilla in the mist," he was damn lucky the police didn't put him to sleep permanently with a choke hold, right then and there. This is what the jury of good white folks was saying, no matter how it's sugar-coated for you otherwise. That jury said no matter how you brutalize a Black man, you aren't really brutalizing him, because he's not a man, because he is not human. Some white people would rather save whales or snail darters, spotted owls and the Amazonian rain forest than get off

Black people's asses. It's true; as true as the day is long. Some white people implement programs to save these animals, and at the same time they'll stand by and watch programs implemented to destroy the minds, bodies, and souls of Black folk.

When you tell people their lives mean nothing, they very quickly find a way to make you realize you're wrong about that.

A change is gonna come. Oh yes it will. One way or another.

On the way to the airport, the limo went down La Brea, along the outer, western edges of the community known as South-central Los Angeles, a community made up of Latinos and whites as well as the African-Americans who get all the bad ink. I noticed a bank had been completely torched on one corner. It looked as though somebody had made a building frame out of giant burned matches, like in a Daffy Duck cartoon, and that charred frame was all that was left of it except for one thing—the massive safe, sitting in the middle of the ruins and surrounded by concrete. Just down the street, the Baldwin Hills Theater was completely untouched, just absolutely undamaged. This is the only Black-owned theater that I know of in the U.S.A. I'd heard that the next week the owners allowed free admission to all showings of all films to all patrons for a few days at the Baldwin, as one gesture of thanks that their business wasn't torched. I thought about the name of the theater. The Baldwin. My man, James.

I also heard that a lot of businesses were burned down by the owners themselves, trying to collect on their insurance, and that most of the deaths were the result of the National Guard and the police shooting people in those seventy-two hours of hell after that deadly verdict came down, when there was total anarchy on the streets of L.A., when everybody in America had to face what had been created in America, what many Republicans of Reagan and Bush stripes, and Democratic liberals alike, had tried to deny for so long. The American system was one of injustice, not justice. And everywhere you went, if you watched any sort of electronic media, the images were there. You saw the last five seconds of Rodney King being handcuffed, after the serious, sadistic beating was over, and then you saw a white truck driver named Reginald Denny, who was being beaten up after being pulled out of truck on the corner of Florence and Normandie. No way are these two images of an equal weight to me.

Later on, police arrested four brothers and charged them with attempted murder and set their bails at an average of $185,-

000, dressed them in those orange coveralls, and jailed them. They said they were looking at possible life sentences, and we started hearing what terrible people they were—bad men. So where was the justice in all that? People said, yes, what they did was bad, what they did was wrong—but it was more wrong for Rodney King to be beaten in first place, because he was beaten while he was being electrocuted by *police officers sworn to uphold the law.* And they never did a day in jail, the police. They weren't even touched by law. They were acquitted of all charges, by law. So, then, what is the law, here in America, after all? What did the law mean? Did it mean death to Black people? Was that the law? We had to ask ourselves these questions now. Was that early, angry Malcolm X right after all as he said it in his righteous anger, right in saying that you, if you are a Black person, would never have peace here, would never have security here, that you would spend a thousand years listening to and being tricked by the lies and false promises of the white man, who doesn't want you to be a law-abiding citizen, who wants you to be a law-breaker, who wants you to be immoral, so he'll have an excuse to come in and bust you upside your head with his clubs?

These were things to think about. The same goddamn videotape that gets ignored so that four policemen can walk is probably going to send four Black men to prison for life. If those young Black men end up getting heavy jail terms, nothing's changed.

I just beat the curfew out of L.A.

No justice, no peace. No justice, no peace.

I went to Cannes for about ten days right after this happened, for the film festival. I had already seen *The Player,* one of the year's entries for the Palme D 'Or, the Cannes version of Best Picture. Robert Altman's film was about the madness that can occur in this business, and I thought it was excellent and funny, and that Tim Robbins, who was kind enough to work with me in a small role in *Jungle Fever,* rocked the house as the lead character, a big-time studio executive named Griffin Mill, kind of the way Anthony Hopkins had rocked the year before as the cannibalistic psychiatrist Hannibal Lecter in *The Silence of the Lambs.* I saw Tim in Cannes, hanging out, and gave him some dap. He and Denzel should be up for the big honor, Best Actor, in '93.

I had a news conference in Cannes, and ripped right into the Simi Valley jury and George Bush. Even my friend Stevie Wonder, who is blind, could have seen what was on that videotape!

If you are Black, it looks like you have no rights in America. And George Bush should have been right in there as soon as it happened, flown in on Air Force One, instead of waiting to see what the political landscape might blow like in a few days. In South Africa, the day before the King verdict, the white government had sentenced a white policeman to death for killing four Black South African people. The operative world is *people.* I never thought South Africa would be ahead of the U.S. in the matter of human rights for Black people. I wish *Malcolm X* could be released tomorrow.

I had just shot some commercials for Nike a couple of weeks before the L.A. uprising, to promote Air Raid sneakers. One of the spots we shot had a *Do The Right Thing* feel to it, a tension between races, represented with some teenagers getting ready to hoop at Spike's "Urban Jungle Gym" by hollering racial insults at each other. Then I came on with the peace sign saying if we're going to live together, we gotta play together. I just had seen that. Felt it. At Cannes, I was asked by a French journalist whether or not *Do The Right Thing* had predicted the revolt, and I told him on the contrary, that film had been taken from events that had already happened in New York City, many times over, the anger left after a deadly session of racist police brutality. I was calling it like it already had been in this case, not as it might be. I was later told that Mickey Rourke was quoted somewhere as saying John Singleton and I were responsible for the riots in L.A. because of the kind of films we'd made. I suggested that just because the French adore his films didn't mean Mickey was an expert on Black folks. I suggested Mickey take a shower and a shave and shut the fuck up. Later on his publicist called and said Mickey had been misquoted.

Anyway, I was in Cannes doing interviews with foreign journalists and having a decent time of it as always, but I couldn't keep my mind off the States, and off *Malcolm X.* But I'll always come to Cannes. This is where *She's Gotta Have It* first broke out in '86. People always want to know how I feel about awards, since I bitched and groaned about *sex, lies and videotape* beating out *Do The Right Thing* for the Palme d'Or, the grand prize at Cannes, back in 1989, and when *Barton Fink* beat out *Jungle Fever* in '91. Well, what I'm trying to do is broaden my market overseas, the entire international scope of my market, get it? I don't think there's a better way of doing that in film than having your work recognized at the Cannes Film Festival. It's like winning an Oscar in the States. What it means is that the studio will run another little marketing campaign for your film, and it will mean more revenue for the picture, by far. That is my position on awards, other than the fact that I think Black people should also have our own, because very often lack of merit ain't the reason you might not get recognized. That's the reason the Black Achievement Awards, the Essence Awards, the Black Filmmakers Awards, and the Soul Train Awards are very important to me, as well. These awards are important because we have to honor our own, if we want to be honored at all. An example of this is Stevie Wonder. I thought he got jerked last year for his songs for *Jungle Fever.* He didn't even get an Academy Award nomination. But he was honored by the Black Oscars. That's an event they have every year, hosted by the actor Bernie Casey, where they honor the Black Academy Award nominees.

Sometimes the best award is like what Sam Jackson is getting now, after finally being recognized for Gator in *Jungle Fever.* What Sam is getting right now, and will continue to get, is work. Work, good work, meaningful work, quality work, well-paid work, is the best award I know about. As for *Malcolm X,* I don't know what kind of awards we'll be up for behind it, I haven't thought about it but some of the few people who have seen it say it should be up for four or five or six Academy Awards. We'll see. I don't know anything but this: The Academy won't be able to deny Denzel Washington. Denzel rocks the world with this performance.

While all this is going on, my Knicks had beaten the Detroit Pistons in a hard five-game set in the NBA playoffs and now faced the world champs, Mike and the Chicago Bulls.

Nobody gave the Knicks a chance, but they went in and beat the Bulls in the first game at Chicago Stadium. I'd seen two games at Chicago Stadium already in this season, but I missed this one. However, I wasn't going to miss any more at home. I got on the plane from Cannes and beat it back to New York, to the Garden, for games three and four—we lost the first, but won the second and the best-of-seven set was tied at two games apiece. My plane back to France left at 10:00 P.M., and the game was over at 9:00. I made it. I went back to Cannes and hung out for a little while doing more interviews, picking up what scuttlebutt I could that might be of some use to me later as I try to expand my horizons in film. Again, we had gone $5 million over budget. Bette Smith and the Completion Bond Co. were trying to cut their losses. They felt it was unfair for them to take the full hit. They wanted Warner Brothers to absorb some of the overage. Warner Brothers wasn't having it. Their position was this: This is your job, we paid you for a service, the film went over budget, it's not our concern, later for you.

This was the dilemma I was in. The Bond Company had fired my editors, Warner Brothers legally said they couldn't fund me or they would be in breach, and I myself was tapped. I got paid 3 million bananas for *X*; 2 million of those went directly back into the film, so I didn't have it either. I couldn't ask the editors to work for free, they had to be paid. I was up the creek without a paddle or a boat. I was in the water and I can't swim, I was going down. I prayed on it, then drew on Malcolm X for inspiration. I had been studying him for two years doing this film. Malcolm always talked about, DO FOR SELF. The BLACK MAN has to learn to stand on his own two feet. DO FOR SELF. I took a page out of the MALCOLM MANUAL. I know BLACK FOLKS with money. I would appeal directly to their BLACKNESS, to their sense of knowing how important this film is. How important MALCOLM X is to us. How important it is that this film succeed. I got down and came up with a list of all the people I knew that I should contact. Let the record state, the first call went out to Bill Cosby. I was in L.A. at the time staying at the Chateau Marmont. Luckily, I was able to track him down in New York. I was straight with him. I told him the deal. At first, Bill said he was tapped. I think he thought I was asking for a million, which I wasn't. Bill said, "How much you need?" I said the amount, he said call my accountant, the check will be at your hotel that night. It was simple as that. Even though, I knew what had to be done it was still nonetheless a hard thing to ask people for money, especially, the type of money I was asking for. When I approached everyone I told them it wasn't to be considered a loan, nor an investment, this was a gift. The only thing I've ever asked Michael Jordan for is for some tickets, that's it. I didn't feel good asking him, begging him, if you will, for the bread, but I had no choice. What's great is that folks responded. Not everyone I approached gave. A lot more said yes than no but it's important to emphasize the positive. Bill Cosby, Oprah Winfrey, Michael Jordan, Janet Jackson, Prince, Magic Johnson, Tracy Chapman, and Peggy Cooper-Cafritz didn't have to give me shit, not a red cent but they chose to. Too often we hear and too often we believe that Black folks never get together, never come together, never are unified, well this wasn't the case with *Malcolm X.* Here was a group, A WHO'S WHO, all African-Americans, all have much bank and all gave their money. These folks saved *Malcolm X*. It was their money that kept us to continue to work on the film. Before things were finally worked out between Warner Brothers and the Completion Bond Co. two months elapsed. For two whole months, we were alone, stranded, cut-off, no funding, no money, and it was prominent African-Americans that financed this film. There has been a lot of speculation about how much I was able to get, well, you can guess all you want. I'm not telling.

With our "Black" money, we got on the good foot, still editing the picture. Warner Brothers and the Completion Bond Co. knew we were still proceeding but they had no idea who was paying for it. I got the idea to announce this whole thing on May 19, on what would have been Malcolm's sixty-eighth birthday. We held a press conference at the Schomburg Library in Harlem, all the major press was invited and it became a big news story. It was definitely a historic event, it was a precedent, this had never been done before, and the world needed to be told. We can do for ourselves, here was a concrete example of it. Who's to say the next time I don't go directly to the same individuals to finance my next film, bypassing Hollywood. Who's to say that these individuals or other people like them don't get together and start pooling their wealth, pooling their resources and talents. It can be done. I don't and I'm not waiting on white folks. If you know only one thing about Malcolm, that should be it.

Malcolm X will be the sixth film we've done in seven years, and, frankly, I'm tired. I'm whipped! It is a physically and mentally draining effort, making films. I'll still direct in the future, no question about that, but right now I think what I want to do most is executive produce some projects that I have in mind. If all goes well, I've got an agreement I'll enter into with my old friends at Universal, a contract that will allow me to be executive producer on any number of projects.

Universal always was my favorite shop among the Hollywood studios that I worked with, and my experience with *Malcolm X* at Warner Brothers (the Plantation) has done nothing to change the studio rankings in my mind. It should be a good year for Warner Brothers, though. They've got *Lethal Weapon 3* with Danny Glover and Mel Gibson and Joe Pesci ready for release, and despite how I might feel about the film itself, I know it will make money for Warner Brothers. Then *Batman Returns* opens in June. Then, to cap it off, *Malcolm X* opens the weekend before Thanksgiving. Warner Brothers should have no complaints about their 1992. But I hope my deal and my new home will be at

Universal. I also want to make sure we get Forty Acres and a Mule Musicworks off the ground running, and I've already put in some promotional appearances with some of the talent we have on the label. I'm looking forward to that as well. I'm just looking forward. The future isn't set in stone, but these are the things I'd really like to get down on.

The sixth game of the Knicks-Bulls series at the Garden was a throw down. Patrick Ewing came off the bench on an injured leg, a bad ankle sprain, sort of the way Willis Reed had played on a bad knee in 1970 against the Lakers. Patrick scored 27 points. The Knicks ran the Chicago Bulls out of New York, 100–85, before the Bulls ran the Knicks back to New York in a seventh-game blowout at Chicago Stadium to end the series in Chicago's favor, four games to three. I went to both games. It had been a good run.

I'd run with the bulls myself, the Pamplona bulls that is, in Pamplona, Spain, in the ritual running of the bulls, the spring before this. I'll tell you, my life sometimes seems like a long jolt of ironies, character establishments, and foreshadowings and turnabouts and plot twists and fighting wars and battles—sometimes it's like a movie itself. I'm constantly rewriting scenes in it. Right now, I'm working on an ending. A somewhat happy ending. Somewhat. I want to and will continue to make films for the rest of my life. I've been blessed. I'm doing what makes me the happiest. Nothing in this world gives me the feeling I get from cinema.

MALCOLM X

Screenplay
by

James Baldwin
Arnold Perl
and
Spike Lee

Based on the
Autobiography of Malcolm X
As told to Alex Haley

*REVISED 4/15/91 – BLUE
**REVISED 7/4/91 – PINK
***REVISED 8/8/91 – YELLOW
****REVISED 8/12/91 – GREEN
*****REVISED 8/24/91 – GOLDENROD
******REVISED 9/9/91 – BUFF
*******REVISED 9/10/91 – SALMON
********REVISED 9/11/91 – CHERRY
*********REVISED 9/16/91 – IVORY
**********REVISED 10/22/91 – GREY
***********REVISED 11/16/91 – TAN
************REVISED 11/25/91 – LILAC
*************REVISED 12/3/91 – GREEN

Fourth Draft
Forty Acres and A Mule Filmworks, Inc.
Brooklyn, N.Y.
Ya-Dig Sho-Nuff
By Any Means Necessary
WGA-East #061569-00

170.

FADE IN:

1   EXT. ROXBURY STREET – THE WAR YEARS – DAY

It is a bright sunny day on a crowded street on the black side of Boston. PEOPLE and KIDS are busy with their own things.

SHORTY bops his way down the street. He is a runty, very dark young man of 21 with a mission and a smile on his face. He wears the flamboyant style of the time: the whole zoot-suit, pegged legs and a wide brim hat with a white feather stuck in the hat band.

2   OMIT

3   OMIT

4   OMIT

5   EXT. STREET – DAY

FOLLOW SHOT. Shorty dodges through the crowd with his packages. His smile is one of anticipation. He nods to a PAL without stopping; eyes a COUPLE OF CHICKS dancing on the street, but is not dissuaded.

6   INT. BARBER SHOP – DAY

Shorty has his jacket and hat off, his sleeves rolled up. He is like a surgeon preparing for an operation. His equipment is spread out on a table: can of lye, large mason jar, wooden stirring spoon, knife, the eggs. His actions have the character of a ritual: each thing being done just so, in time-honored fashion.

He slices the potatoes and drops the thin slices into the mason jar. He adds water and makes a paste of the starch.

Behind Shorty is a spirited barbershop conversation. ONE MAN is getting a haircut; TWO OTHERS are watching (TOOMER, JASON) one of them from behind a newspaper. A middle-aged barber, CHOLLY, is doing most of the talking.

                    CHOLLY
    After I hit the number that woman wasn't no good to me at
    all.

The men laugh.

ANGLE – Shorty pries open the can of lye, whiffs it. It's good and strong. He pours some in the mason jar, stirring with the wooden spoon. He cracks the eggs into the mixture and stirs. He waits as fumes rise and feels the outside of the jar as it gets hot.

6   CONT'D

ANOTHER ANGLE – The barbershop SEEN from a door, slightly
ajar. A wooly head, entirely in shadow, peers out.

> CHOLLY'S VOICE
> She says I'm cheap cuz I won't cop her a diamond ring. Had
> the indignation to call me a cheap black sunovabitch to
> boot.

> TOOMER
> And when a black woman call you a cheap black sunova-
> bitch you've been called a cheap black sunovabitch.

Cholly is annoyed. It's *his* story.

> CHOLLY
> Will you let me tell it?

ON SHORTY – He opens the bulky package he has been carrying,
unfolds a large rubber apron and gets into it. Now he dons a pair of
rubber gloves.

> SHORTY
> Where's Homeboy?

He is all ready; one of his hands is filled with a huge glob of Vaseline. His manner is indignant as if he were asking the whereabouts
of an exasperating child.

> CHOLLY
> Red's in the head, man.

> TOOMER
> You mean hiding in the head.

> CHOLLY
> Hey, Red. Your man's here and waiting on you.

His hands full, Cholly opens the door with his feet and MALCOLM
comes out, a big, gawky, bright-faced country boy, wearing down-
home clothes and an expression of apprehension.

> TOOMER
> Gonna get that first conk laid on, hunh, Homeboy?

> CHOLLY
> Man, don't scare him more than he's scared already. Ain't
> too bad . . .

Malcolm allows himself to be led to an empty chair, where Cholly
drapes him with a double sheet, tucking it tightly around his neck
and adding a protective collar of paper.

6   CONT'D

                              CHOLLY (contd)
          . . . Like anything else. First time a chick gets her cherry
          popped, she might put up a little fight. But pretty soon you
          can't give her enough. Right, Homeboy?

CLOSE – MALCOLM

Malcolm gulps, his eyes on the fuming mason jar.

Shorty starts massaging a great quantity of Vaseline into Malcolm's scalp covering his neck and ears as well. All the men have
gathered around, involved in the ritual. For Malcolm it is closer to
being a kind of execution.

                              CHOLLY
              Git his forehead and eyebrows.

                              SHORTY
                 I know what I'm doing.

Shorty applies the Vaseline to that area. Now he brings over the
steaming jar and places it nearby.

                            SHORTY (contd)
          Listen. You pull my coat if it's still stinging when I get
          through 'cause this shit can burn a hole through cement.

                              CHOLLY
              Hold tight, baby, and keep your eyes shut.

Malcolm nods his, clenches his eyes and grits his teeth. Shorty
applies the congolene with a comb, working it into Malcolm's hair.

CLOSE – MALCOLM

                             MALCOLM
          I thought you said it was gonna sting . . . this ain't nothin'.

For a moment nothing happens, then the heat hits him. He yells,
tries to catch his breath: his head is on fire.

                           MALCOLM (contd)
          You motherfucker. You're killing me. I'm burning up. My
          damn head is on fire.

He nearly leaps out of the chair, but the barber restrains him.

Shorty, utterly unmoved by the outburst, continues working the
congolene into his hair.

Before we began preproduction, we went into the recording studio. Here, film composer Terence Blanchard listens to Miki Howard lay down her vocal track. In the film Miki has a cameo as Billie Holiday. The song is "I Cover the Waterfront."

DAVID LEE

Malcolm transforms into Red, Hayseed to Hustler.

Shorty ready for the big time: white girls, pigs feet, and a conk.

The first day of shooting. Ernest Dickerson and I line up a shot.

Denzel's hair got conked this scene. We're trying to figure out if we've got everything we need before we get his hair done.

DAVID LEE

Shorty and Red, zooted to the T!

DAVID LEE

Final instructions with Denzel and Theresa Randall, who plays Laura. This scene is supposed to take place in Cape Cod; we were in the Bronx. Didn't lose anything.

The Lindyhoppers: Lindy, the Jitterbugs, jitt as the Lionel Hampton Band (Ricky Gordon) wails out "Flying Home."

Denzel and I during the filming of "Flying Home." The last two takes we shot of this sequence were reverse masters, I mean everybody was in the shot. Black folks were cutting up, dancing, clapping, stomping their feet. There was so much good energy in there I thought the roof was going to be blown away. It's a great feeling to be part of. And that doesn't happen a lot, either.

Malcolm and his white girlfriend, Sophia (Kate Vernon), as they first meet.

Roger Smith in the tense Russian-roulette scene with a coke-crazed Red. You might remember Roger as Smiley—the deaf and mute guy from *Do The Right Thing.*

They threw the book at us. Red and Shorty are sent up to the river to the Big House. The Slammer. The Pen. The Joint. The jig was up.

DAVID LEE

First Malcolm, then Red, now Satan in prison, he refuses to say his number.

DAVID LEE

Baines (Albert Hall) gives Malcolm some of the teachings in the prison yard.

The Honorable Elijah Muhammad comes to visit Malcolm in prison as a vision. Al Freeman, Jr., was one of the several people we cast who were dead ringers for the real life people they were portraying.

DAVID LEE

Giving the Teachings.

Newlyweds Betty Shabazz (Angela Bassett) and Malcolm.

This is one of my favorite pictures from the shoot: (left to right) Reverend Al Sharpton, myself, Denzel Washington, and Bobby Seale. In this scene, the Reverend and ex–Black Panther Chairman Bobby Seale play activists competing with Malcolm for the citizens of Harlem.

The Monster Rally was shot at the 145th Armory. We were short of extras, and our friends at WLIB and WBLS put out a call through the airwaves, saying we desperately needed bodies. People rolled out of bed, school, work, or the street to help participate.

Seeing Denzel, oops, Malcolm, I mean Denzel like this on the set every day was scary.

6   CONT'D

Malcolm breaks out of the chair wildly. But the three men drag him
to a basin where Shorty has attached the shower spray. His cries
filling the room, Malcolm is ducked under the spray. Shorty starts
rinsing out his hair.

SHORTY
Don't fight me, man. Let me git it out.

Malcolm is a little relieved, he tentatively opens his eyes, then he
feels the congolene again and there is another outburst. Shorty
forces his head under the spray, spurts the water all over his head,
wetting Malcolm and the shop in the process.

7   OMIT

8   OMIT

9   INT. CLOTHING STORE – DAY

SHORTY
Well, Homeboy, you almost there. Turn around.

Shorty is supervising as Malcolm tries on a zoot suit. He slips into
the jacket . . .

Shoes-off, Malcolm steps into the tight-fitting peg-legged pants
. . . . . . dons a wide-brimmed hat with a bright blue feather. . . .
Finally, fully outfitted, he leans forward toward his new image in
the full-length mirror, twirling a long, dangling key chain.

SHORTY
Well, all right, then.

MALCOLM
Well, all reet, then.

The transformation is complete. The two laugh and slap hands.

10 EXT. ROXBURY STREET – DAY

Malcolm and Shorty come strutting down the street: two conked-
zoot-suited sharpies. Hometown boy has departed. And the
CHICKS on the street notice them, especially Malcolm, the taller of
the two, the lighter-skinned, the more dominant. They walk im-
periously past, fully aware of their impact.

CLOSE SHOT – MALCOLM

FREEZE FRAME. He becomes a STILL.

10   CONT'D

> VOICE OF MALCOLM X
>
> When my mother was pregnant with me, she told me later,
> a party of Klansmen on horseback surrounded our house
> in Omaha.

10A   ANGLE. KLAN on horses in front of house.

> VOICE OF MALCOLM X (contd)
>
> They brandished guns and shouted for my father to come
> out. My mother went to the door where they could see her
> pregnant condition . . .

ANGLE. A pregnant Louise Little on porch.

> VOICE OF MALCOLM X (contd)
>
> . . . and told them my father was in Milwaukee, preaching.

ANGLE. The Klan breaks all the windows in the house then rides off
into the glorious D.W. Griffith *Birth of a Nation* moonlit night.

CLOSE – LOUISE LITTLE

> VOICE OF MALCOLM X (contd)
>
> The hooded Klansman said the good, white Christians
> would not stand for his troublemaking, and to get out of
> town.

ANGLE. The terrified Little children look out a broken window at
their mother.

ANGLE. AN OLD FRAME HOUSE IN OMAHA

> VOICE OF MALCOLM X (contd)
>
> They broke every window with their rifle butts before rid-
> ing off into the night, their torches flaming.

ANGLE. FRONT PORCH OF THE LITTLE HOUSE – AN EMPTY
ROCKER ON IT.

> VOICE OF MALCOLM X (contd)
>
> My father was not a frightened Negro as most were then
> and as many still are today. He was six feet four and very
> black . . .

10B   CLOSE – EARL LITTLE

He looks directly into the camera, wearing a Baptist Minister's
robe.

10B   CONT'D

> VOICE OF MALCOLM X (contd)
> . . . and had a glass eye. He believed, as did Marcus Gar-
> vey, that freedom, independence and self-respect could
> never be achieved by the Negro in America . . .

10C   CLOSE – EARL LITTLE

He wears a Garvey hat, ornate with gold braid.

> VOICE OF MALCOLM X (contd)
> . . . that, therefore, black men should leave America and
> return to the land of their origin.

10D   ANGLE. Earl Little, in a wagon with little Malcolm.

CLOSE – EARL LITTLE

> VOICE OF MALCOLM X (contd)
> My father dedicated his life to his beliefs because he had
> seen four of his six brothers die violently . . .

10E   WIDER ANGLE. WE SEE Earl in front of a podium in church. He is
preaching.

> VOICE OF MALCOLM X (contd)
> . . . three killed by white men and one lynched. There are
> nine children in our family.

ANGLE. The nine Little children.

CLOSE – LOUISE LITTLE

She is a pretty, mature woman and white-looking.

> VOICE OF MALCOLM X (contd)
> My mother was an attractive woman, an educated woman,
> a strong woman.

10F   CLOSE – LOUISE AND EARL

A posed wedding picture, serious but sweet.

> VOICE OF MALCOLM X (contd)
> She was very light, her mama was raped by a white man.
> One of the reasons she married my father was because he
> was so black, she disliked her complexion and wanted her
> children to have some color.

CLOSE SHOT

10F CONT'D

Flash bulb of camera flashes.

11 OMIT

12 OMIT

13 OMIT

14 OMIT

15 INT. ROSELAND STATE BALLROOM – NIGHT

CLOSE – MALCOLM AND SHORTY

They both were posed for a picture. The music "FLYING HOME" is blaring as LIONEL HAMPTON and his band is killing. The music is WILD, the dancing is frantic, the clothes are OUT, and the crowd is predominately BLACK, although there is a peppering of WHITES, especially white chicks. And Malcolm is a little bug-eyed as he nudges Shorty, watching mixed couples on the floor.

A BOY in extreme zoot-suit flips him; a WHITE GIRL in long blond hair wigs him. Malcolm is a little open-mouthed.

A VOICE
SHOWTIME, SHOWTIME!

ANGLE – THE BALLROOM – NIGHT

People start moving off the floor, making room for the showtime dancers. The music begins to get faster and more furious.

CLOSE – HAMPTON'S BAND – NIGHT

It is a fast Lindy. People start clapping to the beat as they form a U around the DANCERS, with the band at the open end.

16 INT. THE DANCE FLOOR

TWO COUPLES are on the floor, dancing wildly. They are quickly joined by a half dozen OTHERS. These are the best dancers and constitute the main event of a Saturday night black dance.

People crowd and push to get better vantage points and the competition is under way.

ANGLE ON THE CROWD

It is dominantly black, but there are some whites in the audience, mostly women. One is SOPHIA, a spectacular blonde with a degree of refinement, something of a thrill-seeker. Many of the men try to

16   CONT'D

catch her eye, but for the moment Sophia is just watching, looking for no one in particular, but nonetheless looking.

ANGLE – COUPLE ON THE DANCE FLOOR

Getting ready to enter the fray, the GIRL takes off her shoes and bounces out on the floor barefoot with her partner. Their advent is greeted with cheers and ad libs. Clearly the crowd has its favorites.

WIDER SHOT

The music gets faster and the dancing takes on a more frantic and more remarkable quality.

FOLLOW SHOT – MALCOLM

He is looking for his partner, the girl he brought and now he sees her. He makes his way through the watching audience.

CLOSE – LAURA

She is a fine chick, cool and beautiful. She smiles as she sees Malcolm approaching.

TWO-SHOT. Laura and Malcolm stand together, delighted to be with one another, starting to move to the music, as they watch the dancers.

> MALCOLM
> Come on, baby, let's show 'em how.

Laura smiles shyly; she's willing.

> MALCOLM (contd)
> You better get out of them shoes, girl.

Laura laughs, goes quickly to a bench and changes into a pair of sneakers.

17   INT. THE DANCE FLOOR

Because of the competition, Laura and Malcolm begin at high speed. In a moment they are executing the most intricate steps of the "flapping eagle" and the "kangaroo." Malcolm starts boosting her over and around his hips, then boosting her over his shoulders. Laura is the perfect partner. She loves it.

ANGLE WITH THE CROWD

So does the crowd, who loves new stars. There are ad lib remarks: "Go, man, go." "Hey, Red." "Mmmmmm ummm."

17 CONT'D

ANGLE – SHORTY

A big, fat, hefty BLACK WOMAN takes Shorty out to the dance floor, and she takes the lead. As they do the Lindy she is slinging Shorty around like a rag doll. This woman slides him through her legs and Shorty has had enough, he runs off the dance floor, and hides.

TWO-SHOT. Laura and Malcolm are, in the phrase, cooking on all burners now; and when they execute an especially intricate step, even Hamp waves over.

Malcolm is sweating and flushed and enormously elated. He sees that people are watching him, goading him on. He notices that Sophia, in particular, has not taken her eyes off him; she is clapping in time to his steps.

Seeing new stars in the making, the other dancers move to the side of the floor, marking time, yielding the dance floor to them. Laura and Malcolm go into a solo.

ANGLES

The crowd loves it. Malcolm and Sophia are very aware of each other. The finale is the classic drag, with Laura hanging limp around Malcolm's neck as he capers off the dance floor to the spontaneous applause of the audience.

CLOSE SHOT – SOPHIA (SLO-MO)

Clapping enthusiastically—in open admiration.

CLOSE SHOT – SHORTY

Waiting to catch them as they come off. Shorty is whistling and shaking his hand appreciatively. He is also looking out for his dance partner.

> SHORTY
> Hey, man, gimme some skin.

> MALCOLM
> Shorty, this is Laura.

Laura is flushed and out of breath and joyous.

> LAURA
> 'Lo. I've got to freshen up.

> MALCOLM
> Now you come back.

17 CONT'D

Laura laughs as she goes. She surely will be back.

> SHORTY
> That's a fine chick.

> MALCOLM
> Fine as May wine.

> SHORTY
> Except she live on the Hill and got a grandma.

> MALCOLM
> Make it too easy and it ain't no fun.

Then his vision catches Sophia, who is approaching him. She makes a simple, direct gesture, "Want to dance?" Malcolm eyes Shorty and wordlessly glides into Sophia's arms.

ANGLE – THE DANCE FLOOR

Immediately from the glances of the other men at the dance, he is the cynosure of all eyes. He has new status. It's a heady feeling because she is the first white girl he has ever been with socially who is not an obvious whore. He begins to show off a little, cuts a few fine steps.

TWO-SHOT. They are dancing closer than before. Sophia begins to rock his black world.

CLOSE – MALCOLM

Trying to play it cool—but he is beginning to pant. Not from the dancing, but from the situation: a gorgeous white chick asking for it.

> SOPHIA
> Why don't you take your little girl home, Red, and come on back?

He stops in his tracks. He can't believe it.

> SOPHIA (contd)
> Just walk. Don't run. It'll be here when you get back.

He can only grin.

18 EXT. LAURA'S HOUSE – ROXBURY – NIGHT

The porch of a respectable house. Malcolm with Laura; he anxious to get away.

> MALCOLM
> I better not come in.

18 CONT'D

> LAURA
> I ain't stupid.

> MALCOLM
> I mean it's late, baby.

> LAURA
> I know where you're going.

> MALCOLM
> I'm going to bed. I gotta work tomorrow, need my rest.

Laura walks to the door.

> MALCOLM (contd)
> Baby, I'll call you tomorrow.

> LAURA
> What for? I ain't white and I don't put out.

The front door opens, it's Laura's grandmother, MRS. JOHNSON.

> MALCOLM
> 'Night, Mrs. Johnson.

He runs down the porch steps.

19 INT. SOPHIA'S CAR – NIGHT

The lone light emits from the car radio which plays The Inkspots "IF I DIDN'T CARE."

ANGLE – SOPHIA

Sophia pulls her tight sweater over her head to expose two full ripe *white breasts*. Malcolm's eyes are popping out of his head. NOTE: It's very unusual for women not to wear a bra back in that day but you might say Sophia was way ahead of her time.

> SOPHIA
> Malcolm, look at them. Have you ever seen white breasts
> like these?

CLOSE – MALCOLM

He shakes his head.

> SOPHIA (contd)
> Put your black hands on them.

He is paralyzed.

19 CONT'D

> SOPHIA (contd)
> Please do as I say.

Malcolm mumbles something. He then kisses Sophia as if his black life depended on it and he commences to kill it.

> SOPHIA (contd)
> Hey, baby.

She stops him for a moment, but he buries his head in her long neck.

> SOPHIA (contd)
> Am I the first white woman you've been with?

She already knows the answer. He laughs.

> MALCOLM
> Sheeet, you ain't. I had aplenty.

> SOPHIA
> . . . That isn't a whore?

Knowing she's right Sophia becomes the aggressor.

A beat—both panting—then Malcolm stops abruptly. He raises his hand to his face, then to Sophia's hand which is still caressing him.

> SOPHIA
> That's alright. Baby, take your time. Sophia's not going anywhere. I told you to walk, don't run.

> MALCOLM
> Shhhh! I don't like women that talk.

CLOSE – SOPHIA

She shrugs, then moves to embrace him.

> SOPHIA
> Who wants to talk?

The couple starts at it again.

19A INT. MOVIE THEATRE – DAY

On the screen, Bogart and Cagney are blasting away the dirty, flat-footed coppers with machine guns. It's one of those great Warner Brothers gangster B movies, maybe *The Roaring Twenties.*

ANGLE – MALCOLM AND SHORTY

182.

19A CONT'D

Malcolm and Shorty sit, transfixed in their seats.

MALCOLM
Don't you know, you can't hump the Bogart.

SHORTY
Eat lead, coppers.

20 EXT. BOSTON COMMONS – DAY

A bright, sunny day, long shadows in the park. The Commons is
almost empty. Two improbable zoot-suited blacks race past trees,
and run over the grass. Malcolm and Shorty are playing Cops and
Robbers while PASSERSBY stare.

SHORTY
Bang, bang. You're dead.

MALCOLM
Naw, you missed me, copper. Try this on for size.

Malcolm fires an imaginary tommy machine gun at Shorty.

SHORTY
I forgot to tell you I'm wearing a bulletproof vest.

MALCOLM
The hell you are.

SHORTY
I'm tired of always playing the cops. I wanna be Bogart
sometimes.

MALCOLM
You're too small to be Bogart.

SHORTY
I'm not too short to be Cagney.

Shorty shoots Malcolm from behind.

SHORTY (contd)
Pow. Take that.

Malcolm acts as if he's been hit.

MALCOLM
Ahhh! You got me, you dirty, filthy, rotten, stinking copper, only a low-down yellow rat bastard would shoot a man
in the back.

20 CONT'D

Malcolm starts to stagger, this is a long drawn out Hollywood drawn-out death a la Cagney death in *Public Enemy*.

LOW ANGLE – MALCOLM

Malcolm falls directly into the camera, face first, and Shorty stands over him.

> SHORTY
> He use to be a big shot.

21 OMIT

23 OMIT

24 OMIT

25 OMIT

26 EXT. THE TROLLEY TRACKS – NIGHT (REMEMBERED TIME)

MATCH CUT

CLOSE EARL LITTLE

Earl Little's face is in the same exact position as Malcolm's from the previous scene. His mouth opens in terror as the moving trolley comes closer and closer to the black man lying on the tracks.

27 INT. A HEARING ROOM – DAY

A room, clinically empty; table, chair, and MR. HOLWAY. He is putting papers into his briefcase; the hearing is concluded.

> LOUISE
> What you mean took his own life?!

> HOLWAY
> I'm sorry, ma'am. You heard the verdict. A man bash in the back of his head with a hammer, lay down on the tracks and kill himself! We merely act on the verdict. We don't make them.

He is nearly out the door.

> LOUISE
> Do you pay or don't you?

> HOLWAY
> Read the policy, ma'am. It clearly states.

28 OMIT

29   INT. SOPHIA'S APARTMENT – MORNING

Malcolm lies in bed, naked under the sheet. A half-empty whiskey bottle and an ashtray full of butts are on the night table: last night's partying.

                    SOPHIA
        You like 'em scrambled soft or hard, sweetie?

                    MALCOLM
                    C'mere.

WIDEN TO SHOW SOPHIA at the stove fixing eggs. She wears an apron and nothing else. It's a nicely furnished middle-class apartment.

                    SOPHIA
            Sweetie, they're almost ready.

                    MALCOLM
            You hear me, girl?

She shrugs, shuts off the burner, smiles and ambles toward him.

                    SOPHIA
            You the man.

                    MALCOLM
            You better believe it.

She starts to sit down on the bed next to him.

                MALCOLM (contd)
            Sit over there.

He points to a nearby chair. Sophia makes an amiable hand-shrug and complacently goes.

                    SOPHIA
            You evil this morning.

                    MALCOLM
            What's your story, baby?

He doesn't want to hear her; he wants to talk. He goes right on:

                MALCOLM (contd)
        You one of them white bitches can't get enough black dick.
        Is that what you are?

Sophia smiles. She aims to please. Malcolm smacks the bed next to him. She gets up and comes over.

29 CONT'D

>   MALCOLM (contd)
>   Take it off.

She takes off the apron.

>   MALCOLM (contd)
>   Now kiss my feet. Kiss 'em!

CLOSE – SOPHIA

As Sophia bends to do so.

>   MALCOLM
>   Feed me.

ANGLE. Sophia now has the scrambled eggs on a plate at Malcolm's side. She spoons some into his mouth. He chews and swallows slowly, then grabs her head and brings it to his. A long, brutal kiss. Then he pulls her head away by the hair. She looks at him: anything he wants.

>   MALCOLM
>   Yeah, girl; that's your story. When you gonna holler
>   "rape," sister?

>   SOPHIA
>   Me?

>   MALCOLM
>   You will, baby—if the time come.

>   SOPHIA
>   Lemme feed you, sweetie, while they hot.

Malcolm lays back on the pillow and she holds out the eggs to him.

>   MALCOLM
>   Sure wish your mama and papa could see you now. And
>   that ofay you gonna marry.

30 EXT. A BEACH – BRIGHT SUNLIGHT – DAY

Malcolm and Laura are on a deserted Cape beach. They are dressed but have their shoes and socks off, and he has his trousers rolled up. They walk, like birds, avoiding getting their feet wet as the waves roll in.

>   LAURA
>   Malcolm, you can be anything you want. You got class and
>   you're smart.

186.

30 CONT'D

                    MALCOLM
All them books you read and you still don't know nuthin.

                    LAURA
        I do know I love you.

Laura stops him and moves to him. Her kiss is a tender one, explor-
atory. Then Malcolm responds, embracing her fully. Her arms go
around him as they both drop into the sand.

CLOSE – MALCOLM AND LAURA

                    LAURA
Oh, Malcolm, I love you. Please, there's no one around.
Now?

Malcolm turns his head from her, he gets up.

                    MALCOLM
          Let's go.

                    LAURA
Why? Is it because of your white gal? Folks say you're
running around town with her.

                    MALCOLM
Save it, baby. Save it for Mr. Right, 'cause your grandma's
smarter than ya think.

She looks at him.

                    LAURA
She raised me, my mother died when I was six. Is your
mother alive?

                    MALCOLM
        Yeah, she's alive.

31 OMIT

32 OMIT

33 INT. DRUGSTORE – EVENING

Laura is eating a banana split. Malcolm is smoking and drinking
coffee.

                    MALCOLM
You know how dumb I was? I used to think that "Not For
Sale" was a brand name.

33 CONT'D

Laura looks over. She doesn't understand.

34 INT. LITTLE KITCHEN – DAY

Louise's hand reaches for a small sack of flour stamped "Not For Sale." She brings it down on the table with a hard, controlled whap.

> MISS DUNNE'S VOICE
> I did knock.

Louise doesn't look up.

> LOUISE
> Did you hear me say come in?

WIDEN TO SHOW Louise with a WHITE SOCIAL WORKER, MISS DUNNE, complete with pad, pencil and goodwill. Huddled out of sight, but nonetheless visible, are five small BLACK CHILDREN.

> MISS DUNNE
> There's no point in fighting about it. I'm sorry. May I sit down?

Louise is very aware of the children and struggling for self-possession.

> LOUISE
> As you nice enough to ask, we'll git you one.

One of the children brings over a chair. Miss Dunne sets out her papers.

> MISS DUNNE
> It's the same questions, Mrs. Little. Since the death of your husband—

> LOUISE
> Murder.

> MISS DUNNE
> —there is a serious question as to whether—

> LOUISE
> These are my children. Mine. And they ain't no question. *None.*

> MISS DUNNE
> I think sometimes, Mrs. Little, candor is the only kindness.

34 CONT'D

PAN THE CHILDREN'S FACES

> MISS DUNNE (contd)
> All of your children are delinquent, Mrs. Little, and one, at least, Malcolm is a thief.

> LOUISE
> Get out.

> MISS DUNNE
> (still sitting)
> Your control over your children, therefore—

> LOUISE
> Did you hear me?!

> MISS DUNNE
> You'll regret this, Mrs. Little.

> LOUISE
> If you don't move out through that door, you're going to be past all regretting.

The terror-stricken children huddle together.

FREEZE FRAME. It becomes a still.

> MALCOLM'S VOICE
> We were parceled out, all five of us. I went to this reform school and lived at this woman's house. She was in charge.

34A A SMALL CLEAN ROOM WITH A COT, A CHAIR AND A BUREAU.

> MRS. SWERLIN
> (motherly, friendly)
> This is your room, Malcolm. I know you'll keep it clean.

34B A DINING ROOM TABLE. FIVE WHITE BOYS AROUND IT.

> MRS. SWERLIN
> This is Malcolm, our new guest. We'll treat him like a brother.

34C A CLASSROOM.

> MALCOLM'S VOICE
> I was special. The only colored kid in class. I became a sort of mascot. Like a pink poodle.

34D KIDS PLAYING IN THE SCHOOL YARD.

> MALCOLM'S VOICE
> I didn't know then that I was a nigger.

MALCOLM PLAYING BASKETBALL.

34E MALCOLM SPEAKING BEFORE HIS CLASS.

34F MALCOLM DOING HOMEWORK.

34G A HORSE HAVING ITS TEETH EXAMINED.

> MRS SWERLIN
> He's bright.

> MALCOLM'S VOICE
> They talked about me like

34G CONTD

MRS SWERLIN (contd)	MALCOLM'S VOICE (contd)
Good grades.	I wasn't there. Like I was some
Fine athlete.	kind of pedigreed dog or a horse.
President of his class.	Like I was invisible.

35 INT. OSTROWSKI'S CLASSROOM – DAY

OSTROWSKI is talking to Malcolm, it's after school, the classroom is empty.

> OSTROWSKI
> The important thing is to be realistic. We all like you. You know that. But you're a nigger and a lawyer is no realistic goal for a nigger . . .

> MALCOLM
> But why, Mr. Ostrowski? I get the best grades. I'm the class president. I want to be a lawyer.

36 INT. THE DRUGSTORE – P.M.

Laura and Malcolm. Neither is talking. She is simply watching him as he sips his coffee and puffs on a cigarette.

36A INT. OSTROWSKI'S CLASSROOM – DAY

> OSTROWSKI
> . . . Think about something you can be. You're good with your hands. People would give you work. I would myself.

36A CONT'D

> OSTROWSKI (contd)
> Why don't you become a carpenter? That's a good profes-
> sion for a nigra. Wasn't your pa a carpenter?

Malcolm is silent.

> OSTROWSKI (contd)
> Jesus was a carpenter.

36B INT. THE DRUGSTORE – P.M.

CLOSE – LAURA

> LAURA
> It's not the end of the world, Malcolm.

37 OMIT

38 EXT. A SIGN – BLINDING SUNLIGHT – DAY

It reads "KALAMAZOO STATE HOSPITAL FOR THE MENTALLY INSANE"

39 INT. A ROOM IN THE HOSPITAL – DAY

The room is totally white and Louise sits in a white smock at a window in a rocking chair.

CLOSE LOUISE

As she rocks.

> LOUISE
> I said it just as plain, I said, don't let them feed that boy no
> pig, because he got enough of the devil in him already. I
> told her she ain't got no reason talk to me that way cuz' my
> hair blow in the wind. You want my skin. All right, I'll give
> it to you. I'll scrape it off. See how you like it.

ANGLE – Louise starts to sing a Negro spiritual.

CLOSE – MALCOLM

He has been standing there in deep pain all along.

THE SOUND OF A SPEEDING TRAIN IS HEARD.

40 EXT. THE YANKEE CLIPPER – DAY

The crack train of the New York, New Haven & Hartford speeds through the New England countryside.

41   INT. GALLEY OF TRAIN – NIGHT

THREE ELDERLY BLACK WAITERS and Malcolm wearing a sand-
wichman's uniform are crowded around a portable radio in the
galley where food is prepared. The four stand around TULLY, a
bland-faced personification of fine Pullman service. They are all
listening to the JOE LOUIS–BILLY CONN heavyweight championship fight.

                         TULLY
            Nigger, shut up so we can hear.

                        MALCOLM
                       C'mon, Joe.

                       WAITER #1
                    Turn it up, Tully.

                         TULLY
                It is up. Fool be quiet.

                       WAITER #2
                Tully, move the antenna. . . .

Tully turns some knobs.

                       WAITER #3
                   This Mick is tough.

                         TULLY
        Joe is just playing possum. He's waiting for an opening.

The waiters are acting as if they are at ringside.

                    RADIO ANNOUNCER
A left jab to the jaw and a right cross, scored by Louis and
Conn is hurt, as Louis rips a right to the jaw. Conn is
staggering, but he won't go down. Conn bops a left hook,
he's reeling around the ring. Louis hooks a left and a right
to the jaw and Conn is down.

The waiters are going crazy.

                    RADIO ANNOUNCER
He's taking the count, four, five, six, seven, he's on his
back, eight, nine, he's getting up, no! The referee says it's
over. The bout has stopped.

The waiters are all jumping up and down when the galley door
opens. MR. COOPER, the white man in charge of the kitchen, pops
his head in.

41   CONT'D

                          COOPER
                  What in hell's going on?

In a moments notice Tully and the others have resumed their cus-
tomary servient roles.

                          TULLY
                  Nothing, Mr. Cooper.

                          COOPER
              Got a lot of hungry customers out there.

                          TULLY
              Yes sir, Mr. Cooper, soup done finished.

                          MALCOLM
                  On my way, Mr. Charlie.

Cooper eyes him narrowly.

                          COOPER
              The name is Mr. Cooper and don't you forget it. Mr.
              Cooper.

                      RADIO ANNOUNCER
              The winner and still champion, Joe Louis, but what a fight
              Billy Conn gave.

42   OMIT

43   OMIT

44   OMIT

45   INT. A PASSENGER TRAIN – DAY

      As Malcolm hefts his sandwich basket and a large container of
      coffee down the aisle, hawking as he goes.

                          MALCOLM
              Get your good haaaam and cheeeeese sandwiches. I got
              coffee, I got cake and I got ice cream too. Right chere.

ANGLE FAVORING A WHITE CUSTOMER, BLADES.

                          BLADES
              Hey, boy. Gimme a cheese on white and coffee.

Malcolm's mood is exuberant: the fight is still in his ears. He makes
the delivery with a flourish and a smile.

45 CONT'D

MALCOLM
Yes, sir. Best in the house.

BLADES
You mighty pleased with yourself, boy.

MALCOLM
Yes, sir. I aims to please.

BLADES
I like you, boy.

45A INSERT – FANTASY PROJECTION. Malcolm picks up a slab of cream pie and pushes it in Blades' face.

45B BACK TO THE PASSENGER CAR

Normality again: Malcolm finishes serving him with complete servility. He pulls out a bill.

BLADES
Keep the change.

And takes a satisfying bite out of his thin sandwich.

46 EXT. THE RAILROAD TRACKS IN HARLEM – P.M.

As the Clipper surfaces in Harlem, pulls up to the 125th Street station.

47 EXT. 125TH STREET STATION – P.M.

Malcolm, out of uniform and dressed in his zoot suit, comes down from the Park Avenue station in Harlem. He is hit with the sights and sounds. Everything delights him: the noise, the lights, the women, the pimps, the signs, the windows, the crowds, the laughter, the music.

48 OMIT

49 OMIT

50 OMIT

50A ANGLE – CROWD

A CROWD OF PEOPLE run by Malcolm yelling and screaming.

CROWD
The Brown Bomber, The Brown Bomber, Joe Louis, the heavyweight champion of the world. Joe got the belt back. Lawd have mercy. Great day in the morning.

50A CONT'D

ANGLE – MALCOLM

He runs after them.

50B EXT. 125TH AND LENOX AVENUE

All traffic has stopped, there is a huge spontaneous celebration going on. Black folks are everywhere, it seems as if all of Harlem is out on the streets. The citizens of Harlem are hugging, kissing, drinking, dancing, folks are hanging from street lamps, yelling out their windows, holding up hand-made JOE LOUIS banners, every-one has great reason to be joyous. The heavyweight champion of the world is a BLACK MAN—JOE LOUIS, THE BROWN BOMBER, he has regained his championship.

CLOSE – MALCOLM

Malcolm quickly looks at his watch, he's running late for his train, as he fights his way through the crowd like a salmon going up-stream, the CAMERA CRANES up to see him eventually get lost in a sea of BLACK HUMANITY "cutting loose."

FADE OUT.

51- OMIT

56- OMIT

FADE IN:

57 EXT. SEVENTH AVENUE – NIGHT

Malcolm, newly conked and sharp as a tack (zoot suit, trouser crease like a knife's edge, orange knob-toed shoes) walks toward his goal: Small's Paradise.

The street is crowded with PEOPLE, KIDS and HUSTLERS.

YOUNG HOOKER
Slow down, daddy, what's your hurry? Lemme show you somepin brand new.

Malcolm smiles "No thanks"; keeps moving.

HUSTLER
Hey, man, hundred-dollar ring—diamond; and a ninety-dollar watch. Take the both of them for a quarter; twenty-five bucks.

Malcolm waves; he's not having any. Goes on.

58   EXT. SMALL'S PARADISE – NIGHT

Before entering, Malcolm sharps himself a bit, picking off some lint, cocking his hat. And enters.

59   INT. SMALL'S PARADISE – NIGHT

The restaurant is crowded, both at the bar and at the tables beyond. The immediate impression is of subdued well-being, of decorum, of easy affluence. This is the world Malcolm wants into. He digs it, drinking in its details.

ANGLE – BAR

A big man, FOX, accidentally bumps into Malcolm almost knocking him over.

> MALCOLM
> The word is excuse me.

> FOX
> Look, country boy, you shouldn't have been in my way.

Everyone becomes quiet in the bar.

> FOX (contd)
> So what are you gonna do? Go run home to your Mama.

Malcolm grabs a bottle off the bar counter and with lightning speed brings it crashing down on Fox's head. As he lays on the floor with head bleeding, Malcolm kicks him in the stomach *two times*. It's done, the fight is over and people pull him off of Fox.

> MALCOLM
> Don't ever again in life step on my Florsheims again, and never talk-bout my mother.

ANGLE WITH MALCOLM AND THE BARTENDER

> MALCOLM
> Gimme a whiskey.

The BARTENDER pours him a double.

> MALCOLM
> I ordered a single, Jack.

> BARTENDER
> The double's on that gentleman. Jack!

He points.

ARCHIE AT THE TABLE – FROM MALCOLM'S POV

59   CONT'D

The elderly man nods. He is big, he is very black. The same color
as Malcolm's father.

CLOSE – MALCOLM

He raises his glass, toasts Archie and downs it. Then leaning into
the bar, asks:

                    MALCOLM
              Who is he, man?

                    BARTENDER
            That's West Indian Archie.

                    MALCOLM
              Whut's he do?

The bartender would not normally answer this, but Malcolm is the
man of the moment, so the bartender speaks:

                    BARTENDER
              This and that.

Malcolm nods, then looks over again at Archie—in appreciation.
Archie wiggles a finger for him to come over.

59A   AT ARCHIE'S TABLE

Malcolm is standing.

                    ARCHIE
        Sit down. We ain't fixing to eat you. You look brand new in
        town. Pretty handy with a bottle.

                    MALCOLM
              He had it coming.

Malcolm sits. There are no introductions. He just nods at SAMMY
and CADILLAC.

                    ARCHIE
              What they call you?

                    MALCOLM
            Red, and I ain't no punk.

                    ARCHIE
        You better not be. 'Cause if a cat toe you down in this town,
        you better stand up or make tracks.

> SAMMY
> Man live by his rep.

> ARCHIE
> That's a fact. What you do, boy?

> MALCOLM
> I'm working trains. Selling.

> ARCHIE
> Bet you like that shit.

> MALCOLM
> Keeps me out of the army.

> ARCHIE
> When they want your ass, won't nothing keep you out.

> MALCOLM
> Not this boy . . . I ain't fighting their war. I got my own.
> Right chere. Heard tell you're a good man to know.

> ARCHIE
> Heard where?

> MALCOLM
> Where I come from. Boston.

Sammy and Cadillac are watching a little skeptically. Archie is
flattered.

> ARCHIE
> Sombitch and I ain't never been to Beantown.

> MALCOLM
> Man's rep travels.

> ARCHIE
> How 'bout that?

Then seeing Sammy and Cadillac's dubious visages, Archie adds:

> ARCHIE (contd)
> You ain't bullshitting me, is you, boy?

> MALCOLM
> My papa taught me one thing: don't never bullshit a West
> Indian bullshit artist.

Archie laughs. Even Sammy smiles. Cadillac still holds his judgment.

                         ARCHIE
              Is your papa West Indian?

                         MALCOLM
              No, my mama. She's from Grenada.

                         ARCHIE
              I like you, country.

                         SAMMY
              Only where'd you get them goddam vines.

                         CADILLAC
              And them shoes. Oh, my.

                         ARCHIE
              Yeah, got to do something about you.

                         SAMMY
              You putting a hurtin' on my vision.

Sammy covers his eyes. Malcolm plays off the insults.

                         MALCOLM
              Where can I get a hold of you.

                         ARCHIE
              YOU can't. I'll get a hold of you.

                         MALCOLM
              Lemme write it down for you.

Malcolm reaches for a pencil.

                         ARCHIE
              Don't never write nothing down. File it up here, like I do.
                         (touching his head)
              'Cause if they can't find no paper they ain't got no proof.
              Ya dig?

                         MALCOLM
              Yes, sir.

Archie looks at him sharply.

                         ARCHIE
              Boy, look me in the face.

Malcolm does so.

                         ARCHIE (contd)
              Did you just now con me?

59A   CONT'D

A pause.

                    MALCOLM
                  Yes, sir.

                    ARCHIE
                    Why?

                    MALCOLM
    'Cause I want in. And it don't take a lot to know you there
    daddy.

Archie and Sammy laugh at his directness. Cadillac smiles.

Archie pushes back his chair, about to get up.

                    ARCHIE
          I got me a little run to make.

Malcolm has suddenly been excluded and he wants desperately
back in.

                    MALCOLM
          Can I run with you, Mr. Archie?

Archie eyes him, weighing him seriously.

                    ARCHIE
    I like your heart and I like your style. You might just do,
    Little. Lessen you got to git back to that train job.

                    MALCOLM
    I done told the man what he could do with his train.

                    ARCHIE
                    When?

                    MALCOLM
                  Just now.

The three established hustlers smile at the newcomer in their
midst.

                    ARCHIE
          Come on, baby. We going shopping . . .

60   OMIT

61   OMIT

62   OMIT

63 INT. ARCHIE'S ROOM – NIGHT

Malcolm is looking at himself in a mirror in Archie's room. He has on the full outfit now, together with a new white on white shirt and a Sulka tie. Looks great.

> ARCHIE
> Just the middle button, baby. Just the middle one.

Malcolm buttons the jacket and turns around, demonstrating for Archie's inspection.

> ARCHIE (contd)
> You looking good, Little. Real clean. Clean as the Board of Health. But you missing something.

> MALCOLM
> What?

> ARCHIE
> Frisk me, baby. Give me a real pat down.

Malcolm doesn't understand, but he senses something—and becomes excited. Archie has walked over to him.

> ARCHIE (contd)
> Go ahead. Do me.

Malcolm frisks him carefully: pats his sides, his pockets, under his arms, his legs. Archie is clean to the touch.

> ARCHIE (contd)
> (triumphantly)
> And I'm still carrying.

He smacks the small of his back. Then, reaching under his coat, he takes a revolver out from the middle of his back. And hands it to Malcolm.

CLOSE – MALCOLM

Holding the deadly instrument, fascinated by it, hefting it, feeling its power.

> ARCHIE
> It's yours, baby. Put it on.

Malcolm slips it carefully into the small of his back, behind his trouser belt. His first gun: the feeling shines in his eyes, Bogart has become a black man.

> ARCHIE (contd)
> How's it feel?

63   CONT'D

                         MALCOLM
                    Solid, daddy.

                         ARCHIE
          Okay, baby. Now you outfitted. You ready to tackle the
          street?

                         MALCOLM
                 Let 'em come. I'm ready.

64   INT/EXT. VARIOUS LOCATIONS – SERIES OF CLOSE SHOTS

     A FIVE-DOLLAR BILL. CAMERA GOES IN for the last three digits.

64A THE STOCK MARKET BOARD at the end of a day's trading. GO IN
     for the last three numbers.

64B PREACHER in a pulpit, reading from the Bible.

                         PREACHER
          Let us turn to the Gospel according to St. John. Chapter 3,
          Verse 23.

                         A VOICE
                        3, 2, 3.

     Malcolm scribbles the number onto a piece of paper.

64C CLOSE – A CASH REGISTER

     Ringing up an amount: $2.98.

                         A VOICE
                        2, 9, 8.

     Malcolm's hand writes out the number.

64D CLOSE – TRAIN TERMINAL SIGN

     It reads "New York to Chicago." PAN DOWN TO SHOW "Train
     arrives 1:05."

                         VOICE
                        1, 0, 5.

     Archie with Malcolm as the latter writes down "1, 0, 5."

                         ARCHIE
               I told you less paper, less trouble.

                         MALCOLM
                  I'm working on it.

64D   CONT'D

> ARCHIE
> I keep all my numbers in my head. I've never written any
> down.

He taps his head.

64E   CLOSE – FACE OF AN ELDERLY WOMAN

> ELDERLY WOMAN
> I saw it in my dream. 5, 5, 5. And last week my sister had
> a dream and she hit.

64F   CLOSE – FACE OF AN ELDERLY BARBER

> BARBER
> I got it from Ching Chow. It got to be 2, 5, 1.

65   OMIT

66   OMIT

67   OMIT

68   OMIT

68A   INT. MOVIE THEATRE – NIGHT

CLOSE – MALCOLM

WE ARE TIGHT ON Malcolm's intense face, he is pulling on a fat
joint. We hear BOGART blasting his way out of a police blockade.

A phone rings.

69   OMIT

70   OMIT

71   INT. ARCHIE'S ROOM – NIGHT

There is music playing. Wordlessly, Archie sprinkles a few grains
of fine crystal onto a round shaving mirror. He slides it across a
table to Malcolm and hands him a short straw. Sophia sits next to
Malcolm; she and Archie are already high. Malcolm leans over the
mirror, placing the straw in his nostril.

TIGHT CLOSE SHOT – MALCOLM'S FACE

In the mirror (something satanic about him)—as he sniffs the cocaine well into his nose.

71   CONT'D

A beat as he leans back waiting for the drug to take hold, Malcolm looks into dressing mirror.

                    ARCHIE
                    It hit?

                    MALCOLM
                    Nnnnnnn!

Malcolm with gun in hand does his Bogart gangster imitation.

                    ARCHIE
          Ain't nuthin' in the world to give you that real deep cool.
          Like girl. You there?

                    MALCOLM
          I'm there, daddy. Wheww. I'm cool enough to kill.

                    ARCHIE
                    Bet you are.

CLOSE – MALCOLM

FREEZE FRAME

                    SOPHIA'S VOICE
                    Malcolm, you're so funny.

She continues to laugh.

BACK TO REAL TIME.

                    MALCOLM
                    You got any money.

Before Sophia can answer he grabs her pocketbook, dumping all the contents on the floor but the dough.

                    SOPHIA
          Baby, I was gonna give it to you.

                    MALCOLM
          Well, bitch you move too slow.

                    ARCHIE
          Sometimes you got a big ugly mouth.

                    MALCOLM
          Yeah, and I'm putting my money where my ugly mouth is.
          I'm putting you back in the numbers right now.

71   CONT'D

MALCOLM (contd)
(to Sophia)
Baby, what's today?

Sophia is not sure of this, or anything else.

SOPHIA
August 2nd. I think. Yeah.

She laughs at her achievement.

MALCOLM
Daddy, put me down for a combination. Combinate me.
daddy: 8, 2, 1. You got me? 8, 1, 2; 1, 8, 2 . . .

With each number he throws a bill at Archie.

MALCOLM (contd)
1, 2, 8; 2, 8, 1. I git 'em all?

ARCHIE
(angrily taking the money)
I'll take your goddam bet.

Malcolm slides his tongue down Sophia's throat.

72   OMIT

73   OMIT

74   OMIT

75   EXT. SMALL'S PARADISE – NIGHT

A miserable night, raining and cold. Malcolm turns into the bar.

76   INT. THE BAR – NIGHT

Shaking off the rain as Malcolm walks through. He is now a familiar figure to the bar's DENIZENS. He is met with ad lib cries: "Hey,
Little," "Have a taste," from the men; and from the women: "Come
here, sugar," "Where you been?"

Malcolm acknowledges the greetings, strolls down in the bar. It's
immediately clear that a subtle change has come over him. He is no
longer the neophyte but a well-groomed, smooth, fully polished
hustler.

ANGLE – BOOTH

Malcolm sits into the booth and motions for the waitress.

76   CONT'D

ANGLE – HONEY

A fine copper tan waitress comes to him.

> **HONEY**
> I thought you said we were going to the movies last night.

> **MALCOLM**
> I say a lot of things.

> **HONEY**
> And like a fool I believe it.

> **MALCOLM**
> Do your job, get me a bourbon on the rocks and a pack of
> Lucky's.

Honey stares at him.

> **MALCOLM** (contd)
> I said now.

She leaves. He leans his head back against the booth—

> **A FEMALE VOICE**
> Daniel come in yet, Honey?

Malcolm turns his head sharply at the sound of the voice. It's
familiar, a sound from the seemingly distant past. He looks toward
the bar and sees the women who asked the question.

LAURA – MALCOLM'S POV

It's Laura, but not the Laura we last saw. She is still young, still
vulnerable, but she is bolder, more self-assured, more vividly
dressed. She is unaware of Malcolm.

> **HONEY**
> Ain't that him now?

ANGLE FAVORING DANIEL. He is a young, cocky, nervous, ginger-
bread colored boy who comes over to her quickly. He goes to the
corner of the bar and quickly grabs Laura's neck and kisses her
hungrily.

> **DANIEL**
> Hey, gorgeous, how you been? Waiting long? Lemme see
> you. Wow!

It's obvious he's a junkie. And in need of a fix. *QUICK!*

76 CONT'D

SHOT – MALCOLM

Honey places his drink and cigarettes before him. He's watching, taking it all in immediately. Laura is clearly crazy about Daniel.

CLOSE – MALCOLM

He looks, then belts down his drink.

CLOSER – LAURA AND DANIEL

Daniel motions to her pocketbook and she takes out a five-dollar bill. He grabs it, and bolts for the door.

WITH MALCOLM AND HONEY

She has been watching Malcolm.

> HONEY
> You know that gal?

> MALCOLM
> Mind your own goddamn business . . . She comes in a lot?

> HONEY
> 'Bout every other night, Red.

> MALCOLM
> With him?

Honey nods.

> MALCOLM (contd)
> She know?

> HONEY
> If she got eyes, she do.

ANGLE – LAURA

Walking toward the door, looking for Daniel. She leaves the bar.

CLOSE – MALCOLM AND HONEY

> MALCOLM
> Is she hooking?

> HONEY
> Not yet. But the way things going, that boy gonna turn her out any day.

Malcolm smacks the table in frustration.

76   CONT'D

> HONEY (contd)
> You stuck on her?

CLOSE – GLASS

Malcolm's glass on the table is trembling.

> MALCOLM
> Shut up, bitch.

He raises his arm to hit her and it is held back before it can find its mark.

> ARCHIE
> Don't do that.

Archie is standing above him. Malcolm nods, and Archie lets his arm go; standing next to him is Sophia.

> ARCHIE (contd)
> Honey, he didn't mean it.

Archie wiggles his fingers and Honey goes, but not before throwing daggers at Malcolm and Sophia. Archie sits down, takes out a cigar. For a good beat there is a coolness between them. Then Malcolm reaches over and lights Archie's cigar. Sophia stares at her man, he then motions for her to sit down beside him.

> ARCHIE (contd)
> Thanks. You got it. Who's beating on you, Red? You look-
> ing a little up tight.

The father-son thing is back, but Malcolm will never again be the student.

> MALCOLM
> Daddy, where's my money?

> ARCHIE
> What you talking?

> MALCOLM
> You owe me six big ones.

Archie looks at him, non-comprehending.

> MALCOLM
> 1, 2, 8 hit, didn't it?

> ARCHIE
> You din't have no 1, 2, 8.

76 CONT'D

> MALCOLM
>
> Was you that high? Old man, I threw the slats at you. I said to combinate me.

> ARCHIE
>
> You never had it.

> MALCOLM
>
> The bitch was there.

Archie doesn't even look at Sophia.

> ARCHIE
>
> Shit, what else she gonna say?

> MALCOLM
>
> Then skip it, man. But you slipping, baby. You done slipped.

Archie is controlling himself. Everyone in Small's is all ears, a falling out between Malcolm and Archie—their reps are at stake.

ANGLE. Archie looks at Sammy. Sammy is neutral. Archie digs in his pockets, comes up with a roll. He peels off six $100 bills and throws them on the table in front of himself, as he gets up.

> MALCOLM
>
> Oh, sit down, man. What you tasting? I'm buying.

> ARCHIE
>
> I ain't drinking hot piss with you. Come on, Sam.

> SAMMY
>
> Be right there.

Archie goes.

> SAMMY (contd)
>
> Twenty-two years he didn't never forget no number.

> MALCOLM
>
> Got to be a first time, daddy-o.

> SAMMY
>
> He gonna check the collector he turn into. His rep is on the line, boy, and so's yours. If you lying one of you is dead.

> MALCOLM
>
> Ain't gonna be this mother.

76 CONT'D

Sammy goes.

> MALCOLM (contd)
> Come on, sweetlips, I got us some g-i-r-l, girl. Let's you and
> me fly.

77 OMIT

78 OMIT

78A OMIT

79 OMIT

80 OMIT

81 OMIT

82 OMIT

83 OMIT

84 OMIT

85 EXT. ONYX CLUB – NIGHT

The well-known 52nd Street nightspot features Billie Holiday. A
stand-up cutout of her is outside.

86 INT. ONYX CLUB – NIGHT

This is a plush nightclub, with a mixed black and white AUDIENCE.
Some of the hustlers from Small's are in evidence.

CLOSE BILLIE

Lady Day starts into "YOU DON'T KNOW WHAT LOVE IS."

ANGLE – TABLE

Malcolm and Sophia high as a kite and on the town.

CLOSE – ARCHIE

He makes his way toward Malcolm's table. There is murder in his
eyes.

ANGLE – TABLE

> ARCHIE
> You're a damn liar.

CLOSE – ARCHIE

86 CONT'D

> ARCHIE (contd)
> You *took* me, you bastard, and now I'm taking you.

ANGLE – TABLE

> MALCOLM
> It's me or you, ain't it, Pops?

> ARCHIE
> You know it.

> MALCOLM
> I'll give you back the 600.

> ARCHIE
> I don't want your money.

> MALCOLM
> I'm wearing, Archie.

> ARCHIE
> There's two guns on you.

His eyes gesture. Malcolm looks:

MALCOLM'S POV

Sammy at the nearby bar: his hand in his coat pocket.

CLOSE – ARCHIE

His hand is also in his pocket.

> MALCOLM
> And every cat's watching, ain't they? It's a toe-down.

> ARCHIE
> That's what it is. Walk on out.

> MALCOLM
> Let Billie finish.

> ARCHIE
> Now.

Archie backs away from the table, his gun on Malcolm.

ANGLE. As Sammy moves a step toward Malcolm, Malcolm rises in his seat.

> SOPHIA
> You had the number.

86   CONT'D

> MALCOLM
>
> Baby, I got to let this old man win. Keep the faith, and tell Billie I'll see her later.

CLOSE – BILLIE

She knows what's going on.

ANGLE – Sammy and Archie are walking behind Malcolm, when he pushes a waitress into their path with drinks flying everywhere, Malcolm darts away.

87   INT. ENTRANCE TO THE TOILET

He races into the men's room.

ANGLE. Archie and Sammy run after him.

88   INT. MEN'S ROOM – NIGHT

There is an open window. Archie is leaning out, looking both ways.

89   EXT. OUTSIDE THE MEN'S ROOM WINDOW – NIGHT FROM ARCHIE'S POV

A tiny alleyway. No one is visible.

> ARCHIE
>
> The dirty yellow rat bastard.

90   INT. MEN'S ROOM – NIGHT

> SAMMY
>
> Don't push it. You way ahead. You back on top. That boy loves you, man.

> ARCHIE
>
> What you say?

> SAMMY
>
> He gave it to you, Archie. He did.

91   EXT. THE STREET NIGHT

Malcolm comes running out of an alleyway and onto the street. He stops to catch his breath, to regain his composure. He is shook up, frustrated, but mostly saddened. He then runs down the block and into a CLOSEUP.

91A INT LITTLE HOUSE – LANSING MICHIGAN – NIGHT (REMEM-
BERED TIME) – *FINAL FLASHBACK*

CLOSE EARL

Earl is sitting up in bed, he wakes his sleeping wife Louise, next to
her is a baby in a crib, another child. Malcolm sleeps between Earl
and her.

91AA ANGLE – HOUSE

Outside the house are 5 members of THE BLACK LEGION. They are
dressed in the style of the KKK, but in black sheets rather than
white. WE SEE gasoline cans being passed around.

> EARL
> Somebody out there. Wake the children.

Earl starts to put on his overalls and reaches for his gun which sits
on a nearby chair when an explosion of flames greets the house.

> EARL (contd)
> Everybody out. OUT! OUT! Get the kids.

ANGLE – CHILDREN'S BEDROOM

Flames roar through the room and the Little kids are hysterical.
Louise rushes in and pushes them past the fire, she has infant in
hand covered in a blanket.

91C EXT. HOUSE – NIGHT

The entire house is in flames. The Little family stands in front of it,
just out of harm's way.

ANGLE – BLACK LEGION

They sit on their horses watching the results of their work.

CLOSE – BLACK LEGION LEADER

> BLACK LEGION LEADER
> Boy, good thing we're good Christians. Nigger, it's time for
> you to leave this town.

CLOSE – EARL

> EARL
> This here is 'pose to be a free country.

CLOSE – BLACK LEGION LEADER

> BLACK LEGION LEADER
> Rev, we warned you 'bout that Garvey preaching, stirring
> up the good nigras here. Boy, next time you're a dead
> nigger.

91C   CONT'D

CLOSE – EARL

EARL
I ain't a boy. I'm a man, and a real man don't hide behind
no bedsheets.

Earl takes his pistol out from behind his back and fires above their
heads.

EARL (contd)
Take these here bullets for dem sheets.

ANGLE – BLACK LEGION

The bullets send the Black Legion flying into the glorious D.W.
Griffith moonlit night.

ANGLE – HOUSE

The burning house collapses behind the Little family.

ANGLE – EARL AND LOUISE

LOUISE
Earl, I know you a better shot than that. You shoulda
killed 'em all, shot 'em dead.

EARL
Just wanted to scare 'em, they won't be bothering us no
more.

CLOSE – YOUNG MALCOLM

Young Malcolm stares at his father while the house still burns
behind him, no doubt drawing on the great courage displayed by
his father.

EARL
They won't be here no time soon. I'm a MAN.

91D   EXT. STREET – LANSING – NIGHT (REMEMBERED TIME)

It's raining cats and dogs and it's foggy. We hear a big thud, then
a grunt and Earl Little falls across the trolley tracks, the sound of
men running away is heard in the distance.

ANGLE – A STREETCAR APPROACHES

ANGLE – EARL ON TRACKS

He has been beaten to a bloody pulp.

ANGLE – CLOSER SHOT OF STREETCAR APPROACHING

91D CONT'D

CLOSE – EARL

He opens his one good eye.

CLOSE – STREETCAR MOTORMAN

He sees something ahead in the fog and rain.

ANGLE – MOTORMAN'S POV

CLOSE – HAND REACHES BRAKE LEVER

CLOSE – STREETCAR WHEELS STOPPING, SPARKS FLY

CLOSE – MOTORMAN

Winces and then makes the Sign of the Cross.

ANGLE – LONG SHOT OF PASSENGERS

Jumping out of the streetcar to attend to Earl.

> PASSENGER'S VOICE
> Somebody get a doctor.

> MOTORMAN'S VOICE
> No doctor, get him a priest.

> VOICE OF MALCOLM X
> My father's skull, on one side was crushed in, and then
> laid across some tracks, for a streetcar to run him over.
> His body was cut almost in half. My father, Earl Little lived
> two and a half hours in that condition. Negroes were
> stronger than they are now.

92 INT. A CAR – NIGHT

Shorty is driving with Sophia in the front seat. Malcolm is in the
back. They are in the country—outside New York.

> SHORTY
> Man, I'm glad we got you out of there. With West Indian
> Archie on your ass, your name on the wire—Boston the
> best goddam place in the world for you—things are too hot
> and it's not even summer.

Malcolm has withdrawn within himself. He takes out a packet of
cocaine and sniffs it.

> SOPHIA
> We'll take it easy. I got a place fixed up on Harvard Square.
> How's that sound?

92 CONT'D

> SHORTY

Yeah. Cool it and lay dead for a while, Homeboy. And don't worry none.

The drug takes hold. Malcolm is out of it.

> SHORTY (contd)

I'll stake you, baby. I got my band. I'm blowing great sax. Hell, you ain't even heard us—

He and Sophia keep talking it up, trying to bolster Malcolm.

CLOSE – MALCOLM

Stoned, his nose running, Malcolm stares out of the window at the receding landscape. FREEZE FRAME.

> VOICE OF MALCOLM X

Like every hustler I was trapped. Cats that hung together trying to find a little security, to find an answer—found nothing. Cats that might have probed space or cured cancer—(Hell, Archie might have been a mathematical genius)—all victims of whitey's social order.

Music of a dance combo heard in BG.

> VOICE OF MALCOLM X (contd)

Three things I was always scared of: a job, a bust and jail. I realized then I wasn't afraid of anything. I didn't care.

93 OMIT

94 INT. HARVARD SQUARE APARTMENT – DAY

Shorty, Sophia and PEG face Malcolm—stoned in a chair. PEG is 17, Sophia's kid sister and Shorty's date.

> SHORTY

You got to eat somethin', Red.

> SOPHIA

You want eggs, baby?

> MALCOLM

Yeah and get a slave, too, huh, baby?

> SHORTY

I ain't doing bad.

> MALCOLM

Man, the name musicians ain't got shit. How you gonna have something? I need a stake, a bundle, a grand. My

94   CONT'D

MALCOLM (contd)
woman can't afford it; my homey ain't got it. How about
you baby? What you got?

Peg smiles, afraid of Malcolm.

SHORTY
Jesus, Red, she's just a kid.

MALCOLM
Jesus ain't got nothin' to do with this.

Shorty eyes him with amazement. The degree of Malcolm's deprav-
ity surprises even him.

MALCOLM
Surprise you, baby? Well, that's the way it is. What kind
of scratch you got on you? Turn out. Let me have it. All of
you—

Glances exchanged among Shorty, Sophia and Peg. Shorty reaches
into his pocket.

95   INT. HARVARD SQUARE APARTMENT – NIGHT

Malcolm with Sophia, Shorty and Peg around him.

MALCOLM
We gone rob this town blind. Anybody want out say so.

Nobody answers; they'll go with Malcolm.

MALCOLM (contd)
Okay. I got the stake and I got a fence. I need a driver.

PEG
How about Rudy?

SHORTY
Yeah, Rudy.

MALCOLM
Who's Rudy?

JUMP CUT:

95A   SAME LOCATION – LATER

RUDY is with them. He is a good-looking, very-light skinned black,
tough as they come.

RUDY
I'm half wop, half nigger and ain't afraid of no one.

95A CONT'D

> MALCOLM
> What can you do?

They are in the process of appraising each other, seeing which one
has the bigger penis.

> RUDY
> You name it, feller.

> SHORTY
> Rudy does catering. Rich joints on Beacon Hill.

> MALCOLM
> That ain't bad.

> SHORTY
> Tell him about Baldy.

> RUDY
> Yeah. This rich ofay, like he's 60. I give him a bath on
> Friday.

Peg and Sophia are listening, a little horrified.

> RUDY (contd)
> Then I put him to bed and pour talcum powder on him like
> a baby. He gets his jollies off.

> MALCOLM
> So what about him?

> RUDY
> So? The man got silver, china, rugs—

> MALCOLM
> Might be all right.

> RUDY
> Might be, shit. Man, I know this town. I got my own fences.
> Who the hell are you? Who put you in charge?

Malcolm smiles easily.

> MALCOLM
> You want to be the head man?

> RUDY
> That's right.

95A   CONT'D

> MALCOLM
> Head nigger in charge?

> RUDY
> I'm the man.

> MALCOLM
> Okay, baby. Let's flip for it. Flip this.

He takes out his gun, a .32 revolver. He dumps the shells on the table, then reinserts one shell and twirls the barrel.

> MALCOLM (contd)
> I'll flip first.

He puts the revolver to his own head.

> PEG
> Don't.

Malcolm squeezes the trigger. It clicks. Now he twirls the barrel again and hands the gun to Rudy.

> MALCOLM
> Your flip, baby.

Rudy is staring at him; so are they all. Malcolm puts the gun to his temple again.

> SOPHIA
> Red, for God's sake—

He pulls the trigger a second time. Click. Now he twirls it again.

> SHORTY
> Christ, Red, no—

> PEG
> I can't stand it.

Malcolm puts the gun to Rudy's head.

> MALCOLM
> Your turn, Rudy. You want me to flip for you?

> RUDY
> Jesus Christ, no. Okay, okay. You got it, you got it! You're the boss.

A beat.

95A   CONT'D

MALCOLM
Don't never try to cross someone who ain't afraid to die.

SHORTY
You the man!

Nodding accord from Rudy and Shorty. Sophia can hardly stand.

MALCOLM
All right. We'll start with Old Talcum Powder. You draw
the house, where everything is. You and Peg go out and
buy them tools like I told you. We hit tonight on account of
in the daytime some of us got that high visibility. Ya dig?

ANGLE. Rudy is at a table drawing a diagram; the girls have left.
Shorty and Malcolm alone at a window.

SHORTY
What did you do, Homey, palm it?

MALCOLM
Yeah.

He breaks open the gun—the bullet is in the next slot to be fired.

MALCOLM (contd)
Palmed it right in the goddam chamber.

SHORTY
Jesus Christ, Homey, you are nuts.

Malcolm starts laughing: a silent, hysterical laugh.

96   EXT/INT. A BEACON HILL HOUSE – NIGHT

The robbery, IN QUICK CUTS:

—A door lock is picked by Sophia.

96A   —Pencil flashlight passes an upstairs window.

96B   —Rudy in the car.

96C   —Silver removed from a drawer by Shorty.

96D   —Peg walking down the street, as lookout.

96E   —Malcolm takes off his shoes.

96F   —The sleeping OLD MAN, OLD TALCUM POWDER, as Malcolm
takes a watch, a wallet from within inches of his pillow. Then, more
boldly, picks up the man's hand and removes a ring from one of his

96F CONT'D

fingers. Shorty watching with bated breath, he's about to have a
heart attack.

97 INT. MANSION – DAY

A Boston matron, MRS. CRAWFORD, is showing the girls her collection of U.S. silver. In a fine New England home.

> PEG
> Beacon Hill survey.

> SOPHIA
> We're doing a survey for the Atheneum Society—We won-
> dered if you'd permit us to include your collection in the
> catalog of Great New England Antiques—?

> MRS. CRAWFORD
> Now these are my prizes. My Paul Revere silver coffee
> service.

SHOT—AN ARRANGEMENT OF MUSEUM-QUALITY PIECES

> PEG
> Lovely, just lovely.

Sophia is casing the room carefully as the matron continues.

> MRS. CRAWFORD
> And my husband's collection of scrimshaw should be in-
> cluded.

> SOPHIA
> May we see it?

> MRS. CRAWFORD
> Won't you step this way?

97A OMIT

98 OMIT

98A OMIT

101 INT. A COURTROOM – DAY

The prisoners face the bench: Peg, Sophia, Shorty, Rudy and Malcolm.

> VOICE OF MALCOLM X
> The average first offender gets two years for burglary. We
> were all first offenders. That's what Sophia and Peg
> drew—

101   CONT'D

                    JUDGE
Two years in the Women's Reformatory at Framingham.

              VOICE OF MALCOLM X
But our crime wasn't burglary. It was balling white girls.
They gave us the book.

                    JUDGE
Burglary, count one—8 to 10 years; count two, 8 to 10
years; count three, 8 to 10 years . . .

He continues giving them 8 to 10 years, behind Malcolm's comment:

              VOICE OF MALCOLM X
Fourteen counts of 8 to 10 years.

                    JUDGE
The sentences to run concurrently.

              VOICE OF MALCOLM X
Shorty thought he hit us with 114 years till I explained
what concurrently meant. It meant a minimum sentence
of 10 years hard labor at the Charlestown State Prison.
The date was February 1946. I wasn't quite 21. I had not
yet begun to shave.

CAMERA HAS GONE IN for a TIGHT CLOSE SHOT of Malcolm's face:
a hardened hustler, pimp, dope peddler and now jailbird at the ripe
old age of 20. FREEZE FRAME.

                                        CUT TO BLACK.

FADE IN:

102   INT. THE CELL CORRIDOR – DAY

It is the afternoon lockup: about 3:30 P.M. The line of PRISONERS
stands in front of their cells, as two guards, WILKINS and BARNES,
one white, one black, slowly walk past the P.M. check.

The procedure is routine, done without emotion, as it is done three
times a day: the black guard calls out the prisoner's name, the
prisoner answers with his number, then steps into his cell. Where-
upon the white guard slams the door shut and locks it.

                 GUARD WILKINS
                    Jackson.

102   CONT'D

> PRISONER
> A 231549.

Door is slammed and gate locked.

CLOSE – MALCOLM

Each time a gate is locked his tension increases. His face is a mask hiding his fury, violence and the hunger of an advanced junkie who has not had a fix in over a week.

> GUARD WILKINS
> Crichlow.

> SECOND PRISONER
> A 5991301.

Same procedure.

ANGLE. SHOOTING PAST MALCOLM, FAVORING TWO OTHER PRISONERS. The guards are approaching Malcolm's cell. Past Malcolm are two experienced PRISONERS who have been watching Malcolm during the scene. They whisper surreptitiously without moving their bodies, and barely moving their lips. One of the prisoners is PETE, a huge barrel of a man, a lifer—beaten by the system and a lifetime of incarceration. The other is BEMBRY, a man of no great physicality, but who possesses immediately the gift of leadership. It is clear that Pete and others look up to him with great respect.

> PETE
> Looka Satan.

> BEMBRY
> I see him.

Bembry's language is very unhip. He speaks carefully. He respects words and he respects himself, something which sets him apart from all the other prisoners.

> PETE
> He 'bout to bust.

> BEMBRY
> No, he's not gonna bust. But he's not gonna fix his face to please them, neither.

ANGLE. The check-in has reached the man next to Malcolm.

102   CONT'D

> GUARD WILKINS
> Harrington.

> THIRD PRISONER
> B 775717.

> GUARD BARNES
> Yeah. Lucky Seven.

Door slammed and locked.

CLOSE SHOT – MALCOLM

The guards are now in front of him.

> GUARD WILKINS
> Little.

Malcolm doesn't move.

> GUARD BARNES
> State your number.

Malcolm doesn't answer, doesn't blink.

> GUARD WILKINS
> Little.

ANGLE. Bembry in the FG of the scene.

> BEMBRY
> He's a new fish, Mr. Barnes. Give him a break.

It's a bold step by Bembry and the prisoners look over at him with admiration. Barnes accepts the irregularity and calls over to Bembry.

> GUARD BARNES
> Okay, I'll give him a break. Now state your number, Little.

CLOSE – MALCOLM

> MALCOLM
> I forgot it.

CLOSE SHOT – BEMBRY

Shaking his head in anguish. He knows what's coming.

ANGLE. Barnes makes a small gesture and Wilkins seizes Malcolm, grabbing his head and uniform at the same time. Stenciled on the chest of his faded dungarees is Malcolm's number. The guard bends

102 CONT'D
Malcolm's head to the number, shoving the material in Malcolm's
face.

> GUARD WILKINS
> Can you read, boy? Thass your number.

> GUARD BARNES
> Now say it.

> MALCOLM
> I'm Malcolm Little, not no goddam number.

> GUARD WILKINS
> Oh, yes you is, baby; thass all you is.

And slams Malcolm hard. He slumps to the floor.

> GUARD BARNES
> Two days in the hole. Take him.

Wilkins drags Malcolm off as Barnes resumes the roll call.

> GUARD BARNES (contd)
> Burnham.

> FOURTH PRISONER
> A 551613, sir.

> JUMP CUT:

103 INT. A SOLITARY CELL – DAY

Only the faintest light comes into the hideous room, which consists
of a mattress and a slop bucket. If Malcolm were to stretch out his
arms, he could touch both walls. He lies half on the stone floor, half
on the mattress.

A clang as the heavy door is opened.

> GUARD CONE
> Time's up. Get on your feet.

Malcolm stands.

> GUARD CONE (contd)
> Little, state your number.

A beat as Malcolm stares at the man, refusing to answer.

> GUARD CONE (contd)
> You just drew two more days.

103   CONT'D

And slams the door shut.

104   INT. SOLITARY – NIGHT

It is almost pitch black. We can almost smell the stench of the room.
Malcolm sits stony-faced, his back against a wall.

> TRUSTEE'S VOICE
> Water.

The long spigot of a watering can is pushed through an opening in
the cell door. Malcolm, animal-like, leaps at it and bends the spout,
almost wrenching it off in his fury.

105   OMIT

106   INT. SOLITARY CELL – DAY

TWO-SHOT – A WHITE CHAPLAIN AND MALCOLM

> CHAPLAIN GILL
> Do you know what a friend you have in Jesus, son?

> MALCOLM
> Preacher, take your tin Jesus and the Virgin Mary, both,
> and shove 'em.

Door slam.

107   INT. SOLITARY – NIGHT

Malcolm is alone at the bars: the hope of freedom filling his mind.

Malcolm pulls at the bars, tries to shake them in impotent fury. He
pounds the walls. Empty, sick, defeated, his nails scratching the
walls, he slides to the floor of the cell.

It is the low point of his life: nowhere to turn, nothing to hope for.

108   INT. SOLITARY – LATER

Guard Cone is shaking him into consciousness.

> GUARD CONE
> All right, Little. Get up.

Malcolm just about makes it. The guard is in half-focus.

> GUARD CONE (contd)
> State your number.

He is beaten.

108 CONT'D

MALCOLM
A 859912.

A shower is heard.

109 INT. SHOWER ROOM – DAY

Malcolm stands with bowed head as the hot water cascades over his broken body. He lets it run and run, but it cannot really touch his problems. On a nearby bench are his clothes, his towel and the makings for a conk: lye, Vaseline, comb, etc.

He turns for a moment as he sees he is being watched by someone. It's Bembry standing nearby. Malcolm turns away, trying to find solace in the water. He wants no part of the world or anyone, just to be left alone.

BEMBRY
I know how you feel. Like you want to lay down and die.

Malcolm shows no flicker of interest or understanding.

BEMBRY (contd)
I brought you something.

He puts down a small matchbox on the bench next to Malcolm's things. Malcolm eyes him like a snake—but the punishment has reduced him to deep insecurity and his belligerence is more cautious than angry.

MALCOLM
Who the hell are you?

BEMBRY
Put it in a cup of water. It's nutmeg.

MALCOLM
Man, what do you want?

BEMBRY
You need something. It's not a reefer, but it'll help some.

MALCOLM
Man, get outa my face. I ain't nobody's punk.

But he steps out of the shower, fills a tin cup with water and empties the contents of the matchbox into it. And drinks it down quickly.

109   CONT'D

> BEMBRY
> Sit down or it might knock you down.

Malcolm sits, toweling himself as the spice hits him. For the first time he smiles; this is the first relief he has tasted in prison. He looks at Bembry wonderingly, unable to figure him out.

> MALCOLM
> If you ain't trying to punk me, what's your hype?

> BEMBRY
> I can show you how to get out of prison. And it's no hype.

> MALCOLM
> Talk, daddy, I'm listening. Hey that ain't bad. You got some more?

> BEMBRY
> That's the last stuff you'll ever get from me.

> MALCOLM
> What did you give it to me for then?

> BEMBRY
> 'Cause you needed it. 'Cause you couldn't hear me without it.

This is a new breed of cat; Malcolm has never met anyone like him. He eyes him closely, as he slips into his clothes.

> MALCOLM
> What in the hell are you talking about?

He begins to conk his hair, but is paying attention to what Bembry is saying.

> BEMBRY
> I think you got more sense than any cat in this prison. How come you are such a fool?

Malcolm looks over, piqued.

> BEMBRY (contd)
> Nobody can bust out like Bogart does it, in the movies. Because even if you get out, you are still in prison.

Malcolm is putting the conk into his hair now.

> MALCOLM
> You ain't lying.

109   CONT'D

                          BEMBRY
When you go busting your fists against a stone wall, you're
not using your brains. 'Cause that's what the white man
wants you to do. Look at you.

These last words are spoken sharply with disgust. Malcolm turns
his hands massaging the conk into his hair.

                       BEMBRY (contd)
               Putting all that poison in your hair.

                          MALCOLM
Man, you been locked up too long, everybody conks. All
the cats.

                          BEMBRY
               Why? Why does everybody conk?

                          MALCOLM
'Cause I don't want to walk around with my head all
nappy, looking like—

                          BEMBRY
Like what? Looking like me? Like a nigger?! Why don't you
want to look like what you are? What makes you ashamed
of being black?

                          MALCOLM
               I ain't said I'm ashamed.

He turns the water on to wash out the conk—which has begun to
burn. Bembry restrains him, holding his arm.

                          MALCOLM
               Leggo. I got to wash it out.

                          BEMBRY
               Let it burn. Maybe you'll hear me then.

But it is burning now.

                          MALCOLM
               Man, you better get off me.

He wrenches away from Bembry and puts his head in the water.

                          BEMBRY
Sure, burn yourself, pain yourself, put all that poison into
your hair, into your body—trying to be white.

109   CONT'D

MALCOLM
Man, I don't want to hear all that.

BEMBRY
I thought you was smart. But you just another one of them
cats strutting down the avenue in your clown suit with all
that mess on you. Like a monkey. And the white man sees
you and he laughs. He laughs because he knows you ain't
white.

Malcolm is drying his hair, finishing his conk. But some of what
Bembry has said disturbs him.

MALCOLM
Who are you?

Malcolm is completely humiliated. Bembry sees this and stops the
barrage.

BEMBRY
The question is, who are you? You are in the darkness, but
it's not your fault. Elijah Muhammad can bring you into
the light.

MALCOLM
Elijah who?

BEMBRY
Elijah Muhammad can get you out of prison. Out of the
prison of your mind. Maybe all you want is another fix. I
thought you were smart.

And he is gone. Malcolm stands looking after him, a long thoughtful
moment. He is pulling the comb through his hair.

110   INT. PRISON LICENSE SHOP – DAY

PRISONERS are working on a beltline that stamps out and finishes
license plates. Bembry is on the stamping machines, working as he
talks to the other prisoners. Malcolm is painting the plates, a little
removed from Bembry, but listening with interest. Barnes, with
rifle, idles by a window.

A whistle sounds, ending the work shift. The inmates quickly file
out into the yard. Bembry stays. Malcolm is half decided.

GUARD BARNES
You taking the yard?

110   CONT'D

> BEMBRY
> I'm staying.

Barnes gestures to Malcolm.

> MALCOLM
> Me too.

He goes.

> BEMBRY
> What you sniffing around for? I told you I gave you your
> last fix.

> MALCOLM
> I ain't never seen a cat like you. Ain't you scared talking
> like that in front of an ofay?

> BEMBRY
> What's he gonna do to me he ain't already done?

> MALCOLM
> You the only cat don't come on with that "Whatcha know,
> daddy" jive; and you don't cuss none.

> BEMBRY
> I respect myself. A man cuss because he hasn't got the
> words to say what's on his mind.

> MALCOLM
> Tell you this: you ain't no fool.

> BEMBRY
> Don't con me. Don't try . . .

> MALCOLM
> Okay, okay.

> BEMBRY
> Don't con me.

> MALCOLM
> What do you do with your time?

> BEMBRY
> I read. I study. Because the first thing a black man has to
> do is respect himself. Respect his body and his mind. Quit
> taking the white man's poison into your body: his ciga-
> rettes, his dope, his liquor, his white woman, his pork.

110   CONT'D

MALCOLM

That's what Mama used to say.

BEMBRY

Your mama had sense because the pig is a filthy beast:
part rat, part cat, and the rest is dog.

Malcolm has been pondering all this and now grows animated as he
thinks he has come to the essence of a hustle.

MALCOLM

Come on, daddy, pull my coat. What happens if you give all
that up? You get sick or somethin'? I pulled a hustle once
and got out of the draft.

BEMBRY

I'm telling you God's words, not no hustle. I'm talking the
words of Allah, the black man's God. I'm telling you, boy,
that God is black.

MALCOLM

What? Everybody knows God is White.

BEMBRY (contd)

But everything the white man taught you, you learned. He
told you you were a black heathen and you believed him.
He told you how he took you out of darkness and brought
you to the light. And you believed him. He taught you to
worship a blond, blue-eyed God with white skin—and you
believed him. He told you black was a curse, you believed
him. Did you ever look up the word black in the dictionary?

MALCOLM

What for?

BEMBRY

Did you ever study anything wasn't part of some con?

MALCOLM'S VOICE

What the hell for, man?

BEMBRY

Go on, fool; the marble shooters are waiting for you.

MALCOLM

Okay, okay. Show me, man.

110A   CLOSE SHOT – A DICTIONARY

WE CAN READ the fine print of the definition:

DICTIONARY

Black, (blak), adj. Destitute of light, devoid of color, enveloped in darkness. Hence, utterly dismal or gloomy, as "the future looked black."

MALCOLM'S VOICE
You understand them words?

BEMBRY'S VOICE
Read it.

PULLBACK TO SHOW Bembry and Malcolm in a small PRISON LIBRARY. No one else is in the book-lined room.

MALCOLM
I can't make out that shit.

BEMBRY
Soiled with dirt, foul; sullen, hostile, forbidding—as a black day. Foully or outrageously wicked, as black cruelty. Indicating disgrace, dishonor or culpability.

DICTIONARY
See also *blackmail, blackball, blackguard.*

MALCOLM
Hey, they's some shit, all right.

BEMBRY
Now look up "white."

Bembry turns the pages of the dictionary to "w."

BEMBRY (contd)
Read it.

CLOSE SHOT – DICTIONARY DEFINITION OF "WHITE"

MALCOLM'S VOICE
White (whit), adj. Of the color of pure snow; reflecting all the rays of the spectrum. The opposite of black, hence free from spot or blemish; innocent, pure, without evil intent, harmless. Honest, square-dealing, honorable.

Malcolm stumbles through the definition as well as he can. Bembry takes over the reading, giving it ironic emphasis.

110A CONT'D

> MALCOLM
> That's bullshit. That's a white man's book. Ain't all these white man's books.

SHOT – THE SHELVES OF BOOKS

> BEMBRY
> They sure ain't no black man's books in here.

> MALCOLM
> Then what you telling me to study in them for?

> BEMBRY
> You got to learn everything the white man says and use it against him. The truth is laying there if you smart and read behind their words. It's buried there. You got to dig it out.

> MALCOLM
> Man, how'm I gonna know the ones worth looking at?

Bembry smiles at Malcolm. He is a remarkable man who always takes careful measure of his listener. He never talks down to his audience; he talks to them. (A manner Malcolm later will adopt.) Bembry can talk funky or salty or, as we will see, in the cadence and eloquence of the Bible. Right now he goes into street talk.

> BEMBRY
> I'll pull your coat, daddy. 'Cause lots of these can't nobody read, be he black or white or a Ph.D. with their suspenders dragging the ground with degrees.

Malcolm laughs. He likes and admires the man. Then caught by a passage he does not understand:

> MALCOLM
> Man, I'm studying in the man's book. I don't dig half the words.

> BEMBRY
> Look 'em up and find out what they mean.

> MALCOLM
> Where am I gonna start?

> BEMBRY
> Start at the beginning. Page one, the first one. Here—

110A CONT'D

CLOSE SHOT

As Bembry's hand opens the book to page one.

CLOSE IN ON A PICTURE OF AN AARDVARK WITH ITS DEFINITION

> MALCOLM
> Aardvark, noun. An earth pig; an ant-eating African mam-
> mal. Man, that sounds like the dozens.

ANGLE – TWO-SHOT

> BEMBRY
> Read it and keep on reading.

Malcolm's finger runs down to the next definition:

> DICTIONARY
> Abacus, noun. An ancient and primitive Chinese counting
> device.

> BEMBRY
> If you take one step toward Allah, He will take two steps
> toward you.

111 OMIT

112 OMIT

113 INT. MALCOLM'S CELL – NIGHT

He is reading on his bunk as Barnes walks by. The lights in the cell
go out. Malcolm looks up, annoyed at being interrupted. He shifts
his position to the floor of the cell so that he can catch the dim light
coming from the corridor and goes on with his reading.

CLOSE SHOT – THE BOOK

Malcolm is studying the dictionary, the last of the "a's": the words
azimuth, Azores, Aztec, azure, etc. He reads a word, then holds his
hand over the printed definition to test himself, half-mouthing its
meaning. Malcolm is also copying the dictionary in a school book
word for word.

114 INT. LIBRARY – DAY

There are several books on the desk before Malcolm. WE SEE their
titles: W.E.B. DuBois's *The Soul of Black Folks,* Carter G. Wood-
son's *Journal of Negro History,* Durant's *Story of Philosophy,* H.G.
Wells's *Outline of History,* Spinoza, Thoreau, etc.

114 CONT'D

> GUARD BARNES'S VOICE
> Closing. Knock it off.

Malcolm is surprised the time has gone so fast. He gathers up his books with care. He cherishes them, putting them back on the shelf carefully.

> GUARD BARNES
> Hey, you studying to be the first colored President of the United States?

115 INT. LICENSE SHOP – DAY

The machines are idle; no one is in the room but Malcolm. He starts to reach inside his jacket when Barnes sticks his head in.

> GUARD BARNES
> You taking the yard or not?

> MALCOLM
> I'm staying.

> GUARD BARNES
> Then give me a butt.

Malcolm takes out a half-filled pack of cigarettes, about to offer one, then pauses. Malcolm hands him the pack of cigarettes.

> MALCOLM
> Take 'em. I don't smoke no more.

He takes the pack happily and goes. Malcolm reaches into his jacket again, takes out a book. WE SEE its title: Mahatma Gandhi's *My Struggle.* He sits next to the license press to read.

116 EXT. THE PRISON YARD – DAY

A baseball game is in progress. A BLACK TEAM is playing a WHITE ONE. Most of the CONVICTS are watching the game; partisanship at every pitch. A base hit gets a big reaction.

ANGLE – MALCOLM AND BEMBRY

They are out along the right field wall. They walk throughout the scene.

ANGLE – The ball is hit over the fence for a home run. There is a big cheer from the black prisoners. Pete, the batter, trots proudly around the bases.

116   CONT'D

MALCOLM

Ole Pete ain't much in the head, but he can lay in there
with the wood.

BEMBRY

Lemme tell you about history: black history. You listening?

TWO-SHOT – Malcolm still watching the game.

MALCOLM

You pitch, baby; I'll ketch.

BEMBRY

The first men on earth were black. They ruled and there
was not one white face anywhere. But they teach us that
we lived in caves and swung from trees. Black men were
never like that.

Malcolm is listening to Bembry's intent statement.

BEMBRY (contd)

We were a race of kings when the white men went around
on all fours.

There is a crack of the bat and Malcolm turns to watch another base
hit, by a black convict, stir the crowd.

MALCOLM

This a helluva game. Somethin's going on.

He sees a black convict, CHUCK, nearby and calls over:

MALCOLM (contd)

Hey, whatsa score?

CHUCK

10 to 1; we murdering them, Din't you hear?

MALCOLM

What?

CHUCK

The Brooklyn Dodgers brought up Jackie Robinson and we
pounding the hell out of them, celebrating.

MALCOLM

How 'bout that?

116   CONT'D

> BEMBRY
>
> Sure, white man throw us a bone and that's supposed to
> make us forget 400 years.

> MALCOLM
>
> A black man playing big league ball is something.

> BEMBRY
>
> I told you to go behind the words and dig out the truth.
> They let us sing and dance and smile—and now they let
> one black man in the majors. That don't cancel out the
> greatest crime in history. When that blue-eyed devil locked
> us in chains—100,000,000 of us—broke up our families,
> tortured us, cut us off from our language, our religion, our
> history.

SHOTS OF THE FACES OF THE BLACK BALL PLAYERS AND THE
CONVICTS

In the stands, cheering and joyous.

> BEMBRY (contd)
>
> Do they know who they are? Do you know where you came
> from? We are the Original People.

Malcolm is listening to him now.

> BEMBRY (contd)
>
> What's your name, boy?

Malcolm is startled; answers like a boy.

> MALCOLM
>
> Little.

> BEMBRY
>
> No. That's the name of the slave-master who owned your
> family. You don't even know who you are. You're nothing.
> Less than nothing. A zero. Who are you?

CLOSE SHOT – MALCOLM

Wrapped in thought.

ANGLE ON MALCOLM

> MALCOLM
>
> I'm not Malcolm Little and I'm not Satan.

116   CONT'D

                    BEMBRY
            Who are you?

CLOSE – MALCOLM

Malcolm cannot answer because he truly does not know.

A ball is hit. Malcolm watches its flight—but his face is fixed somewhere between understanding and anger: it is the face of the future
leader.

                    BEMBRY
        I told you we are a nation, the lost Tribe of Shabazz in the
        wilderness of North America.

117   INT. ANOTHER PART OF THE PRISON – LATE AFTERNOON

The rays of the sun come through bars that cut across Malcolm and
Bembry's face.

                    BEMBRY
        Allah has sent us a prophet, a black man named Elijah
        Muhammad. For if God is black, Malcolm—

                    MALCOLM
            Then the devil is white.

                    BEMBRY
        I knew you'd hear me. The white man is the devil. All white
        men are devils.

                    MALCOLM
            I sure met some.

                    BEMBRY
        No. Elijah Muhammad does not say "that white man is a
        devil." He teaches us that the white man is *the* devil. All
        white men.

CLOSE SHOT – MALCOLM

Listening.

                    BEMBRY
        Have you ever known a good white man in all your life?
        Think back, did you ever meet one who wasn't evil?

A prison whistle is heard.

118   OMIT

119   OMIT

120   INT. A NICHE IN A PRISON WALL – P.M.

Malcolm and Bembry standing close together. The feeling is of someone taking communion: with Bembry the minister and Malcolm the communicant. Their voices are little more than whispers.

> BEMBRY
> The body is a holy repository.

> MALCOLM
> I will not touch the white man's poison: his drugs, his liquor, his carrion, his women.

> BEMBRY
> A Muslim must be strikingly upright. Outstanding. So those in the darkness can see the power of the light.

Malcolm lifts his head.

> MALCOLM
> I will do it.

> BEMBRY
> But the key to Islam is submission. That is why twice daily we turn to Mecca, to the Holy of Holies, to pray. We bend our knees in submission.

Bembry kneels in a praying position. Malcolm stands.

> MALCOLM
> I can't.

> BEMBRY
> For evil to bend its knee, admit its guilt, implore His forgiveness, is the hardest thing on earth—

> MALCOLM
> I want to, Bembry, but I can't.

> BEMBRY
> —the hardest and the greatest.

> MALCOLM
> I can't.

> BEMBRY
> For evil to bend its knee, admit its guilt, implore His forgiveness, is the hardest thing on earth—

120   CONT'D

                          MALCOLM
          I want to, Bembry, but I can't.

                          BEMBRY
          —the hardest and the greatest.

                          MALCOLM
          I don't know what to say to Allah.

                          BEMBRY
          Have you ever bent your knees, Malcolm?

Malcolm laugh-snorts:

                          MALCOLM
          Yeah. When I was picking a lock to rob somebody's house.

                          BEMBRY
               Tell Him that.

                          MALCOLM
               I don't know how.

                          BEMBRY
          You can grovel and crawl for sin, but not to save your soul.
          Pick the lock, Malcolm; pick it.

                          MALCOLM
          I want to. God knows I want to.

121   INT. MALCOLM'S CELL – NIGHT

Malcolm holds a letter in his hand. He reads it carefully. He has
read it several times before.

                    VOICE OF MALCOLM X
          I received a letter that day from the Honorable Elijah
          Muhammad. The Messenger of Allah wrote me, a nobody,
          a junkie, a pimp and a convict.

                    VOICE OF ELIJAH
          I have come to give you something which can never be
          taken from you: I bring you a sense of your own worth, the
          worth of one human being. The knowledge of self.

The room becomes transformed. It is suddenly suffused with light.
And standing in the cell with Malcolm is ELIJAH MUHAMMAD. He
has materialized, but he can be seen through. He is MALCOLM'S
HALLUCINATION.

121   CONT'D

>   VOICE OF MALCOLM X
>   It was like a blinding light and I became aware that he was
>   in the room with me. He wore a dark suit and on his face
>   I saw a pain so old and deep and black I could scarcely look
>   at him. I knew I was not dreaming. He was there.

>   ELIJAH
>   I tell you that the most dangerous creation of any society
>   in the world is the man with nothing to lose. You do not
>   need ten such men to change the world. One will do. The
>   Earth belongs to us, the Black man and whatever is
>   around it, and on it and in it. Praises are due to him for-
>   ever for bringing to us again, ourself and our property, the
>   UNIVERSE OF SUN, MOON, AND STARS.

>   VOICE OF MALCOLM X
>   And suddenly as he came, he was gone.

The hallucination disappears.

>   VOICE OF MALCOLM X (contd)
>   And then I could do it.

Malcolm goes down on his knees. There are tears in his eyes as he
begins praying:

CLOSE – MALCOLM

>   MALCOLM
>   Allah Akbar: all praise to Him who is all-seeing, all-under-
>   standing.

He continues to pray.

>   VOICE OF MALCOLM X
>   We are told that Saul, on the road to Damascus, heard the
>   words of truth, he fell from his horse. I do not liken myself
>   to Paul, but I understand. It happened to me.

122   INT. BEMBRY'S LIVING ROOM – NIGHT

A poorly furnished, small, but immaculate room. There are two
couches, a table set for eating, and, on the walls, a portrait of Elijah
and a Muslim banner. It is dinner time in a Muslim home.

SIDNEY, aged 20, a perfect specimen of the Fruit of Islam, stands
behind his chair, waiting. Their mother, LORRAINE, a woman of
Bembry's age, is seated, but she, too, awaits Bembry.

122   CONT'D

SHOT – BEMBRY

> BEMBRY
> In the name of Allah, the beneficent and the merciful to whom all praise is due.

At the window Bembry saying the evening prayers.

> BEMBRY'S VOICE
> Dear Brother Malcolm: I am back in the bosom of Islam, praise Allah . . .

He comes to the table, nods and sits. Sidney respectfully sits after him. Food is passed. It is simple fare: natural foods, milk, greens. The portions are small. They eat in silence, but there is warmth and love at this table.

> BEMBRY'S VOICE (contd)
> . . . We don't have much, but what we have is yours. Lorraine and my two sons join with me in saying that when you come out, which will not be too long, come straight to us.

123   INT. PRISON BARBER SHOP – DAY

Malcolm is reading Bembry's letter as he waits his turn. There is a WHITE CONVICT in the chair, just being finished by a WHITE BARBER – SIMMONS. A BLACK BARBER – SLIM sits by. Both are convicts. NOTE: Malcolm now wears glasses, all that reading in his badly lit cell has ruined his eyes.

> BEMBRY'S VOICE
> You write thanking me. Don't thank me. Praise Allah. He did it all.

> SIMMONS
> Next.

Malcolm starts for the chair. Simmons moves away to light a ciga-rette as Slim takes over.

> MALCOLM'S VOICE
> Dear Bembry. Please thank the Honorable Elijah Muham-mad for the money and tell him I have not written him because I have not yet proven myself.

124   INT. SMALL'S PARADISE – NIGHT

Archie and Cadillac are reading a letter they have received. They look at each other incredulously.

124 CONT'D

> MALCOLM'S VOICE
> But I have written everyone else.

125 INT. ANOTHER PRISON – DAY

Shorty is waving a letter he has received to his CELLMATE.

> SHORTY
> Look like Homey got himself a brand new hype.

126 INT. ELIJAH'S OFFICE – DAY

An immaculate room, well furnished. ELIJAH sits in a chair as Bembry stands reading Malcolm's letter.

> BEMBRY
> "I wrote the Mayor, the Governor and the President, but for some reason I haven't heard from them" . . .

Bembry laughs; Elijah smiles.

> MALCOLM'S VOICE
> Tell the Messenger of Allah that I have dedicated my life to telling the white devil the truth to his face. I greet you with the ancient words: "As Salaam Alikum."

> ELIJAH
> Wa-Alaikum Salaam.

> MALCOLM'S VOICE
> P.S. I finally worked my way through the "Z's" . . .

127 INT. PRISON CHAPEL – NIGHT

TITLE – 6 YEARS LATER

A GROUP OF PRISONERS, mostly white, but with a goodly smattering of black convicts, are listening to a lecture by CHAPLAIN GILL.

> CHAPLAIN GILL
> Are there any questions?

ANGLE. Malcolm seated next to a black convict, raises his hand. It's the only hand up. The Chaplain searches for another questioner, but there aren't any.

Pete, sitting next to Malcolm, whispers.

> PETE
> Watch out, baby, this cat is heavy on religion.

127   CONT'D

> CHAPLAIN GILL
> I see this has become a struggle between good and evil.
> Satan has a question.

There is laughter from the convicts.

> MALCOLM
> Yes it is, Chaplain Gill. But I wouldn't want to say which
> one of us is what.

Laughter, especially from the black convicts.

> CHAPLAIN GILL
> Why don't you just ask your question.

> MALCOLM
> You've been talking about the disciples. What color were
> they?

> CHAPLAIN GILL
> I don't think we know for certain.

There are reactions from the convicts. Malcolm is sharply challenging a white man about color.

> MALCOLM
> They were Hebrew, weren't they?

> CHAPLAIN GILL
> That's right.

> MALCOLM
> As Jesus was. Jesus was also a Hebrew.

> CHAPLAIN GILL
> Just what is your question?

> MALCOLM
> What color were the original Hebrews?

> CHAPLAIN GILL
> I told you we don't know for certain.

> MALCOLM
> Then we don't know that God was white.

There is a strong reaction to this.

> CHAPLAIN GILL
> Now just a moment, just a moment—

127 CONT'D

MALCOLM

But we do know that the people of that region of Asia
Minor, from the Tigris-Euphrates valley to the Mediterra-
nean, are dark-skinned people. I've studied drawings and
photographs and seen newsreels. I have never seen a na-
tive of that area who was not black.

CHAPLAIN GILL
Just what are you saying?

MALCOLM
I'm not saying anything, preacher. I'm proving to you that
God is black.

127A INSERT FLASH – A BLOND, BLUE-EYED JESUS ON THE CROSS
(Note: Try to get footage from *The Last Temptation of Christ* [Wil-
lem Dafoe])

MALCOLM'S VOICE
God is black.

128 INT. ELIJAH'S OFFICE – DAY

Malcolm opens the door, the room is dark and he sees a small,
slight man standing against the window, he doesn't move. This is
the same man who appeared in Malcolm's cell, this is the Honorable Elijah Muhammad. Malcolm slowly moves toward him; he is
completely humbled in his presence.

CLOSE – ELIJAH

He turns from the window to Malcolm.

ELIJAH
My son, you've been a thief, drug dealer and a pimp and
the world is still full of temptation. When God bragged how
faithful Job was, the devil argued that only God's protective hedge around him kept him pure, the devil said remove the hedge and he will curse his maker. Malcolm,
your hedge has been removed and I believe you will remain faithful.

CLOSE – MALCOLM

He cannot say anything and he drops his head, he is overwhelmed
with heartfelt emotion.

129   INT. BEMBRY'S LIVING ROOM – P.M.

In contrast to the peaceful family scene, the room is a beehive of
activity. Sidney is turning out leaflets on a mimeograph machine;
Lorraine is busy making up a mailing list using 3 × 5 file cards;
Bembry is recruiting on the telephone.

MALCOLM
How many you turning out?

SIDNEY
500.

MALCOLM
Make it 1000. We got a lot of fishing to do.

SIDNEY
Brother Malcolm, I want you to meet Brother Earl. He just
joined the Nation.

Earl moves toward Malcolm and extends his hands. Malcolm
shakes it firmly.

MALCOLM
We can always use another good brother.

EARL
I'm a willing servant for Allah.

129A   EXT. CHURCH – DAY

Sunday service has let out and Malcolm, Earl, and Sidney are
"fishing." They're trying to convert the Black Christians. Malcolm
speaks, while the others hand out leaflets.

MALCOLM
You think you are Christians, and yet you see your so-
called white Christian brother hanging black Christians on
trees. You say that white man loves you and yet he has
done every evil act against you. He has everything while
he is living and tells you to be a good slave and when you
die you will have more than he has in Beulah's land. We
so-called Negroes are in pitiful shape. Get off your knees
praying to a picture of a white, pale blond, and blue-eyed
Jesus. Come out of the sky. Build heaven on earth. Islam
is the black man's true religion.

130   EXT. STREET CORNER, 125TH AND SEVENTH AVENUE – DAY

Malcolm is talking to a CROWD from a ladder.

MALCOLM

And that the white man is the devil. Yes, God is black and
you are made in His image and don't know it. That's how
brainwashed you are.

The crowd is listening, caught up in Malcolm's intensity.

MALCOLM (contd)

My brothers and sisters, they tell you you will sprout
wings when you die and fly to heaven. The Honorable Elijah Muhammad tells you that's pie in the sky.

ANGLE ON SIDNEY

Amid the listeners, watching their response.

MALCOLM'S VOICE

Have you ever seen a black man who wasn't down on his
knees begging the Lord to give him in heaven what the
white devil enjoys right here on earth?

CLOSE SHOT – SEVERAL LISTENERS

They turn from Malcolm, moving a few steps away, and now are
the audience on an adjacent SPEAKER. He is a young firebrand:

SPEAKER

The Harlem Council fights for rat control, for rent control
and for community control of our schools.

PAN CONTINUES to take in ANOTHER SPEAKER, a few feet away.
WE SEE the street corner is Harlem's Hyde Park, with half a dozen
SPEAKERS haranguing the crowd with half a dozen panaceas. That
Malcolm is just one among many:

SECOND SPEAKER

If the man behind the counter ain't black, don't go in.
Boycott the man. Be black. Think black. Buy black.

ANGLE – MALCOLM

MALCOLM

Come to our Temple and hear the truth. Because, brother
and sister, you are dead. Yes you are, mentally dead,
spiritually dead, morally dead. And we are here to resur-
rect the black man back from the dead.

131   EXT. OPEN AIR "MAID'S MARKET" – DAY

A place where black women come to offer themselves for day work.
SEVERAL ARE SEEN. A WHITE WOMEN comes up to one to interview her (bargain with her). Malcolm's voice is heard before he is
seen, speaking to the women from a ladder.

> MALCOLM'S VOICE
> My beautiful sister, for you are beautiful. Beautiful be-
> cause you are black. Because black is beautiful. You work
> in the white folks' kitchen so I don't have to tell you that
> they're devils.

CLOSE – MALCOLM

> MALCOLM (contd)
> And you are putting yourselves on the auction block, let-
> ting them examine you like a horse, like a slave. The Hon-
> orable Elijah Muhammad teaches that you are black and
> should be proud . . .

FACE OF ONE BLACK WOMAN, beginning to shake her head in
accord.

132   INT. TEMPLE #7 – NIGHT

The SAME WOMAN, now at a Muslim meeting. The faces of other
listeners (from the church and from the maids' market) are scat-
tered in Malcolm's audience.

The headquarters itself shows the progress Malcolm has made. It
is better furnished, larger, and the chairs are filled. Bembry, Sidney, and Lorraine are in the back of the room, pleased with the
growth. Malcolm stands at a podium.

> MALCOLM
> We're not American, we're Africans who happen to be in
> America. We were kidnapped and brought here against
> our will from Africa. We didn't land on Plymouth Rock,
> brothers and sister. Plymouth Rock landed on us.

Reactions: laughter, interest. Ad lib "That's the truth."

> MALCOLM
> Put an end to your begging. No more "Please, Mr. White
> Man, Lawdy boss, brush me another crumb from off your
> table, kindly, sir." We are a nation, a great nation and
> don't need a thing from them.

132 CONT'D

Malcolm scanning the faces of his audience as they react. He sees
someone he knows and blurts out boyishly (and winningly):

MALCOLM (contd)
Shorty!

The crowd turns to Shorty, sitting embarrassedly in the audience.

MALCOLM (contd)
Come on up here, man, and give us some skin. Here's a
man, brothers and sisters, who shot up with me, who
robbed with me, and did time in the white devil's jailhouse.
Stand up, Shorty, and be counted—

But Shorty is trying to hide from the spotlight. Malcolm comes
down from the platform and walks to him.

MALCOLM (contd)
Folks, the brother is shy and needs special attention. So
would you excuse us, while Brothers Sidney and Earl take
up the collection.

He embraces Shorty as the crowd laughs appreciatively and Brothers Sidney and Earl have a chuckle themselves.

133 INT. MUSLIM CAFETERIA – NIGHT

Shortly and Malcolm sit at a table. Shorty has a cup of coffee in
front of him.

SHORTY
I got to hand it to you, Homey. That's the best preacher
hype I ever did hear.

MALCOLM
It isn't a hype, Shorty. And I meant what I said: join us.

SHORTY
Come on, baby. I don't pay that shit no mind.

MALCOLM
The Honorable Elijah Muhammad says you should pay it
all your mind. If you got a mind.

SHORTY
Baby, I love you. Take it easy, greasy. How about a snort?

MALCOLM
I've been clean for twelve years, Shorty.

133 CONT'D

> SHORTY
>
> You is something, Homeboy. My trouble is—I ain't had enough stuff yet, I ain't et all the ribs I want and I sure ain't had enough white tail yet.

> MALCOLM
>
> How's the rest of the gang? You seen anyone?

> SHORTY
>
> Well, Sammy's dead. Yeah, fell over in the bed with a chick twenty years younger than him. Had twenty-five grand in his pocket.

133A INSERT FLASH – Sammy, he's dead on top of TEENAGE WHORE who is screaming, trying to push that dead weight off her.

> MALCOLM
>
> How about Old Cadillac?

133B INSERT FLASH – Cadillac is an old junkie, past reclaiming, sitting staring in a MENTAL WARD, twitching, nose running.

> SHORTY'S VOICE
>
> Hooked on horse. Been in and out of Lexington five times.

> MALCOLM'S VOICE
>
> You seen Sophia?

133C INSERT FLASH – Sophia is a bored housewife, she's in the kitchen cooking while her husband hides behind the *Wall Street Journal*.

133D BACK TO THE BAR

> SHORTY
>
> I ain't seen Archie, but the vine tells it he's living some- where's in the Bronx. If you can call it living.

134 INT. A DINGY ROOM – DAY

A knock on the door rouses Archie, by now an old and dying man. All the vigor is gone, all the life has ebbed out.

> ARCHIE
>
> Git the hell away, you bitch, I'll pay you tomorrow.

Door opens, Malcolm enters.

> MALCOLM
>
> Hello, Archie.

134   CONT'D

Archie sits up from his bed and stares. He tries to bring back some
of his old juice, tries to stand up.

> ARCHIE
> My man, Red. Come on in, man.
> (then giving up)
> Hey, I can't make it.

Malcolm has to help him lie back.

> MALCOLM
> Take it easy, baby.

> ARCHIE
> That really you, Red?

The contrast is shocking: Malcolm tall and straight; Archie ruined.

> MALCOLM
> You saved my life, Archie. Running me out of Harlem.
> When I think how close we came to gunning each other
> down, I have to thank Allah.

> ARCHIE
> I wasn't gonna shoot you, baby. It was just my rep, that's
> all. And don't shit me now, but did you have that number?
> Tell me.

> MALCOLM
> I don't know. It doesn't matter. The thing is we got to get
> you back on your feet.

> ARCHIE
> Yeah. I got a couple a new angles ain't been figured yet. All
> I need's a stake and a chance—

> MALCOLM
> Can you use a few bucks? I ain't got much, but—

> ARCHIE
> No, man, I'm doing okay. Thanks.

> MALCOLM
> Take it easy. Lay down and don't think about it.

> ARCHIE
> Yeah.

> MALCOLM
> You could of been something, Archie, but the devil got to
> you.

134 CONT'D

The old man is asleep.

MALCOLM (contd)
You know all the angles except how to live.

135 EXT. A STREET IN HARLEM – NIGHT

Malcolm walks thoughtfully down the street; Archie is still on his mind, as he passes prostitute after prostitute. Once beautiful women now selling their bodies. He passes Laura, she has been turned totally out and she looks the part, there is no way he can recognize her. We do though.

CLOSE – LAURA

She has just gotten a "white john, and leads him into an alley."

MALCOLM'S VOICE
Women who could be mothers, teachers, scientists . . .

ANGLE – ALLEY

Laura kneels down to unzip her John's pants.

MALCOLM'S VOICE (contd)
Who is going to raise our children?; men who might have been astronauts, composers, engineers; Who is going to be the head of the households?—

136 INT. TEMPLE #7 – NIGHT

Malcolm is addressing a HUGE AUDIENCE. His tone is more intense, more personal than before, because of his recent encounters. In the audience, sitting with Bembry, is BETTY, a lovely dark-skinned woman. Her interest in Malcolm (true, also, for most of the other unmarried sisters) is more than religious.

MALCOLM
—and what has the white devil made of them: dead souls. Oh, my he has no conscience. He should fall on his knees and say, "My kind commits history's greatest crime against your kind every day of your life." But does he? No. He scorns you, splits your head with his nightstick and calls you nigger. If you've had it, then stand up and come forward. If not us, then who? If not now, then when?

ANGLE – THE AUDIENCE

Many stand, some walk toward the podium speaking his name: "I'm with you, Brother Malcolm," "Praise Allah," "Me, Brother Malcolm."

136 CONT'D

CLOSE – BETTY AND BEMBRY

There is applause; some of the audience get to their feet—Malcolm acknowledges their approval, trying to quiet them, but caught up in the heady excitement of leadership.

CLOSE – BETTY AND BEMBRY

Both are moved by Malcolm's performances.

> BETTY
> (whispering)
> He ought to try to make it a little easier, Brother Bembry.

> BEMBRY
> Why don't you try telling him that, Sister Betty?

137 INT. A LARGE ANTEROOM IN TEMPLE #7 – NIGHT

The Muslim movement has grown enormously. The activity in this anteroom, leading to other rooms off it, shows that. Betty and Bembry stand before a Directory announcing activities in the Temple: MONDAY – Fruit of Islam Meeting; TUESDAY – Unity Night; WEDNESDAY – Student Enrollment; THURSDAY – Muslim Girls Training; FRIDAY – General Civilization Class; SATURDAY – Swahili, etc.

A stir of people and activity as Malcolm enters the anteroom. He excuses himself from a group of MUSLIMS, making his way toward Bembry.

> MALCOLM
> (little out of breath)
> Brother Bembry, can we fix it so our loudspeaker is heard
> on the street?

> BEMBRY
> I'm sure we can. This is a new sister, Sister Betty.

Malcolm nods at her; she nods in return.

> BEMBRY (contd)
> The Sister lectures our Muslim women in hygiene and diet.

Malcolm mutters "very good," but his mind is clearly on a million other details.

> BEMBRY (contd)
> The Sister stresses care of the body and regular eating
> habits.

137   CONT'D

Malcolm is still distracted.

                    BETTY
    The Sister wonders if the Brother knows what Harriet Tub-
    man did between taking souls to the Promised Land?

Malcolm is stopped. He looks at Betty.

                    MALCOLM
                    What?

                    BETTY
                    She ate.

Malcolm laughs.

                    BETTY (contd)
    And the Sister suggests he put his actions where his mouth
    is.

Malcolm's laughter is heard, in response.

138   INT. MUSLIM CAFETERIA – NIGHT TWO-SHOT – BETTY AND MAL-
      COLM

                    MALCOLM
    Sure I'll speak to your class. But I'm a hard man on
    women. You want to know why?

                    BETTY
                    If you want to tell me.
                                        CUT TO:

138A   EXT. ELIJAH'S GARDEN – DAY

Malcolm sits next to the Honorable Elijah Muhammad. The student
and the teacher.

                    MALCOLM
                    If you want to tell me.

                    ELIJAH
    Women are deceitful. They are untrustworthy flesh. I've
    seen too many men ruined or tied down or messed up by
    women.
                                        CUT BACK TO:

138B   BETTY AND MALCOLM

Betty says nothing, she merely pushes the salad plate a little toward him. The food has thus far gone untouched. Malcolm continues.

138B   CONT'D

CLOSE – MALCOLM

> MALCOLM
> Women talk too much. To tell a woman not to talk is like telling Jesse James not to carry a gun or a hen not to cackle. And Samson, the strongest man that ever lived, was destroyed by the woman who slept in his arms.

> BETTY
> Shall I tell my sisters that we oppose marriage?

CUT TO:

138C   CLOSE – ELIJAH

> ELIJAH
> No. We are not Catholic priests. We do not practice celibacy. If a woman is the right height for a man, the right complexion, if her age is half the man's plus seven, if she understands that man's essential nature is strong and woman's weak, if she loves children, can cook, sew and stay out of trouble—

CUT TO:

138D   CLOSE – BETTY

> BETTY
> I think you've made your points, Brother Malcolm.

> MALCOLM
> What points?

> BETTY
> That you haven't time for either marriage or eating—

Malcolm chuckles a bit.

> BETTY (contd)
> —and that women aren't the only ones who talk a lot.

Now he bursts out laughing.

CLOSE – BROTHERS SIDNEY AND EARL

They are alarmed at Brother Minister's behavior.

TWO-SHOT – BETTY AND MALCOLM

> BETTY
> If you'll start eating, there is a question I have. Go ahead. Start.

138D CONT'D

He takes a forkful of the salad.

> BETTY (contd)
> Considering today's standards of animal raising and curing meats, I don't fully understand the restriction on pork.

> MALCOLM
> Let me explain. No. I'll do better than that. I'll show it to you. Scientifically. But it's demonstration purely in the interest of science, you understand?

> BETTY'S VOICE
> Yes, I understand, Brother Malcolm. Purely scientific.

139 INT. MUSEUM OF NATURAL HISTORY – DAY

Before a comparative evolutionary display showing the skeletons of various animals, Malcolm is holding forth. Betty is dressed in a vivid, becoming red dress.

> MALCOLM
> Notice especially the claw, the jaw and the skull formation. This is the rat. This the mole. Here you have the aardvark and the boar . . .

CLOSE ON THE SKELETONS

> MALCOLM'S VOICE
> . . . All members of the pig-rodent family.

> BETTY
> I see your point.

> MALCOLM
> So it is not a matter of the breeding conditions or preparation of the meat. The meat itself is foul.

ANGLE. As they saunter out, passing the huge skeletons of prehistoric animals now.

> BETTY
> Could we sit down someplace?

> MALCOLM
> I'm sorry. I've had you on your feet for hours.

139   CONT'D

                           BETTY
          You've been on your feet for days. And didn't even finish
          your salad.

140   INT. SODA FOUNTAIN – DAY

                           WAITER
          You're the strawberry soda and you're the hot fudge sun-
          dae.

He plunks down the order before Betty and Malcolm. Malcolm
takes a long, long satisfying pull on his straw. Then he sighs:

                           MALCOLM
          That's something I haven't done in fifteen years.

                           BETTY
                           What?

                           MALCOLM
          Sat down with a pretty girl and had an ice cream soda.

                           BETTY
                     How do you like it?

                           MALCOLM
                        Delicious.

She laughs. He blushes.

                       MALCOLM (contd)
                 Let's talk about you for a change.

                           BETTY
                There's nothing to talk about.

                           MALCOLM
          Oh, yes, there is. I know a lot about you. Brother Bembry
          briefed me.

                           BETTY
               Oh? Purely scientific interest I'm sure.

                           MALCOLM
                         (a beat)
          You're from Detroit, near where I come from. You majored
          in education at Tuskegee. You're studying nursing and
          having trouble with your family.

140 CONT'D

> BETTY
> I can handle it.

> MALCOLM
> They want you to quit the Muslims or they won't pay your tuition, isn't that it?

> BETTY
> You have enough worries of your own.

> MALCOLM
> No, good Sisters are rare. We need every one. Tell me something: how tall are you?

> BETTY
> Why do you ask?

> MALCOLM
> Just an idle question.

> BETTY
> If it's just idle, I won't answer it.

She takes a bite of her sundae.

> BETTY (contd)
> But Brother Bembry says I'm tall enough for a tall man.

> MALCOLM
> How old are you, Betty?

> BETTY
> There's a few things you don't know about women, Brother Malcolm. They're possessive and vain.

> MALCOLM
> Are you?

> BETTY
> And dogged when I set my mind to something.

> MALCOLM
> What have you set your mind to?

> BETTY
> Being a good Muslim, a good nurse and a good wife.

Malcolm takes a good look at the lovely woman in front of him, then a long sip from his ice cream soda.

> SIDNEY'S VOICE
> Brother Malcolm.

140 CONT'D

Betty sees him first.

> BETTY
> It's Sidney.

ANGLE. As Sidney runs to them at the table:

> SIDNEY
> Brother Johnson was attacked by the cops.

> A MAN'S VOICE
> There was a scuffle. The Brother was watching.

141 EXT. SIDE STREET IN HARLEM – P.M.

Malcolm listening as SEVERAL WITNESSES simultaneously describe the attack. A small angry CROWD has gathered. The most animated one is BENJAMIN, a very dark young black teenager, we will soon meet him later.

> BENJAMIN
> The cop says, "Move on."

> MAN
> The Brother didn't scatter fast enough for the ofay.

CLOSE – MALCOLM

> BENJAMIN
> Crack. He bled like a stuck hog.

> MAN
> Watcha gonna do?

> VOICE FROM THE CROWD
> (deprecatingly)
> He'll rap a little. He's a Muslim. And make a speech.

> ANOTHER VOICE FROM CROWD
> Muslims talk a good game, but they never do nothing, unless somebody bothers Muslims.

Malcolm's face goes taut. He nods sharply at Sidney, as Benjamin watches them both.

> MALCOLM'S VOICE
> I demand to see Brother Johnson.

142 INT. POLICE STATION – LATE P.M.

Malcolm facing a DESK SERGEANT, TWO UNIFORMED COPS and a PLAINCLOTHESMAN off to one side.

142 CONT'D

> SERGEANT
> Who the hell are you?

> MALCOLM
> I'm from Muslim Temple 7.

> COP
> Never heard of you.

> MALCOLM
> Where is he?

The police respond with a squeeze play intended to intimidate Malcolm:

> SERGEANT
> Nobody here by that name.

> PLAINCLOTHES
> What's your name, feller?

He feels the power play and stiffens in resistance.

> MALCOLM
> I'm Minister Malcolm X. Two witnesses saw him brought in. He was not brought out.

> PLAINCLOTHES
> You heard the Sergeant. Outside.

Malcolm stands his ground coolly.

> MALCOLM
> Take a look out that window. I intend to see Brother Johnson.

The cops eye each other. Plainclothes walks to the window.

143 EXT. THE STREET OUTSIDE – LATE P.M.

Across from the station is a phalanx of some FIFTY MEN of the Fruit of Islam. All are dressed in dark suits with white shirts. They stand in military formation: eyes forward, every face burning. People from the neighborhood have formed a crowd behind and around them. WE MAKE OUT Benjamin among the crowd.

143A INT. – POLICE STATION – NIGHT

> PLAINCLOTHES
> Who the hell are they?

143A   CONT'D

> MALCOLM
> Brothers of Brother Johnson.

> PLAINCLOTHES
> Eddie, let's see that blotter.

TWO-SHOT – FAVOR MALCOLM

As the cops examine the police blotter.

> SERGEANT
> Yeah. We got a Muslim. The relief must of put it down.

> PLAINCLOTHES
> But you can't see him. You ain't his lawyer.

> SERGEANT
> No lawyer, no see.

> MALCOLM
> Until I'm satisfied Brother Johnson is receiving proper medical attention, no one will move.

Cops eye each other. Plainclothes nods slightly, he has to give in, Malcolm is not playing.

144   INT. A LOCKUP – SAME

The back of Malcolm's head, as he examines Brother Johnson. As he comes up OUT OF FRAME, WE SEE that Johnson has been badly beaten.

> MALCOLM
> (shaking)
> Only a pig could do a thing like that.

> PLAINCLOTHES
> Watch your tongue, boy.

> MALCOLM
> Don't you call me boy, you pig. Letting a man bleed like that.

Sergeant puts a restraining hand on Plainclothes.

> MALCOLM (contd)
> That man belongs in a hospital. Get an ambulance. Now!

145   EXT. THE STREET – LATER (DARKER)

As Johnson's body, on a stretcher, is hurried into an ambulance. The crowd has grown in proportions. There are ad libs: "Goddam

145 CONT'D

pigs,'' ''Damn police brutality,'' ''Least they got him out of the meat house.''

Malcolm with the Sergeant and a LIEUTENANT, as the ambulance pulls away.

> LIEUTENANT
> All right, break it up. You got what you wanted.

> MALCOLM
> I'm not satisfied.

Malcolm starts walking down the center of the street, after the ambulance.

> MALCOLM (contd)
> To the hospital.

The Fruit of Islam fall in behind him, marching slowly. It takes on the start of a march as the neighborhood people fall in behind them. People (especially kids) race with them on the street and on the sidewalk.

ANGLE – BENJAMIN

Benjamin fights his way through the crowd trying to walk beside Malcolm, the Brothers in the Fruit stop him and Benjamin drops back.

146 EXT. LENOX AVENUE – NIGHT

Now the march has taken over the broad avenue. COPS are forced to redirect traffic, holding up crosstown cars as the group walks solemnly by. The people walking behind have swelled it to a huge demonstration. Their faces reflect their anger and their satisfaction that, for once, something is being done about what has happened.

147 EXT. HARLEM HOSPITAL – NIGHT

LONG SHOT SHOWS the Muslim men in perfect order, calm with their arms folded across their chests, waiting. Their eyes are on Malcolm as he walks toward the hospital entrance.

SHOTS

—of the growing crowd.

—of the nervous cops, including some big brass.

147 CONT'D

—of kids watching from a rooftop.

—of Benjamin trying to emulate the Fruit of Islam.

148 EXT. OUTSIDE HARLEM HOSPITAL – NIGHT

Malcolm is standing in front of the Fruit of Islam men, as HIGH-RANKING POLICE OFFICER GREEN comes over.

> CAPTAIN GREEN
> All right, that's enough. I want these people moved out of here.

> MALCOLM
> They're all disciplined men. They're doing nothing except waiting.

SHOT

The unruly crowd behind the Fruit of Islam. They are restive, milling, ugly.

> CAPTAIN GREEN
> What about them?

> MALCOLM
> That's your headache, Captain. And if he dies, I pity you.

149 EXT. OUTSIDE HARLEM HOSPITAL – NIGHT

> DOCTOR
> He'll live. He's getting the best care we can give.

> MALCOLM
> Thank you, Doctor.

> DOCTOR
> I had to put a plate in his head.

> MALCOLM
> (to Captain)
> You bastards.

> CAPTAIN GREEN
> All right, okay. Now disperse this mob.

MEDIUM SHOT – MALCOLM, FRUIT OF ISLAM AND CROWD

It's clear the decision is in one man's hands, Malcolm's.

CLOSE SHOT – MALCOLM

He makes a gesture with his hand, the Fruit of Islam disperse.

149   CONT'D

ANGLE. People moving away, going home. Only one person remains from the Fruit of Islam and the crowd, it's Benjamin.

CLOSE – CAPTAIN GREEN

> CAPTAIN GREEN
> That's too much power for one man to have.

149A   INT. MUSLIM CAFETERIA – NIGHT

Everyone is in a somber mood over the evening's events.

ANGLE – TABLE

Malcolm sits with Brothers Earl and Sidney.

> SIDNEY
> Brother Minister, we need to strike back.

> BROTHER EARL
> Put fear into those devils.

> MALCOLM
> I want to also, but until we are instructed by the Messenger to do so, we will just wait and pray.

> BROTHER EARL
> I'm tired of praying.

> MALCOLM
> That's enough, Brother Earl.

ANGLE – ENTRANCE

Benjamin comes into the cafeteria and everyone looks at him. He sees Malcolm sitting and moves toward his table.

ANGLE – TABLE

Brothers Sidney and Earl get up to intercept him but Malcolm waves him through. Benjamin stands.

> MALCOLM
> Sit down, son.

Malcolm pours some cream into his cup of black coffee, then also some white sugar.

> MALCOLM (contd)
> There is only one thing I like integrated. My coffee.

Benjamin laughs.

149A   CONT'D

> MALCOLM (contd)
> What can I do for you?

> BENJAMIN
> Mr. X, I was out there tonight. I saw what you did. I want
> to be a Muslim. I ain't never seen a Negro stand up to the
> police like that.

ANGLE – SIDNEY AND EARL

They exchange dubious looks.

> MALCOLM
> Do you know what it means to be a true Muslim?

Benjamin hesitates.

> MALCOLM (contd)
> Do you?

> BENJAMIN
> Not exactly, but I want to be one, like you.

> MALCOLM
> I admire your enthusiasm but you should never join any
> organization without first checking it out thoroughly.

Benjamin is crushed and he starts to get up.

> MALCOLM (contd)
> We need more young warriors like yourself, stick around
> and we shall see if your heart is true.

> BENJAMIN
> Mr. X, I won't make you out a liar.

150   INT. TEMPLE #1 – DETROIT – DAY

CLOSE – NEWSPAPER HEADLINE *(DAILY NEWS)*

MALCOLM X WINS $70,000 JUDGMENT FOR BEATEN NEGRO

An AIDE of Elijah puts down the newspaper and shakes Malcolm's
hand.

> AIDE
> The Honorable Elijah Muhammad would like to see you
> now.

151 INT. ELIJAH'S OFFICE – DAY

Elijah is sweeping the floor with a plain hand broom. Malcolm enters the room, is surprised and waits at the door. The two are alone together.

ELIJAH
If I surprise you, let me explain. Menial work teaches us humility.

MALCOLM
Let me do it then.

ELIJAH
No, each of us must relearn that work is the only worthwhile thing. Allah has given you a great gift. Use it wisely, never forgetting that we are nothing, while He is all.

MALCOLM
Allah Akbar.

The sweeping done, they stand together near a table at a window.

ELIJAH
Tonight I shall introduce you as my National Representative. It will be a difficult task. Your assignment is to build temples all over this nation. More work than you have ever done in your life and you will be in the public eye. My son beware of those cameras, they are just as bad as a narcotic.

ANGLE – AIDES and OTHERS come into the room now. They are listening.

ELIJAH (contd)
Yes, the white devil will watch your every step. Even your own Brothers will become jealous, and hostile, go slowly. So I offer you a parable—regarding your work.

Elijah picks up a glass and sets it before Malcolm.

ELIJAH (contd)
Here is a glass, dirty and its water foul. If you offer it to the people and they have no choice, they must drink out of it. But if you present them with this glass—

He is holding a clean glass, with clear water in it.

ELIJAH (contd)
—and let them make their decision, they will choose the pure vessel. Islam is the only religion which addresses the

151 CONT'D
ELIJAH (contd)

needs and problems of the so-called Negro, especially in the ghettos—Islam is the only way out from drugs, crime, unemployment, prostitution, alcohol, gambling, fornication and adultery.

Elijah holds up the clear glass.

VOICE OF MALCOLM X

This sweet, gentle man gave me the truth from his own mouth. And I adored him, in the sense of the Latin root of the word. Adorare, to worship and to fear. He was the first man I ever feared—not fear such as the one has of a gun— but the fear one has of the power of the sun, I pledged myself to him, even if it cost me my life.

152 INT. A HOSPITAL WARD – DAY

Betty is administering to a PATIENT, as a phone is heard ringing. It's answered. ANOTHER NURSE motions Betty to the phone. She finishes with her patient and goes quickly.

BETTY
Hello.

MALCOLM'S VOICE
Sister Betty?

BETTY
Yes.

153 EXT. A PAY PHONE AT A GAS STATION – DAY

MALCOLM
I'm in Detroit.

BETTY
I know.

MALCOLM
At a gas station.
(a beat)
Will you marry me?

BETTY
Yes.

MALCOLM
Did you hear what I said?

153   CONT'D

> BETTY
> Yes I did. Did you hear my answer?

> MALCOLM
> I think so. Can you catch a plane?

> BETTY
> Yes. Did you eat?

> MALCOLM
> I love you.

154   INT. BEMBRY'S BEDROOM – NIGHT

Betty and Malcolm sit on the floor in the dimlit room, very close.

> MALCOLM
> It won't be easy.

> BETTY
> Just hold me.

> MALCOLM
> It will be rough.

> BETTY
> Hush your mouth.

> MALCOLM
> I'll be away alot.

> BETTY
> You're with me even when you're away.

He embraces her. Then Betty laughs.

> BETTY (contd)
> I never told you, but when I first saw you on the podium,
> cleaning your glasses, I felt sorry for you. Nobody as
> young as you should be that serious. But I don't think that
> anymore.

> MALCOLM
> What do you think?

> BETTY
> The simplest thing in the world: I want to have a lot of
> babies with you. Dear Heart, I love you.

Full embrace.

154 CONT'D

BEMBRY'S VOICE
We're waiting on you folks. You trying to starve us?

155 INT. BEMBRY'S LIVING ROOM – NIGHT

Malcolm has just cut the cake and handed a slice to Betty. Amid laughter and great warmth, Sidney unfurls the front page of the *Messenger,* the Muslim newspaper. Headline reads: "MALCOLM X WEDS BETTY SAUNDERS." Betty kisses her husband and Bembry, Lorraine, Earl, Sidney, Peter and VARIOUS BROTHERS AND SISTERS applaud.

We notice the subtle change in the apartment: it is more comfortable; there is even evidence of some small luxury: a TV set, a new settee, etc.

156 EXT. RALLY – HARLEM – DAY

Malcolm is speaking to a GOOD SIZED AUDIENCE:

MALCOLM
I must emphasize at the outstart, that the Honorable Elijah Muhammad is not a politician, so I'm not here this afternoon as a Republican, nor a Democrat, not as a Mason nor an Elk, not as a Christian nor a Jew, not as a Catholic nor a Protestant, not as a Baptist nor a Methodist, not even as an American. For if I was an American the problem that confronts our people today would not exist. So I stand here as what I was when I was born: A BLACK MAN!

CROWD REACTIONS

MALCOLM (contd)
Before there were any such things as Democrats or Republicans, we were black. Before there were any such things as Masons or Elks, were black. Before there were any such things as Jews or Christians we were black people. In fact long before there was ever any such place as America, we were black people . . . And after America has long passed from the scene there will still be BLACK PEOPLE.

CLOSE – BENJAMIN

He is neatly dressed in white shirt, jacket and tie, a fine young Muslim.

BENJAMIN 2X
Take your time.

157 INT. CHICAGO TEMPLE – NIGHT

The Honorable Elijah Muhammad sits on the stage to the right of Malcolm. This is a larger audience.

MALCOLM

What kind of black people does the Honorable Elijah Muhammad speak for? Black people who are jobless . . . the black masses who are poor, hungry, and angry, the black masses who are dissatisfied with the slums and ghettos in which we have been forced to live . . . the black masses who are tired of listening to the promises of white politicians to correct the miserable living conditions that exist in our community . . . the black masses that are sick of the inhuman acts of bestial brutality practiced by these semi-savage white policemen that patrol our community, like the occupation forces of a conquering enemy army . . . the black masses who are fed up with the anemic, Uncle Tom leadership set up by the white man to act as a spokesman for our people and to KEEP US SATISFIED AND PACIFIED WITH NOTHING!

CROWD – REACTIONS

CLOSE – MALCOLM

MALCOLM

If the black man cannot go back to his own people and his own land, Elijah Muhammad is asking that a part of the United States be separated and given to the Muslims so they can live separately.

CLOSE – ELIJAH

MALCOLM (contd)

The Honorable Elijah Muhammad is the only man the white people can deal with in the solving of problems of the so-called Negro . . .

CLOSE – MALCOLM

MALCOLM (contd)

as Elijah Muhammad knows his problems.

158 INT. BETTY'S BEDROOM – NIGHT

A modest room. She is rocking a cradle with her foot as she writes:

BETTY'S VOICE

Attallah is fine. Our firstborn is an angel and a beauty. And misses you as I do. But the news that you've dedicated four new temples is almost as good as having you with us.

158A INT. HOTEL ROOM – NIGHT

Malcolm sits in front of a television screen and watches the evening news. The following speech will be INTERCUT with

A SERIES OF OLD NEWSREEL FOOTAGE – BLACK & WHITE

(newsclips from Birmingham, Selma, Mississippi, and elsewhere):

158B —POLICE using dogs against DEMONSTRATORS.

158C —The Reverend Dr. Martin Luther King marching.

158D —Cattle prods used against MEN, WOMEN and CHILDREN.

158E —The Reverend Dr. Martin Luther King singing "We Shall Overcome."

158F —PREGNANT WOMAN knocked down by high-pressure water hoses.

158G —The Reverend Dr. Martin Luther King leading a crowd in prayer.

158H Students sitting in at a counter.

158I The smoldering ruins of Birmingham's 16th St. Baptist church.

158J

> MALCOLM/HIS VOICE
>
> The white people who are guilty of white supremacy try and hide their own guilt by accusing the Honorable Elijah Muhammad of teaching black supremacy when he tries to uplift the mentality, the social, and economic condition of black people in this country. And the Jews, who have been guilty of exploiting the black people economically, civilly, and otherwise, hide their guilt by accusing the Honorable Elijah Muhammad of being anti-Semitic simply because he teaches our people to go into business for ourselves and trying to take over the economic leadership in our own community. The black people in this country have been the victims of violence at the hands of the white man for 400 years, and following the ignorant Negro preachers, we have thought that it was God-like to turn the other cheek to the brute that was brutalizing us. 100 years ago they use to put on a white sheet and use a bloodhound against Negroes. Today they've taken off sheets and put on police uniforms, they've traded in the bloodhounds for police dogs. And just as Uncle Tom back during slavery used to keep the Negroes from resisting the bloodhounds or resisting the Ku Klux Klan by telling them to love their enemy

158J CONT'D

> MALCOLM/HIS VOICE (contd)
> or pray for those who use them as spitefully today. The
> Honorable Elijah Muhammad is showing black people that
> just as the white man and every other person on this earth
> has God given rights, natural rights, civil rights, and any
> other kind of rights that you can think of when it comes to
> defending himself.

159

A-C INT. TV STUDIO

CLOSE SHOT – MALCOLM'S FACE

With a studio mike around his neck, he's on a panel show.

ANGLE – MODERATOR

> MODERATOR
> Mr. X, before we start our discussion tonight The Black
> Muslims: Hate Mongers, would you mind explaining for us
> the meaning of your name, which is the letter X.

ANGLE – PANEL

Opposing Malcolm is DR. PAYSON, a NAACP-type NEGRO.

CLOSE – MALCOLM

> MALCOLM
> Yes sir. As you know, during slavery time, the slavemas-
> ters named most of the so-called Negroes in America after
> themselves. Mr. Elijah Muhammad teaches us once you
> come into the knowledge of Islam, you replace your slave
> name with an X. Since we've been disconnected, cut off
> from our Eastern culture for so long that we don't know
> the names we originally had, we will use X until we get
> back to the East.

ANGLE – MODERATOR

> MODERATOR
> Thank you. Now Dr. Payson.

CLOSE – DR. PAYSON

> DR. PAYSON
> Mr. X is a demagogue. He has no place to go, so he exagger-
> ates. He's a disservice to every good law abiding Negro in
> the country. Can I ask you a question?

ANGLE – MALCOLM

                              MALCOLM
                         Please, go ahead.

CLOSE – DR. PAYSON

                             DR. PAYSON
            Mr. Malcolm X, why do you teach black supremacy? Why
            do you teach hate?

CLOSE – MALCOLM

                              MALCOLM
            For the *white* man to ask the black man if he hates him is
            just like the rapist asking the raped, or the wolf asking the
            sheep, "Do you hate me!" The white man is in no moral
            position to accuse anyone of hate.

ANGLE – PANEL

                             MODERATOR
            Certainly Mr. X, you must admit there has been progress.

                              MALCOLM
            I'll talk about "progress" in a minute, but let me finish
            with my brother.

Malcolm gestures to the Negro panelist, the BLACK MEMBERS of
the TV audience are lapping it up. Betty and Earl also sit in the TV
studio audience.

                          MALCOLM (contd)
            Stop me if I'm wrong. I "polarize the community." I "er-
            roneously appraise the racial picture."

                             DR. PAYSON
                        You put it very well.

                              MALCOLM
            You left one phrase out. Another educated Kneegrew said
            to me and I quote: "Brother Malcolm oversimplifies the
            dynamic interstices of the Negro subculture." Would you
            agree?

                             DR. PAYSON
                            Entirely.

                              MALCOLM
            Well, I have this to say. Do you know what a Negro with a
            B.A., an M.A. and a Ph.D. is called—by the white man? I'll
            tell you? He's called a nigger.

159, A-C   CONT'D

There is some blanching and guffawing from the audience. The moderator is totally embarrassed, Betty roars.

> MALCOLM (contd)
> And I'm not finished. To understand this man—

He points a sharp finger at the Negro Panelist.

> MALCOLM (contd)
> —you must know that historically there are two kinds of slaves. House Negroes and Field Negroes. The house Negro lived in the big house; he dressed pretty good; he ate pretty good and he loved the master. Yeah, he loved him more than the master loved himself. If the master's house caught fire, he'd be the first to put the blaze out. If the master got sick, he'd say: "What's a matter, boss; we sick?" WE sick! If someone said to him, "Let's run away and escape. Let's separate." He'd say, "man are you crazy? What's better than what I got here?" That was the House Negro. In those days he was called the House Nigger. Well, that's what we call them today because we still got a lot of House Niggers running around.

There is applause from the blacks in the audience. Moderator tries to regain control.

159D   INT. ELIJAH'S OFFICE – DAY

CLOSE – THE HONORABLE ELIJAH MUHAMMAD

He is enjoying this display by his prize student, the CAMERA PANS to a CLOSE SHOT of BEMBRY and the same cannot be said.

159E   BACK TO STUDIO

> MODERATOR
> I think, perhaps, Dr. Payson has something to—

> MALCOLM
> Don't you want to hear about the Field Nigger?

> DR. PAYSON
> Let him finish.

> MALCOLM
> Thank you. Now the Negro in the field caught hell all day long. He was beaten by the master; he lived in a shack, wore castoff clothes and hated his master. If the house

159E   CONT'D

MALCOLM (contd)

caught fire, he'd pray for a wind. If the master got sick, he'd pray that he'd die. And if you said to him, "Let's go, let's separate"; he'd yell, "Yeah, man, any place is better than this." You've got a lot of Field Negroes in America today. I'm one.

BROTHER BENJAMIN
Tell it.

MALCOLM

—there's another one. The majority of black Americans today are Field Negroes. They don't talk about OUR progress, about OUR government, OUR navy, OUR astronauts. Hell, they won't even let you near the plant.

159F   INT. ELIJAH'S OFFICE – DAY

Bembry turns off the TV set and he commences to plant the seeds of "betrayal."

CLOSE – BEMBRY

BEMBRY

Your holy apostle, dear Messenger, I am your true servant and the brothers asked me to tell you Malcolm is getting too much press. The brothers think he thinks *he* is the Nation of Islam, that he has aspirations to lead the Nation. It was you who made Malcolm the man he is. You lifted him out of the darkness.

CLOSE – ELIJAH.

ELIJAH

Go and tell the brothers what Brother Minister is doing, has done, has been of great benefit to the Nation.

CLOSER – BEMBRY .

BEMBRY
Great benefit for himself.

159G   BRIEF MONTAGE. *THE RISE OF MALCOLM X*

EXT. STREET – HARLEM – DAY

Malcolm is walking the streets of Harlem like he is campaigning for office. He has Brothers Sidney, Earl, and Benjamin at his side, a CROWD follows him. Malcolm sees a WINO.

159G   CONT'D

                      MALCOLM
Brother Man, put that bottle down, take that poison away
from your lips. That's what the devil wants you to do, stay
high, out of your natural mind. I know, I've been there.

The wino looks at Malcolm and continues to drink his wine.

159H   —Malcolm emerges from a doorway to be met by an army of TV
REPORTERS armed with microphones. He walks; they follow.

159I   —Malcolm walking in Harlem, urging people to lift themselves up,
come to the meetings, etc.

159J   INT. TEMPLE #7

Malcolm sits with Benjamin.

                      MALCOLM
It's time you've received your X. But first you must copy
this letter, exactly as I give it to you; down to the dotted
"i's," crossed "t's," everything. And you must go on a
fast, just water and juices, that's it.

CLOSE – BENJAMIN

He takes the letter from Malcolm and looks at it.

                      BENJAMIN
            I'll have it tomorrow.

                      MALCOLM
Brother Benjamin, do not rush, it has to be exact.

—Benjamin goes off in a corner and very quickly copies the letter,
he's so anxious.

—Benjamin hands Malcolm his letter, Malcolm shakes his head
and hands it back, it's not exact.

159K   EXT. STREET – HARLEM – DAY

Malcolm is talking to a group of PEOPLE who are having a rent
strike.

                      MALCOLM
When you live in a poor neighborhood, you're living in an
area where you have poor schools.

159L   CUTAWAY TO MALCOLM AND BENJAMIN

Malcolm hands him back his letter again. The fast is getting to
Benjamin.

159L   CONT'D

> MALCOLM (contd)
> When you have poor schools you have poor teachers.
> When you have poor teachers, you get a poor education.

159M   CUTAWAYS TO THE DESPAIR OF HARLEM – SLUMS, TENE-
MENTS, GARBAGE, RATS

> MALCOLM (contd)
> Poor education, you only work on poor paying jobs and
> that enables you to live again in a poor neighborhood.

159N   CUTAWAY TO BLACK FACES

> MALCOLM (contd)
> So it's a very vicious cycle. We've got to break it.

159O   INT. MUSLIM CAFETERIA

Benjamin weakly walks toward Malcolm and gives him his letter,
which he takes. The fast is wearing him out.

CLOSE – MALCOLM

Malcolm is inspecting it.

CLOSE – BENJAMIN

His face is filled with apprehension.

ANGLE – MALCOLM AND BENJAMIN

> MALCOLM
> You are now Benjamin 2X.

> BENJAMIN 2X
> All praises are due to Allah. Thank you, Brother Minister.

> MALCOLM
> Come, sit with us.

ANGLE – TABLE

Benjamin 2X sits with Malcolm and Brothers Earl and Sidney.

> MALCOLM
> We are now sitting with Brother Benjamin 2X.

> EARL
> Allah Akbar.

> SIDNEY
> You will be good.

1590   CONT'D

> BENJAMIN 2X
> Brother Minister, can I have something to eat?

Everyone laughs.

> MALCOLM
> Let's get this man some food.

160   EXT. HARVARD SQUARE – DAY

A CROWD OF STUDENTS outside the Law School. The setting is the same as the last time we saw Malcolm and Shorty here, except now the students part for him. Malcolm walks slowly toward the entrance, looking up at the Latin inscription of the building when he is stopped by a WHITE COED.

> COED
> Mr. X, I've read some of your speeches and I honestly believe a lot of what you say has truth to it. I have a good heart. I'm a good person despite my whiteness. What can the good white people like myself, who are not prejudiced, or racist, what can we do to help the cause?

CLOSE – MALCOLM

He stares at her.

> MALCOLM
> Nothing!

CLOSE – COED

She is absolutely crushed and runs away in tears.

161   INT. HARVARD LAW SCHOOL – DAY

Speaking to a packed STUDENT AUDIENCE.

> MALCOLM
> . . . My high school was the black ghetto of Roxbury. My college was the streets of Harlem, and I took my masters in prison. If you look out the window—

161A   SHOT MALCOLM'S OLD GANG HANGOUT

> MALCOLM'S VOICE
> —you can see my burglary hangout. I lived like an animal. Had it not been for the Honorable Elijah Muhammad I would surely be in an insane asylum or dead.

161A CONT'D

ANGLE – The audience carefully listening.

MALCOLM
Mr. Muhammad is trying to get us on God's side, so God
will be on our side to help us fight our battles. When
Negroes stop getting drunk, stop being addicted to drugs,
stop fornicating and committing adultery. When we get off
the welfare, then we'll be MEN. Earn what you need for
your family, then your family respects you. They'll be
proud to say "That's my father." She's proud to say
"That's my husband . . ." Father means you're taking care
of those children. Just 'cause you made them that don't
mean you're a father. Anybody can make a baby, but anybody can't take care of them. Anyone can go and get a
woman but anybody can't take care of a woman. This is the
type of teaching that the honorable Elijah Muhammad
teaches us so we can build the moral fiber of our people.

SHOT OF REPORTERS IN AUDIENCE.

Beginning to scribble furiously.

MALCOLM
I can see the gentlemen of the press, also the FBI and CIA
are with us. Get it straight 'cuz if I said, "Mary had a little
lamb," they'd write Malcolm X lampoons poor Mary.

Loud laughter from the audience. But this response is overwhelmed by the response of ANOTHER, LARGER AUDIENCE.

162 INT. MONSTER RALLY – NIGHT

Malcolm is talking before an all-black audience. It is the largest
rally yet; the hall is packed to the rafters.

MALCOLM
We have built temples in Boston, in Detroit, in Atlanta,
Philadelphia, Washington—100 temples in fifty states.
From a handful we have grown to scores of thousands.

VARIOUS SHOTS OF THE RALLY

HAWKERS setting *The Messenger,* faces of Fruit of Islam near the
podium; Lorraine, Sidney, Earl, Benjamin, and Baines. For the first
time a new note is seen in Baines' face: reserve bordering on re-
sentment. When others around him cheer Malcolm, Baines is cool.
Sidney notices this from his father, but makes no comment.

162 CONT'D

MALCOLM/HIS VOICE

The Honorable Elijah Muhammad teaches us that God is
now about to establish a kingdom on this earth based on
brotherhood and against peace, his history on this earth
has proved that. Nowhere in history has he been brotherly
toward anyone. The only time he has been brotherly toward you is when he can use you, when he can exploit you,
when he can oppress you, when you will submit to him.
And since his own history makes him unqualified to be an
inhabitant or a citizen in a kingdom of brotherhood, the
Honorable Elijah Muhammad teaches us that God is about
to eliminate that particular race from this earth. So since
they are due for elimination, we don't want to be with
them.

ANGLE – CROWD

CLOSE – MALCOLM

MALCOLM (contd)

If the so-called Negro were American citizens we wouldn't
have a race problem. If the Emancipation Proclamation
was authentic, you wouldn't have a race problem. If the
13th, 14th, and 15th amendments to the Constitution was
authentic, you wouldn't have a race problem. If the Supreme Court desegregation decision was authentic, you
wouldn't have a race problem. All of this is hypocrisy.
These Negro leaders have been telling the white man everything is all right, everything is under control. And
they've been telling the white man that Mr. Muhammad is
wrong, don't listen to him. But everything Mr. Muhammad
has been saying is going to come to pass is now coming to
pass and now the Negro leaders are standing up saying
that we are about to a racial explosion. We're going to have
a racial explosion and that's more dangerous than an
atomic explosion.

ANGLE – MALCOLM

MALCOLM (contd)

It's going to explode because black people are dissatisfied.
They're dissatisfied now not only with the white man, but
with these Negroes who have been sitting around here
posing as leaders and spokesmen for black people. Anytime you put too many sparks around a powder keg, the

162 CONT'D

MALCOLM (contd)

thing is going to explode and if the thing that explodes is
still inside the house, then the house will be destroyed. So
the Honorable Elijah Muhammad is telling the white man
get this powder keg out of your house, let the black people
in this country separate from him while there's still time.
And if the black man is allowed to separate and go on onto
some land of his own, where he can solve his problems,
then there won't be any explosion. COMPLETE SEPARA-
TION IS THE ONLY SOLUTION TO THE BLACK AND WHITE
PROBLEM IN THIS COUNTRY!!!

ANGLE – CROWD

A WAVE OF CHEERS AS PEOPLE EXPLODE.

163 INT. AN ANTEROOM OF THE RALLY – NIGHT

The rally is over. A small room packed with PEOPLE congratulat-
ing Malcolm, trying to touch him. He is the hero of the hour. Sidney, Earl, and Benjamin with him, enjoying the accolades and trying to help Malcolm make his way out. Bembry stands apart,
removed and silent.

MALCOLM
Thank you, Brother; Sister, how are you?

SIDNEY
Please make way, please—

ANGLE. A WELL-KNOWN PERSONALITY (DICK GREGORY) is at
the door. He and Malcolm know each other well. Malcolm extends
a palm, but Gregory doesn't slap it.

GREGORY
Can I ask you something?

MALCOLM
Sure, man.

GREGORY
Are you Elijah's pimp?

MALCOLM
What?

GREGORY
(scornfully)
"His greatest greatness."

163   CONT'D

> MALCOLM
> Say what you're saying.

> GREGORY
> If you don't know, man, then I feel sorriest for you.

164   INT. MALCOLM'S HOME – NIGHT

Betty, pregnant with child, is in a chair—a newspaper in her lap. Malcolm is in the other room, putting his last daughter to sleep. We hear him . . .

> MALCOLM (OS)
> Okay, last hug.

ANGLE – BEDROOM

As he enters, a smile on his face, but the concern of the evening clearly imprinted. He sits down heavily. Betty watches him carefully.

> MALCOLM
> Long day. Long night. Long year. Long ten years.

He smiles. She doesn't.

> MALCOLM (contd)
> Why are you looking at me like that?

> BETTY
> Because you're in trouble.

> MALCOLM
> How do you know?

She smiles.

> BETTY
> Dear heart, because I know you.

A pause.

> MALCOLM
> I don't want to bring my troubles home. You know that.

> BETTY
> I'm not made of glass.

> MALCOLM
> I just want to sit here and be still.

164   CONT'D

> BETTY
>
> We've never had a fight. Not a real one. But we're going to have one right now if you don't talk about it.

> MALCOLM
>
> Talk about what?

> BETTY
>
> The talk is everywhere!

> MALCOLM
>
> There's always talk, always been talk, and always will be talk. Don't they say how I'm trying to take over the nation, how I'm getting rich off the nation?

> BETTY
>
> We'll get to that, too, but this isn't just *talk* any more.

She picks up the newspaper and reads from it:

> BETTY (contd)
>
> "Los Angeles, UPI: Elijah Muhammad, 67-year-old leader of the Black Muslim Movement, today faced paternity suits from two former secretaries who charged he fathered their four children . . ."

> MALCOLM
>
> There are always slanders, always lies. You're reading the devil's lies. Can't you see they're trying to bring us down, bring down the Messenger.

> BETTY
>
> "Both women, in their 20's, charged they had had intimacies with Elijah Muhammad since 1957 . . ."

> MALCOLM
>
> I was going to talk to Bembry about it tonight.

> BETTY
>
> To Bembry? Is Bembry your friend?

> MALCOLM
>
> Woman, have you lost your mind? What's the matter with you?

Betty gets up, goes to him gently.

> BETTY
>
> No, what's the matter with you? Wake up! Are you so dedicated that you have blinded yourself? Are you so com-

164 CONT'D

> BETTY (contd)
> mitted you cannot face the truth? Bembry is the editor of
> the newspaper you established. Ask him why your name
> hasn't been in "Muhammad Speaks" in over a year? Ask
> him why you rate front page in every paper in the country,
> but not a single sentence in your own.

> MALCOLM
> (rationalizing)
> I'm not interested in personal publicity. Our people know
> what I'm doing.

> BETTY
> Do you know what Bembry is doing? You're so blind, ev-
> eryone can see this but you!!!

> MALCOLM
> Bembry saved my life. The Honorable Elijah Muhammad
> saved my life.

> BETTY
> A long time ago. You've repaid them many times over. Ask
> them why they have new cars and houses full of new furni-
> ture.

> MALCOLM
> Is that what this is about? Material wealth?

> BETTY
> What do we have, Malcolm. A broken-down jalopy and the
> clothes on our backs. We don't even own our own home.
> What about our children? What about me? You don't even
> own life insurance.

> MALCOLM
> The Nation will provide for you and the children if any-
> thing happens to me.

> BETTY
> Will they? Are you sure? Are you sure or are you blind?

She touches him very gently.

> BETTY
> Dear heart, you have to help me. I'm raising our kids
> practically by myself, while you're running all over the
> world. You don't know how many times the girls ask me
> when is daddy coming home?

164   CONT'D

MALCOLM
What do you want me to do? Our people need me.

BETTY
We need you too!

MALCOLM
What do you want me to do?

BETTY
Open your eyes, you can face death 24 hours a day; but the possibility of betrayal never enters your mind. If you won't do that for yourself do it for us.

164A   DETECTIVE MONTAGE

Malcolm knocks on the door of Evelyn Williams, one of the two secretaries/wives. She opens the door and has child in her arms.

ANGLE – APARTMENT

SISTER EVELYN
Her name is Eva Marie, she's 2 years old. Brother Minister I did nothing wrong. I did nothing to be put in isolation. I believed in him. I believed in the Honorable Elijah Muhammad.

CLOSE – MALCOLM

He cannot believe what he is hearing, but he must. The truth is before his eyes.

MALCOLM
Sister Evelyn, believe in Allah.

CUT TO:

164B   INT. SISTER LUCILLE'S ROSARY APT. – DAY

ANGLE MALCOLM

Malcolm is sitting holding both of the children. Sister Lucille who is pregnant with 3rd child waddles across the room to sit down on the sofa with him. She picks up one of the kids from him.

ANGLE – SISTER LUCILLE

SISTER LUCILLE
This is Saudi, she's 3 and you have Lisha, she's 2. Brother Minister the Honorable Elijah Muhammad is the father of my 3 children.

164B   CONT'D

She touches her pregnant stomach.

> SISTER LUCILLE (contd)
> Brother Minister he often talked about you. He loves you,
> loves you like his own son. Says you are the best, his
> greatest Minister but that someday you would leave him
> and turn against him.

CLOSE – MALCOLM

> MALCOLM
> He told you that?

> SISTER LUCILLE
> Yes sir.

> MALCOLM
> Are you sure?

> SISTER LUCILLE
> Yes I am Brother Minister. All I want is support for my
> children. He should provide for his children. That's all I
> want.

> MALCOLM
> Allah will provide.

165   INT. BEMBRY'S HOUSE – NIGHT

CLOSE SHOT – MALCOLM

He has said everything on his mind and waits for Bembry's answer.

PAN TO BEMBRY

> BEMBRY
> What are you talking about—"blackout"? Some of the
> Brothers are a little jealous. Maybe they think you been a
> little—overpublicized. That's all. Forget it. It's nothing.

Malcolm is listening closely. Bembry puts an arm around him,
man-to-man.

> BEMBRY (contd)
> Now about our coming up in the world a little. You're not
> naive. You're a man of the world. The Movement's grown;
> we've grown with it. You know folks. They want their
> leaders to be prosperous. One hand washes the other.

165 CONT'D

> MALCOLM
> (quoting Bembry back to himself)
> "I'm telling you God's words, not to hustle."

> BEMBRY
> You want a new car? You want a new house? Is that it? It's the money, right?

Malcolm has to control his rage.

> MALCOLM
> We tell the world we're moral leaders because we follow the personal example of the Honorable Elijah Muhammad. It's hard to make a rooster stop crowing once the sun has risen. The sun is up.

We hear rifle shots.

DRUM CADENCE (IT WILL BE THROUGHOUT ENTIRE SCENE)

166 OMIT

167 OMIT

168 OMIT

168A INT. MANHATTAN CENTER – DAY

Malcolm, a last-minute replacement for the ailing Honorable Elijah Muhammad, speaks before a HUGE CROWD.

> MALCOLM
> And what do I say of this so-called national mourning? I say . . . the white man's acts are condemned, not only by our beliefs but by his own.

168B SHOT – AMERICAN FLAGS AT HALF-MAST

> MALCOLM
> Both his Bible and the Holy Koran say: "As you sow, so shall you reap." Both say: "Sow the wind, reap the whirl-wind."

SHOT – AMERICAN FLAGS AT HALF-MAST

> MALCOLM (contd)
> In the soil of America the white man planted the seeds of hate. He allowed the weeds that sprang up to choke the life out of thousands of black men.

168C SHOT – THE KENNEDY FUNERAL CORTEGE

> MALCOLM (contd)
> Now they have strangled one of the gardeners. This is the
> justice of Allah. Wa-Salaam Alaikum.

168D SHOT – AUDIENCE

> AUDIENCE
> Alaikum Wa-Salaam.

168E SHOT – THE LONE, RIDERLESS HORSE

169 INT. MALCOLM WITH REPORTERS – DAY

> REPORTER
> Minister X! Don't you have even a little bit of remorse
> . . . saddened by President Kennedy's assassination?

CLOSE – MALCOLM

> MALCOLM
> Assassination might be too good a word, and might I add
> an Arabic word at that. This was a prime example of the
> devil's chickens coming home to roost. Being an old farm
> boy myself, chickens coming home to roost never did make
> me sad. It always made me glad.

169A On his desk is the black headlines: MALCOLM X CALLS ASSASSI-
NATION "CHICKENS COMING HOME TO ROOST." Elijah's health is
getting worse, his coughing is frequent.

> ELIJAH
> Did you see the papers today?

> MALCOLM
> Yes, sir, I did.

> ELIJAH
> That was a very bad statement. The country loved this
> man, and you have made it hard in general for Muslims.

CLOSE – MALCOLM

He knows what is coming.

CLOSE – ELIJAH

> ELIJAH (contd)
> We must dissociate ourselves from your terrible blunder.
> I'll have to silence you for the next ninety days. You are

169A   CONT'D

ELIJAH (contd)
not allowed to make any statements to the press nor are
you to speak at any temples.

CLOSER – MALCOLM

He looks at Elijah, his leader, his friend, his father and speaks with
total sincerity.

MALCOLM
I agree with you, sir. I submit 100 percent.

ANGLE – ROOM

Malcolm turns around and leaves the room.

ANGLE – DOOR

As the door is being closed, WE SEE Bembry kneeling before Elijah
and kissing his hand. The door closes, the SCREEN IS BLACK.

FADE IN:

170   OMIT

171   OMIT

172   INT. MALCOLM'S HOUSE – NIGHT

Sidney is playing on the floor with the kids. Betty scoops them up.

BETTY
C'mon girls, it's bedtime.

The phone rings. Malcolm answers it. From his expression we
know it is a threat call. He hangs up. Betty leaves with the kids.

SIDNEY
Another one?

MALCOLM
How long has this been going on?

SIDNEY
All day since you and Betty left. Brother Minister, I have
to level with you. They gave me a mission. But I couldn't
do it. I love y'all.

MALCOLM
What mission?

172   CONT'D

SIDNEY
To wire your car so it would explode when you turned the
ignition. The Ministers say you are spreading untruths
about the Messenger. The Ministers say you are a great
hypocrite, Judas, Benedict Arnold. The Ministers say your
tongue should be cut out and delivered to the Messenger's
doorstep.

MALCOLM
What does Sidney say?

SIDNEY
I'm with you Brother Minister.

MALCOLM
No. You'll be marked for death.

SIDNEY
Let me die then.

MALCOLM
I won't let myself come between you and your father. Go
home.

SIDNEY
You're my father.

MALCOLM
And don't come back.

Sidney reluctantly leaves, walks out the door, past Betty. She looks
at him, then Malcolm.

173   INT. HOTEL THERESA – DAY

Malcolm backed by Brothers Earl and Benjamin 2X – faces a room-
ful of SUPPORTERS and REPORTERS.

MALCOLM
Because 1964 threatens to be a very explosive year on the
racial front, and because I myself intend to be very active
in every phase of the American Negro struggle for *HUMAN
RIGHTS,* I have called this press conference, this morning
in order to clarify my own position in the struggle—especially in regards to politics and nonviolence. In the past I
thought the thoughts, spoke the words of the Honorable
Elijah Muhammad, that day is over. From now on I speak
my own words, and think my own thoughts. Internal dif-

173   CONT'D

MALCOLM (contd)

erences within the Nation of Islam forced me out of it. I did
not leave of my own free will. But now that it has happened, I intend to make the most of it. Now that I have
more independence of action, I intend to use a more flexible
approach toward working with others to get a solution to
this problem. I do not pretend to be a divine man, but I do
believe in divine guidance, divine power, and in the ful-
fillment of divine prophecy. I am not educated, nor am I an
expert in any particular field, but I am sincere, and my
sincerity is my credentials. I'm not out to fight other Negro
leaders or organizations. We must find a common solution,
to a common problem. I am going to organize and head a
new mosque in New York City, known as the Muslim
Mosque, Inc. This gives us a religious base, and the spiritual force necessary to rid our people of the vices that
destroy the moral fiber of our community. Our political
philosophy will be black nationalism. Our economic and
social philosophy will be black nationalism. The Muslim
Mosque, Inc. will remain wide open for ideas and financial
aid from all quarters. Whites can help us, but they can't
join us. There can be no black-white unity until there is
first some black unity.

A host of questions fired all at once: How many of Elijah's followers
will join you? etc, etc, etc.

Malcolm calms them:

MALCOLM (cont'd)

There is one further preparation I need. It is a return to the
source of our great religion. I will make a pilgrimage to
Mecca.

174   EXT. JFK AIRPORT – DAY

Malcolm, at the window, as his plane takes off. He is watching
Betty and the children on the Visitors' Ramp. He sees her become
a tiny figure, waving a vivid bandana.

175   EXT. VISITORS' RAMP – DAY

The plane is out of sight. Betty gathers up her children. As they
leave she is subtly surrounded by the protecting BAND OF SUP-
PORTERS, led by Earl and Benjamin 2X.

175A MECCA – THE PILGRIMAGE

MALCOLM GREETED AS HE DESCENDS FROM THE PLANE IN
EGYPT

> MALCOLM'S VOICE
> My darling Betty. Everywhere I go I am welcomed as the
> representative of our people.

175B SHOT OF CIA AGENT

He watches as Malcolm walks between the two pyramids.

> MALCOLM'S VOICE (contd)
> Our fight is known and respected worldwide. Incidentally,
> there's a little white man who follows me wherever I go.

175C SHOT OF MALCOLM

On a camel as he rides toward the Sphinx.

> MALCOLM'S VOICE
> I wonder who he's working for? If I was a betting man, I'd
> say CIA. What's your guess?

175D GROUPS OF BURNOOSED SUPPORTERS ON THE STREETS OF
JEDDA, SAUDIA ARABIA.

> BETTY'S VOICE
> I arrived in Jedda, Saudi Arabia. I have never witnessed
> such sincere . . .

176 INT. AUDUBON BALLROOM – NIGHT

Betty is reading Malcolm's letter to a LARGE AUDIENCE.

> BETTY (contd)
> . . . hospitality and true brotherhood as practiced here in
> the ancient home of Abraham, Mohammad and the great
> prophets of the Scriptures . . .''

177 INT/EXT. MECCA – DAY/NIGHT

—Malcolm, wearing the garb of a pilgrim, walks with a VAST
THRONG OF OTHERS, similarly clad, around the Great Temple. He
wears two white towels, one over his loins, the other over his neck
and shoulder, leaving the right arm and shoulder bare. He wears
simple sandals. The other pilgrims are of various colors: from
white, to yellow, to darkest black.

177A —Malcolm and OTHER PILGRIMS kneeling together on a praying
rug.

177B   —Malcolm and SEVERAL WHITE PILGRIMS eating Muslim-style; breaking a chicken and shaking it.

177C   —Malcolm and OTHERS walking around the Great Kaaba, a black stone set in the middle of the Great Mosque. He falls to his knees. WE SEE what he describes:

> MALCOLM'S VOICE
> Today, with thousands of others, I proclaimed God's greatness in the Holy City of Mecca. Wearing the Ihram garb I made my seven circuits around the Kaaba; I drank from the well of Zem Zem; I prayed to Allah from Mt. Ararat where the Ark landed. It was the only time in my life that I stood before the Creator of all and felt like a complete human being.

178   INT. ELIJAH'S HOME – NIGHT

Elijah and a GROUP OF BLACK MUSLIM LEADERS. Bembry among them, it looks like he is the number two man now that Malcolm has been jettisoned. The Messenger lies in bed, he is having a coughing fit, this is the worst condition he's been in. A DOCTOR orders everyone out the room.

> MALCOLM'S VOICE
> You may be shocked by these words, but I have eaten from the same plate, drunk from the same glass and prayed to the same God with fellow Muslims whose eyes were blue, whose hair was blond and whose skin was the whitest of whites. And we are brothers, truly; people of all colors and races believing in One God and one humanity. Once before, in prison, the truth came and blinded me. It has happened again . . .

179   INT. MALCOLM'S HOME – NIGHT

Betty is with Brothers Earl, Benjamin 2X, and the children. There are now four including another BABY – GAMILAH

> MALCOLM'S VOICE
> In the past, I have permitted myself to be used to make sweeping indictments of all white people, and these generalizations have caused injuries to some white folks who did not deserve them. Because of the spiritual rebirth which I was blessed to undergo as a result of my pilgrimage to the Holy City of Mecca, I no longer subscribe to sweeping indictments of one race. I intend to be careful not to sentence anyone who has not been proven guilty. I'm not a racist

179 CONT'D

> MALCOLM'S VOICE (contd)
>
> and do not subscribe to any of the tenets of racism. In all honesty and sincerity it can be stated that I wish nothing but freedom, justice and equality: life, liberty, and the pursuit of happiness for all people.

179A SHOT. Malcolm is bent over in prayer, lone figure in a huge mosque.

> MALCOLM'S VOICE
>
> My first concern, of course, is with the group to which I belong, the Afro-Americans, for we, more than any other, are deprived of these inalienable rights.

179B SHOT. Malcolm on a plane headed home.

> MALCOLM'S VOICE
>
> I believe the true practice of Islam can remove the cancer of racism from the hearts and souls of white Americans.

180 EXT. JFK AIRPORT – DAY

A TIGHT TWO-SHOT of Malcolm and Betty in an embrace. She breaks from him and whispers: "Go ahead. I can wait now."

181 INT. JFK AIRPORT – DAY

A large PRESS CONFERENCE: mikes of every network, every newspaper and wire service present. Malcolm sports a beard.

> MALCOLM
>
> Let's begin.

> REPORTER #1
>
> Malcolm, you said on your trip abroad you sensed a feeling of great brotherhood.

> MALCOLM
>
> As I recall, I pointed out that while I was in Mecca making the pilgrimage, I spoke about the brotherhood that existed at all levels among all people, all colors who had accepted the religion of Islam. I pointed out that what it had done, Islam, for those people despite their complexion differences, that it would probably do America well to study the religion of Islam and perhaps it could drive some of the racism from this society. Muslims look upon themselves as human beings, as part of the human family and therefore look upon all other segments of the human family as

181   CONT'D

> MALCOLM (contd)
> part of that same family. Today my friends are black, brown, red, yellow and white.

> REPORTER #2
> Malcolm, are you prepared to go to the United Nations at this point and ask that charges be brought against the United States for its treatment of the American Negroes?

> MALCOLM
> Oh yes.

The AUDIENCE applauds.

> MALCOLM (contd)
> The audience will have to be quiet. Yes, as I pointed out that during my trip that nations, African nations, Asian, Latin nations look very hypocritical when they stand up in the UN condemning South Africa and saying nothing about the racist practices that are manifested everyday against Negroes in this society. I would be not a man if I didn't do so. I wouldn't be a man.

> REPORTER #3
> Are you prepared to work with some of the leaders of some of the other civil rights organizations?

> MALCOLM
> Certainly, we will work with any groups, organizations or leaders in any way, as long as it's genuinely designed to get results.

> REPORTER #1
> Does the new beard have any religious significance?

> MALCOLM
> No, not particularly. But I do think that you will find black people in America, as they strive to throw off the shackles of mental colonialism, will also probably reflect an effort to throw off the shackles of cultural colonialism. And then they'll begin to reflect desires of their own with standards of their own.

> REPORTER #2
> One of your more controversial remarks was a call for black people to get rifles and form rifle clubs sometime back. Do you still favor that for self-defense?

181   CONT'D

MALCOLM
I don't see why that should be controversial. I think that if
white people found themselves victim of the same kind of
brutality that black people in this country face, and they
saw that the government was either unwilling or unable to
protect them, that the intelligence on the part of the whites
would make them get some rifles and protect themselves.

REPORTER #2
What about the guns Malcolm?

MALCOLM
Has the white man changed since I went away? Have you
put up your guns? The day you stop being violent against
my people will be the day I tell folks to put away their guns.

REPORTER #3
Then you're still an extremist?

ANGLE – MUSLIM MALE

BENJAMIN THOMAS
Git your hand out of my pocket!

Everyone turns around to the back to see what the commotion is
about. The man who yelled out leaves quickly, we will see him later
on, very soon.

182   INT. MALCOLM'S HOUSE – NIGHT

Malcolm looks out the living room window, he has a rifle in hand.
(NOTE: This is the same pose as the famous photograph of him.) He
doesn't see anyone and closes the curtain. The phone rings.

CLOSE – PHONE

Malcolm picks up the receiver.

VOICE
You're one dead nigger.

ANGLE – BEDROOM

Betty has picked up also and she's listening.

VOICE
You're days on this earth are numbered, brother.

CLOSE – MALCOLM

182 CONT'D

CLICK!

He hangs up.

ANGLE – BEDROOM

Malcolm enters the room and gets into the bed with Betty, he puts his ear down on his wife's pregnant stomach.

She kisses him.

> BETTY
> Get some sleep.

> MALCOLM
> You have to sleep for three.

Malcolm pulls Betty closer to him.

> MALCOLM
> I'm sorry. I haven't been the best husband or father.

> BETTY
> Shhh!

> MALCOLM
> Families shouldn't be separated. I'll never make another long trip without you and the kids. We'll all be together.

> BETTY
> Dear heart, I love you.

> MALCOLM
> We had the best organization that black people ever had and niggers ruined it.

183 EXT. THE HOUSE – NIGHT

It is a cold winter night. A Molotov cocktail is lit and hurled through the front picture glass window.

184 INT. THE HOUSE – NIGHT

One of the children screams.

185 INT. MALCOLM'S BEDROOM – NIGHT

Malcolm grabs his pistol and quickly throws a coat over Betty. She is half-asleep, frightened, trembling and disoriented.

> MALCOLM
> Walk out the back, dear. Hurry.

185 CONT'D

Betty goes. Malcolm runs back for the children.

ANGLE. He reassuringly leads the four children, in their pajamas, through the smoke-filled house.

> MALCOLM
> There's nothing to be afraid of. It might be a little cold. Hang on. We'll be fine.

185A INSERT – FLASHBACK

WE CUT BACK TO Earl Little getting his family out of the burning house in Lansing, Michigan. It should be the same exact scene we saw before earlier in the film.

> EARL
> Everybody out. OUT! OUT! Get the kids.

CUT BACK TO PRESENT

186 EXT. THE HOUSE – NIGHT

Neighbors' lights have gone on. There are shouts: "What is it?" "Fire!" "Bring those children in here."

> MALCOLM
> Call the Fire Department.

186A OMIT

187 EXT. THE HOUSE – NIGHT (LATER)

A hose is playing on the fire. Police cars have arrived. There are TWO REPORTERS with the COPS. Malcolm faces them furiously.

> MALCOLM
> And the fire hit the window and it woke up my second oldest baby, but the fire burned on the outside of the house. It could have fallen on six-, four-, or two-year-old girls. And I'm going to tell you, if it had done it, I'd taken my rifle and gone after anybody in sight.

> REPORTER
> Are the Muslims behind this?

> MALCOLM
> It was bombed by the Black Muslim movement upon the orders of Elijah Muhammad.

> SECOND REPORTER
> Do you know what Muslim headquarters is saying?

187   CONT'D

> MALCOLM
> (with total contempt)
> I can imagine. I did it myself. For the publicity.

187A   EXT. TEMPLE #1 – DETROIT – DAY

Bembry is being interviewed by a reporter.

> BEMBRY
> We feel this is a publicity stunt on the part of Malcolm X.
> We hope this isn't a case of "if he can't keep the house, we
> won't get it either."

187B   EXT. MALCOLM'S STREET – NIGHT

A car comes roaring down the street with rifles sticking out the
windows, and pulls right up in front of Malcolm's house.

ANGLE – HOUSE

Brothers Earl and Benjamin 2X run out of the car up to Malcolm.

> BROTHER EARL
> We called your house, operator said you had requested
> that your phone be turned off.

> BENJAMIN 2X
> Give us the command, Malcolm.

> MALCOLM
> I don't care about myself, my wife and four children were
> sleeping in their beds, they have nothing to do with this.

> BROTHER EARL
> Let's get out of this cold.

Brothers Earl and Benjamin take off their coats and put it over
Malcolm and lead him to a police car.

187C   INT. BASEMENT – DAY

FIVE BLACK MEN sit around a table. They do not speak. They are
Thomas Hayer, Ben Thomas, Leon Davis, William X and Wilbur
Kinley. All are Muslims, all are the ASSASSINS.

CLOSE – 12 – GAUGE SAWED-OFF SHOTGUN ON TABLE

CLOSE – 9MM GERMAN LUGER ON TABLE

CLOSE – .45 AUTOMATIC

ANGLE – THOMAS HAYER

187C   CONT'D

He puts a roll of exposed 35mm film into a sock.

ANGLE – TABLE

> ASSASSINS
> Allah Akbar.

187D   EXT. NY HILTON – DAY ESTABLISHING SHOT

187E   INT. NY HILTON

ANGLE LOBBY

Malcolm is checking in when he is approached by a young WHITE COED.

> COED
> Mr. X. I have a good heart. I'm a good person despite my whiteness. What can the good white people like myself who are not prejudiced do to help the cause of the Negro?

CLOSE – MALCOLM

He looks at her. He thinks. He speaks.

> MALCOLM
> Let sincere white individuals find other white people who feel as they do and teach non-violence to those whites who think and act so racist.

CLOSE – COED

> COED
> I will, Mr. X. I will.

CLOSE – MALCOLM

> MALCOLM
> Let's all pray without ceasing. May Allah bless you.

187F   INT. HOTEL ROOM – NIGHT

Malcolm lies on his bed, and for the first time WE SEE the strain in his face, it has begun to take its toll, he's a haunted man. A doomed man.

ANGLE – MALCOLM

Malcolm dials the phone.

> MALCOLM
> Brother Earl.

187G   INT. HOTEL THERESA – NIGHT

> BROTHER EARL
>
> Malcolm, where are you? We've been calling all over the
> city.

INTERCUT between Malcolm and Brother Earl.

> MALCOLM
>
> I'm gonna try and get some work done tonight.

> BROTHER EARL
>
> Let some of us come down there.

> MALCOLM
>
> No, that won't be necessary. I'll be all right.

> BROTHER EARL
>
> I wish you'd listen to us. What about the meeting tomor-
> row? We need to frisk people.

> MALCOLM
>
> I don't want folks to be searched, it makes people uncom-
> fortable. If I can't be safe among my own kind, where can
> I be? Allah will protect me.

There is silence on the other end.

CLOSE – BROTHER EARL

187K   INT. AUDUBON BALLROOM – NIGHT

The five assassins are casing ballroom. They check the different
entrances, the exits, the bathrooms, staircases while the jam
packed crowd continues to dance the night away.

188   INT. A FRIEND'S HOUSE – NIGHT

Betty is putting her four daughters to sleep when the phone rings.
He picks it up.

> VOICE
>
> That red nigger of yours is dead and so are your bastard
> children.

CLICK.

Betty hangs up the phone and it rings again.

> BETTY
>
> Stop calling us. Leave us alone. Leave us alone. I'll kill
> you. I'll kill you.

188A   CLOSE – MALCOLM

188A CONT'D

> MALCOLM
> Betty it's me. It's me.

INTERCUT between between Malcolm and Betty.

> BETTY
> Malcolm, they keep calling, threatening us. I'm going crazy, when is this going to stop?

> MALCOLM
> Don't answer the phone. It's all right. It's all right. Nothing is gonna happen to anybody.

> BETTY
> Dear heart, where are you?

> MALCOLM
> At the Hilton. The girls asleep?

> BETTY
> I just put them to bed. Can we come to the meeting tomorrow?

> MALCOLM
> I don't think that's such a good idea.

A blue 1962 Cadillac passes a sign that says Patterson, New Jersey.

ANGLE – CAR

The assassins are on their way to the Audubon Ballroom, Wilbur Kinley is behind the wheel, no one is talking.

190 EXT. STREET – DAY

Betty is driving to the Audubon Ballroom, her four daughters are in the backseat making a racket.

190A EXT. STREET – DAY

Malcolm drives to the Audubon Ballroom.

191 INT. AUDUBON BALLROOM – DAY

Brothers Earl and Benjamin 2X along with some others are putting the folding chairs in place for the coming meeting. The audience has not started to come in yet.

192 EXT. GEORGE WASHINGTON BRIDGE – DAY

The assassins are driving over the George Washington Bridge.

192   CONT'D

     ANGLE – CAR

                   KINLEY
     Brothers, the time is fast approaching, it's the hour of the
     knife.

193   EXT. STREET – DAY

     CLOSE – BETTY

     Betty is trying to quiet down her daughters as she drives.

194   EXT. STREET – DAY

     CLOSE – MALCOLM

     Malcolm is in deep thought as he drives.

194A   INT. AUDUBON BALLROOM – DAY

     Betty and her four kids walk into the ballroom and move down the
     center aisle. One of the girls drops her black doll and a young man
     picks it up. The young man is Thomas Hayer, he gives it back to
     her.

                   BETTY
             Say thank you.

                 GAMILAH
             Thank you.

                 THOMAS
             You are welcome.

     ANGLE. The rest of the assassins come in and go to their positions
     along with the rest of the crowd, the place is starting to fill up.

195   INT. BACKSTAGE – DAY

             BROTHER BENJAMIN 2X
             No sign of the minister yet.

               BROTHER EARL
             He'll be here like clockwork.

196   EXT. STREET – DAY

     Malcolm drives past the Audubon Ballroom, people are going in but
     no cops are present.

     ANGLE – CAR

196 CONT'D

Malcolm drives by.

ANGLE – STREET

Malcolm parks his car, it's four blocks away. He turns off the ignition and sits there.

CLOSE – MALCOLM

It's as if he's frozen in his car.

ANGLE – STREET

Malcolm finally gets out of the car, locks the door and walks a couple of steps, then stops.

CLOSE – MALCOLM

Malcolm has stopped in his tracks, like some unseen force has overcome him which prevents him from moving. Malcolm is paralyzed.

CLOSER – MALCOLM'S FACE

His eyes are closed, and the street noise begins to build to a deafening *roar.* Then all of a sudden it stops.

ANGLE – OLD WOMAN

> OLD WOMAN
> Son, you all right?

Malcolm opens his eyes, she has brought him out of it. He looks at her but doesn't answer.

> OLD WOMAN (contd)
> Are you okay?

Malcolm looks at this old woman, who slightly resembles his own mother.

> MALCOLM
> Ma'am, I'm fine.

> OLD WOMAN
> Good. We need you. I recognize you, don't pay them folks
> no never mind, you keep on doing what you doing.

> MALCOLM
> May Allah bless you.

196   CONT'D

> OLD WOMAN
> I'll pray for you too, son. Jesus will protect you.

She walks away, carrying her two shopping bags full of groceries.

197   INT. BACKSTAGE – DAY

Malcolm walks in. Present are Brothers Earl, Benjamin 2X and a secretary SISTER ROBIN.

> MALCOLM
> Is the program ready?

> BENJAMIN 2X
> No, Brother Minister.

> MALCOLM
> Why not? You've had ample time, you and the sister.

> SISTER ROBIN
> I apologize Brother Minister, we'll have it next week.

He is pissed.

> MALCOLM
> Folks are sitting out there *today*, not next week, expecting to hear our program.

> BENJAMIN 2X
> Next week, Brother Minister.

> MALCOLM
> Has the Reverend called? Is he going to show?

> BROTHER EARL
> Reverend Chickenwing called last night and said he wouldn't be able to attend.

> MALCOLM
> So now we have no opening speaker? Why wasn't I informed last night?

> BROTHER EARL
> I called Sister Betty, she didn't tell you?

> MALCOLM
> Since when do you start telling Sister Betty my business? Since when? She has nothing to do with this. You tell me, not her, not anybody else.

197   CONT'D

> BROTHER EARL
> I assumed . . .

> MALCOLM
> What did I tell you about assuming?

Malcolm starts pacing the room, nobody has ever seen him like this before.

> MALCOLM
> Benjamin, you better go out there and explain why the program isn't ready *today*.

Benjamin 2X gets up to leave.

> MALCOLM
> Sister, please go with the brother.

They both exit.

CLOSE – MALCOLM AND EARL

> BROTHER EARL
> Brother Minister, what is wrong?

> MALCOLM
> The way I feel, I ought not to go out there today. In fact, I'm going to ease some of this tension by telling the black man not to fight himself—that's all a part of the white man's big maneuver, to keep us fighting amongst ourselves, against each other. I'm not fighting anyone, that's not what we're here for.

> BROTHER EARL
> Let's cancel.

> MALCOLM
> Is my family here yet?

> BROTHER EARL
> Down front as always.

198   INT. ANTEROOM – DAY

A lone COP in uniform stands in the shadows with a walkie-talkie.

198A INT. BACKSTAGE – DAY

Malcolm is about to go on stage when he sees Sister Robin.

198A   CONT'D

> MALCOLM
>
> You'll have to forgive me for raising my voice to you.

> SISTER ROBIN
>
> Brother Minister, I understand.

> MALCOLM
> (to himself)
> I wonder if anybody understands.

199   INT. AUDUBON BALLROOM – DAY

The place is filled. Betty and the girls sit in a boxed-off section near the platform. Malcolm's bodyguards stand on and around the stand. Benjamin 2X is finishing up his speech when Malcolm walks onto the stage and sits down.

> MALCOLM
>
> Make it plain.

> BENJAMIN 2X
>
> And now, without further remarks, I present to you one who is willing to put himself on the line for you—

CLOSE – BETTY AND THE KIDS

CLOSE – THOMAS HAYER

CLOSE – WILBUR KINLEY

CLOSE – LEON DAVIS

CLOSE – BEN THOMAS

CLOSE – WILLIAM X

CLOSE – MALCOLM X

CLOSE – BENJAMIN 2X

> BENJAMIN 2X (contd)
>
> —a man who would give his life for you. I want you to hear, to listen, to understand one who is a trojan for the black man.

ANGLE – STAGE

A roar greets Malcolm's intro. He shakes hands with Benjamin 2X, then steps toward the podium.

CLOSE – MALCOLM

199 CONT'D

He starts to rearrange his 3 × 5 index cards in his hands.

MALCOLM
Brothers and Sisters, Wa-Salaam Alaikum.

AUDIENCE
Alaikum Wa-Salaam.

SWIFT JERKY PAN OF CAMERA

There is a commotion in the rear of the audience.

BENJAMIN THOMAS
Git your hand out of my pocket.

The bodyguards move toward the rear.

CLOSE – MALCOLM

MALCOLM
Hold it, brothers. Don't get excited. Let's cool it—

ANGLE – WILLIAM X

He stands up from the fourth row with 12-gauge sawed-off shotgun blasting.

CLOSE – MALCOLM

Throws up his hands, grabs his chest and is knocked backward.

SHOTS – PURE PANDEMONIUM

People hit the floor, knock over chairs, stampede for the exits.

ANGLE – BACK OF AUDITORIUM

Wilbur Kinley ignites a smoke bomb.

ANGLE – FIRST RUN

Thomas Hayer and Leon Davis stand up, run toward the stage, and empty their .45's and Luger into the fallen body of Malcolm.

ANGLE – BETTY

She is on the floor covering her children.

ANGLE – AISLE

Hayer and Davis charge up the aisle toward the rear exit, shooting at the crowd.

ANGLE – BODYGUARD

199 CONT'D

He stands in Hayer's way, Hayer fires, he turns, the bullet misses and the bodyguard gets off a shot which hits Hayer in the leg.

ANGLE – HAYER

He stumbles momentarily, then limps on.

ANGLE – STAIRCASE

Hayer is running down the staircase when he is tripped, and goes flying through the air to the bottom of the landing. The crowd starts to beat the shit out of him, kicking him in the head, etc., they're about to tear him apart from limb to limb when a PATROLMAN enters with gun drawn. He shoots gun into air and the crowd backs off and he takes custody of Hayer.

ANGLE – STAGE

One of Malcolm's bodyguards, BROTHER GENE, is over him, giving him mouth-to-mouth resuscitation. Brother Gene stops, Betty moves in and hugs her dying husband.

> BETTY
> Somebody call an ambulance. Somebody call an ambu-
> lance.

ANGLE – ENTRANCE

THIRTY COPS walk in like it's a spring Sunday stroll in Central Park.

CLOSE – MALCOLM

His eyes are glazed over.

> BETTY'S VOICE
> They killed him. They killed him.

200 SHOT – BROTHERS EARL AND BENJAMIN 2X SITTING ON STAGE

200A SHOT – MALCOLM IS RUSHED ON A STRETCHER TO HOSPITAL NEXT DOOR

SHOT – HOSPITAL SPOKESPERSON

> HOSPITAL SPOKESPERSON
> The person you know as Malcolm is no more.

200B   THE STUNNED FACES OF BLACK PEOPLE OUTSIDE THE AUDUBON
       BALLROOM . . .

       —AND IN HARLEM.

       OSSIE DAVIS speaking behind the above:

> OSSIE DAVIS'S VOICE
> Here at this final hour, in this quiet place, Harlem has
> come to bid farewell to one of its brightest hopes extin-
> guished now and gone from us forever.

200C   DOLLY SHOT of the long line of people outside the funeral parlor,
       waiting to see Malcolm's body, where it lies before burial.

> OSSIE DAVIS'S VOICE (contd)
> For Harlem is where he worked, and where he struggled
> and fought. His home of homes, where his heart was and
> where his people are. And it is therefore most fitting that
> we meet once again in Harlem to share these last moments
> with him. For Harlem has ever been gracious to those who
> loved her, have fought for her and defended her honor
> even to death. It is not in the memory of man that this
> beleaguered, unfortunate but nonetheless proud commu-
> nity has found a braver, more gallant young champion
> than this Afro-American who lies before us unconquered
> still. Many will ask what Harlem finds to honor in this
> stormy, controversial and bold young captain and we will
> smile and we will answer and say unto them:

200D   SHOTS – FACES OF HARLEM – PRESENT DAY – THE 90'S

       Ordinary PEOPLE in ordinary pursuits of life, BLACK PEOPLE still
       struggling to stay afloat in a racist WHITE AMERICA that does not
       have their best interests at hand—8 years of Reagan and now at
       least 4 years of Bush.

> OSSIE DAVIS'S VOICE (contd)
> Did you ever talk to Brother Malcolm? Did you have him
> smile at you? Did you ever listen to him? Did he ever really
> do a mean thing? Was he ever associated with violence or
> any public disturbance?

200E   SHOT – STREET SIGN – MALCOLM X BOULEVARD – HARLEM

200F   SHOT – YOUNG AFRO-CENTRIC TEENAGERS WITH MALCOLM X
       T-SHIRTS, HATS, JACKETS, JEWELRY, ETC.

> OSSIE DAVIS'S VOICE (contd)
> For if you did, you would know him and if you knew him,
> you would know why we must honor him.

200G   SHOT – NEWSREEL FOOTAGE OF THE *REAL* MALCOLM X

> OSSIE DAVIS'S VOICE (contd)
> Malcolm was our *manhood,* our living black manhood.
> That was his meaning to his people and in honoring him we
> honor the best in ourselves.

200H   FREEZE FRAME – A CLOSE-UP OF THE REAL MALCOLM X SMIL-
ING RIGHT AT US.

> CUT TO:

200I   SHOT – INT. CLASSROOM BULLETIN BOARD

A picture collage of Malcolm X. It reads P.S. 153—Harlem honors
Malcolm on his birthdate May 19, 1925.

> OSSIE DAVIS'S VOICE (contd)
> And we will know him then for what he was and is. A
> PRINCE, A BLACK SHINING PRINCE who didn't hesitate to
> die because he loved us so.

ANGLE – CLASSROOM

It's a fourth-grade class.

CLOSE – STUDENT

> 1ST STUDENT
> I'm Malcolm X.

CLOSE – STUDENT

> 2ND STUDENT
> I'm Malcolm X.

CLOSE – STUDENT

> 3RD STUDENT
> I'm Malcolm X.

CLOSE – STUDENT

> 4TH FEMALE STUDENT
> I'm Malcolm X.

201   INT. CLASSROOM – SOWETO, SOUTH AFRICA – DAY

CLOSE – STUDENT

> 1ST STUDENT
> I'm Malcolm X.

CLOSE – STUDENT

201   CONT'D

                                     2ND STUDENT
                                     I'm Malcolm X.

CLOSE – STUDENT

                                     3RD STUDENT
                                     I'm Malcolm X.

CLOSE – STUDENT

                              4TH FEMALE STUDENT
                                     I'm Malcolm X.

CAMERA PANS slowly to head of class where the teacher stands, it's NELSON MANDELA.

CLOSE – MANDELA

                                   MANDELA
As Brother Malcolm said, "We declare our right on this earth to be a man, to be a human being, to be respected as a human being, in this society, on this earth, in this day, which we intend to bring into existence by any means necessary."

Ossie Davis Eulogy

Here, at this final hour, in this quiet place, Harlem has come to bid farewell to one of its brightest hopes. Extinguished now and gone from us forever.

For Harlem is where he worked and where he struggled and fought. His home of homes, where his heart was and where his people are. And it is therefore most fitting that we meet once again, in Harlem, to share these last moments with him. For Harlem has ever been gracious to those who have loved her, have fought for her and have defended her honor even to the death. It is not in the memory of man that this beleaguered, unfortunate but nonetheless proud community has found a braver, more gallant champion than this Afro-American who lies before us, unconquered still.

I say the word again as he would want me to. Afro-American. Afro-American Malcolm, who was a master, was most meticulous in his use of words nobody knew better than he the power words have over the minds of men. Malcolm had stopped being negro years ago. It had become too small, too puny, too weak a word for him. Malcolm was bigger than that. Malcolm had become an Afro-American, and he wanted so desperately that we, that all his people, would become Afro-Americans too.

There are those who still consider it their duty as friends of the negro people to tell us to revile him. To flee even from the presense of this memory. To save ourselves by writing him out of the history of our turbulent times.

Many will ask what Harlem finds to honor in this stormy, controversial and bold young captain, and we will smile.

Many will say turn away, away from this man for he is not a man but a demon—a monster—a subverter and an enemy of the blackman. And we will smile.

They will say that he is of hate, a fanatic, a racist who can only bring evil to the cause for which you struggle.

And we will answer and say unto them:

Did you ever talk to Brother Malcolm?
Did you ever touch him or have him smile at you?
Did you ever really listen to him?
Did he ever do a mean thing? Was he ever himself associated with
violence or any public disturbance?

For if you did, you would know him and if you knew him, you
would know why we must honor him. Malcolm was our *man-
hood,* our living black manhood. This was his meaning to his
people, and in honoring him we honor the best in ourselves.

Last year, from Africa. He wrote these words to a friend. "My
journey," he says, "is almost ended. And I have much broader
scope than when I started out, which I believe will add new life
and dimension to our struggle for freedom and honor and dignity
in the States. I'm writing these things so that you will know for
a fact, the tremendous sympathy and support we have among the
African States for our human rights struggle.

The main thing is that we keep a united front, where in our most
valuable time and energy will not be wasted fighting each
other."

However much we may have differed with him, or with each
other about him and his value as a man. Let his going from us
serve only to bring us together now. Consigning these mortal
remains to earth, the common mother of all. Secure in the knowledge that what we place in the ground is no more now a man, but
a seed, which after the winter of our discontent will come forth
again to meet us. And we shall know him then for what he was
and is. A PRINCE, A BLACK SHINING PRINCE who didn't hesi-
tate to die because he loved us so.